VOICES OF GHANA

Literary Contributions to the Ghana Broadcasting System 1955-57

PRINTED BY THE GOVERNMENT PRINTER, ACCRA
for
MINISTRY OF INFORMATION AND BROADCASTING
1958

Contents

		PAGE
A Note of History	Henry Swanzy	12

THE COUNTRYSIDE

The Poetry of Drums	J. H. Nketia	17
Across the Prah	A. A. Opoku	24
The Tale of Ananse and Twala the Thief	T. C. Aninfeng	40
Ananse's Punishment	J. K. O. Lindsay ...	41
Ohia and the Thieving Deer	J. V. Mensah	43
The " Iron Bar "	C. V. Hutchison ...	47
Drum Proverbs	J. H. Nketia	49
Afram	A. A. Opoku	54
Fisherman's Day	S. K. Otoo	66
Komenda Hill	Bossman Laryea ...	71
Ahanamanta (Harmattan) ...	Joseph Ghartey	72
Mami Takyiwa's Misfortune ...	Albert Kayper Mensah ...	74
New Life at Kyerefaso ...	Efua Sutherland ...	77
No Ten Without Nine ...	L. K. Idan	84
Ewe Poetry	I. K. Hoh	86
Akoli the Rich	L. K. Safo	94
	(Trans R. Agodzo)	
Fifteen Poems of Eweland ...	I. K. Hoh	98
Down Below the Volta River ...	Adolph Agbadja ...	105
August Fish	E. K. Martey	108
A Hawker's Day	Richard Bentil	109
Come Back to the Land ...	A. B. Derimanu ...	112
Each for a Purpose	A. B. Derimanu ...	113
The Hausa Trader	J. H. Sackey	114
Wakan Sule (A Song for a Shilling)	Malam Bello Osman ...	116
The Tragedy of Nana Kwame Dziratuo II	Bidi Setsoafia	118

THE TOWN

Tumble-Down Woods ...	G. Adali-Mortty ...	135
Tough Guy in Town	M. Cameron Duodu ...	136
In the Streets of Accra ...	A. A. Opoku	139
Snuff and the Ashes	F. E. K. Parkes ...	143
Radio Dance Hour	Chapman Wardy ...	148
This is Experience Speaking ...	P. K. Buahin	148
Palm Leaves of Childhood ...	G. Adali-Mortty ...	157
Hot Day	Kwesi Brew	57
The Literary Society	Henry Ofori	158

Contents—contd.

		PAGE
It's Ritual Murder	Lionel K. Idan	171
The Wrong Packing Case	F. K. Nyaku	173
Lines on Korle Bu	K. M. Stewart	178
Pay Day	G. R. Hagan	183
The Walk of Life	I. K. Hoh	187
Peace	Lebrecht Hesse	188
Heaven is a Fine Place	Adolph Agbadja	189
Ata	I. K. Hoh	195
Complaint	E. K. Martey	195
To my Mother	E. A. N. Ankrah	196
Oh! my Brother	I. K. Ametsime	197
The Homeless Boy	E. A. Winful	199
The Lone Horse	S. A. A. Djoleto	200
The Perfect Understander	Albert Kayper Mensah	201
The Woods Decay	Kwesi Brew	201
On Parting	Joyce Addo	202
To the Night Insects	Albert Kayper Mensah	203
The Blind Man from the North	Albert Kayper Mensah	204
A Second Birthday	Albert Kayper Mensah	204
In God's Tired Face	Albert Kayper Mensah	204
The Executioner's Dream	Kwesi Brew	205
Had I Known	G. M. K. Mensah	205
Re-incarnation	S. D. Cudjoe	209
Ancestral Faces	Kwesi Brew	209
O Forest, Dear Forest	S. E. Archibald Aikins	210
My Sea Adventure	S. E. Archibald Aikins	212
The Passing of the King	Albert Kayper Mensah	215
Patriotism	Joyce Addo	216
African Heaven	F. E. K. Parkes	217
The Ghosts	Albert Kayper Mensah	219
The Herdsman from Wa	Kwaku Poku	224
Pa Grant *Due*	P. E. A. Addo	228
The Mosquito and the Young Ghanaian	K. A. Nyako	229
Unity in Diversity	F. K. Nyaku	230
The Journey to Independence	I. B. Dadson	231
Ode to the Hon. Dr. Kwame Nkrumah	P. H. Nehrbot	240
The Dawn of the New Era	J. Aggrey-Smith	243
The Meaning of Independence	R. K. Gardiner	251

NATIONAL ANTHEM
THE CONTRIBUTORS

The decorations used in this book are taken from **Adinkira** *stamp patterns. Each has a symbolic meaning, suited to its position in the book.*

I do so want to sing the songs
Of Homowo and
Adae;
Of Aboakyer,
Odwira and
Bakatue.
But I want to sing
In verse, not prose.
The kind of verse
Which opens wide the graves
And sets the wild ghosts free.

    Free,
    Free to fly
    Heaven-bound
    With my songs,
    Which must be heard
    In some
    Far off corner
    In heaven.

But, alas!
I must not write.
For I fear these critics—
Some critics!—
Have left at **home**
Their planes.
And, oh,
They have no wings!

                                                   Frank Parkes

A Note Of History

A brief introduction to this anthology of contemporary writing in Ghana is perhaps necessary, although those who prefer their authors to speak for themselves may omit it altogether. To say that the collection fills a long-felt want is no mere figure of speech. There is, in fact, nothing at the moment in print, apart from political and biographical writing, led by Dr. Nkrumah's *Autobiography*, which attempts to portray, in however modest a way, the life of the people of one of the world's newest sovereign states, and the ninth Dominion. Here we have no Cyprian Ekwensi, no Camara Laye, no Amos Tutuola. Why is this? To understand, it is necessary to delve a little into the past.

The first literary development known to history took place in 1763 when 500 Fante words were consigned to writing by the Rev. W. J. Muller. He was followed by a Danish African, the Rev. Christian Protten, who made a Fante grammar in the succeeding year. After this, the impetus waned. It was not until another century had passed that a Fante primer was produced (in 1860). Again, the effort came from missionaries, for the foundation of all African literatures is due to the desire for evangelisation,—first the translation of the Gospels, then devotional book and hymns, primers and dictionaries. The English missions never believed greatly in literary work—they believed in works, and Freeman, their great apostle, could not even speak Fante, although he was a man of colour, and worked in the Gold Coast for 40 years.

The main impetus in the written word came from the Germans whose missionaries from Basel were the pioneers in most of the Ghanaian languages. Of these, Twi is the most important, since it is spoken by three millions in the forest area, and acts as a lingua franca in the markets of the North. Under the name of Oji, it was reduced to writing in 1842—not an easy task, since it is a phonetic language, with simple monosyllables that can be pronounced in four or five different ways, each with a different meaning. (It is this quality of *singing* that makes drum language possible.) As with all other African languages, it is elliptic and suggestive, strong in concrete words, weak in abstractions and generalisations. Despite these difficulties, the Basel translators on the ridge at Akwapim overlooking the Accra plains, had a long and glorious literary tradition. The names are those of scholars—Widmann, H. N. Riis, above all Johann Gottlieb Cristaller. This remarkable man, who lost his wife in Africa, wrote between 1857 and 1890 no less than 28 books in Twi including the standard Twi-English dictionary, and a translation of the Gospels. Equally important was his initiative in compiling 3,680 **mmebusem** or maxims. But this initiative was never really followed up, although Cristaller had distinguished disciples, like the Rev. David Asante. Indeed, the fact that the missionaries used the Akwapim or southern dialect, as opposed to Akyem Twi, and the language of the Ashanti proved, and still proves, a stumbling block. In the late 20's, a further problem was added. The orthography of the language was altered by another German scholar, Diederich Westermann. His new alphabet (which is used in this book) reproduced with much accuracy the characteristic open vowel and nasal N of the language, at the cost of making the mission presses out of date. Down to the present time, in fact, the main names in the Twi literary scene remain those of scholars: Dr. Eugen Rapp of Mainz University, the late Professor Ida Ward, the great paralysed scholar, C. A. Akrofi of Akropong, and J. H. Nketia, the young musicologist at the University College whose work is slowly emerging from the academic, and who is represented in this book.

The most important creative contribution in Twi may have been the songs of the (Ewe) musician, Ephraim Amu, an early nationalist, who according to legend built a wooden bicycle in the 1920's, and served water in calabashes although he used imported spoons. His song *Yen ara asase* is the nearest approach the country has to a national hymn:

Yɛn ara asase ni
Ɛyɛ abodenne ma yɛn
Mogya na nananom hwiɛgui
Nya de too hɔ maa yɛn.

This is our own land
It is to us a priceless heritage
Our fathers shed their blood
To win it for us.

Fante is the coastal form of Twi, much influenced by borrowings from the European languages—Portuguese, Dutch, and especially English. As we have seen, it did not have the scholarly care lavished on the inland languages. All the same, the usual collection of devotional works were forthcoming, assisted by local scholars. Its translations were more varied—*Sinbad, Merchant of Venice, Rumpelstiltskin*, and 23 *Tales from Tolstoy*. The Fante writing seems also to have what Twi lacks, original writers. The most interesting of these is the Rev. Gaddiel Acquaah, Moderator of the Methodist Church, who only died in 1954. In 1939, he produced the first Fante epic, 1,364 lines on Cape Coast Castle, *Oguaa Aban*, with much local history of early tribes (Etsii, Asebu and Guan), the state dynasty, the star lore of the fisherman, the Ashanti war, the work of the missions:

> Oguaa Aban, Aban nwanwa siarfo,
> Ofi Efutuhen Don John ber do
> Aman horow bɛn na woenndzi no mu
> Ndofir, w'afasu mmbɔ hɔn hu?

> *Cape Coast Castle, marvellous rich encampment,*
> *How many the nations that have entered and left*
> *Your portals since Don John, Chief of Winneba?*
> *How many have not started from your walls?*

This work has convinced many of the younger generation of something they despaired of—that Fante was a rich language with a power of renewal. Next year, Acquaah published Fante **mbebunsem**, in emulation of Cristaller, although his *maxims* came to 3,041.

Besides Gaddiel Acquaah, and his relative Francis Acquaah, a number of writers in Fante flourish at the present time, J. A. Annobil, Henry Martin, and S. K. Otoo who is represented in this collection. Here is a part of a *Prayer for Every Day* by Henry Martin (Kweku Martin).

> Otumfo nye Onnyiewiei Nyankopɔn, yɛda wo ase. Egya Ansa n'egya ahanamanta a okitsa po; Kwamu ewia a ofi mpaampaa; akwantsen kuku a wɔtra wo nyansafo; ɔtakoraa kɛse a wɔko ase mbarimba; Akwambew a wotwa wo nyansafo; kyirefuwa a wonnsi wo pɔw; ɔkwankyen anoma. Samampowmu ɔdasefo, Ahomakor a eyɛ odɔtɔ. Sikampɛtsea a ehyɛ egya ne nsa. Nsu bun a obi nnyim w'ase. Enyienyiakwa a ihu botan do ɔtwe n'ananmɔn. Eminsapɔw mu gyata. Nhyira nka wo dzin.

> *Almighty and everlasting God, we thank thee. Thou art likened to the Corona constellation which makes the warm sea icy; the bright rays of the sun that reach the darkest spot in the forest; the stumpy tree in the road over which only the wise can go; the egg from which no one can tie a knot. Thou bird of the roadway. Thou guide of the dead. The single creeper that constitutes the grove. The ring on the father's finger. The deep water whose bed no one has seen. The vigilant that can trace the footmarks of the duiker on the rock. The lion of Eminsa grove! Blessings be unto Thee.*

With the other language groups in Ghana, one can only deal very briefly. Ga, the language of the people around Accra, has a Bible that dates from 1866, again the work of a German, the Rev. Johannes Zimmermann. The usual devotional books, the usual translations have followed—*Gulliver's Travels*, the works of Shakespeare, even a novel **Adote Eeleykome** (the story of a boy) written in 1950 and used in schools. Ga and its linked language, Adangbe, have some relation to Ewe, across the Volta. Here again, literature began with the labours of a German, the Rev. Bernhard Schlegel, in the 1850's, with a primer, the story of the Gospels, 104 Bible stories. An Ewe Bible only emerged in 1910. But this vigorous people have a number of translations, besides the *Pilgrim's Progress*, the work of Pastor A. Aku. They include many hymns, the *Merchant of Venice*, and *Julius Caesar*. Even more worthy of note, a pioneer in putting the Northern language of Dagbani down on paper was an Ewe school official, Tamakloe, in the early 1920's.

Such then is the background of the writing that is emerging in Ghana. It has still far to go. The Vernacular Literature Bureau, now the Bureau of Ghana Languages, which was founded to provide material for Mass Education, has over 100 manuscripts in Twi alone still awaiting publication. The magazines now published in all the main languages make very slow headway, and Twi is still held up by the conflict between the dialects and alphabets.

What then of expression in English? It is here that one wonders whether the spirit of the people inclines against creative literature, and in favour of polemical and pragmatic writing. A communal society does not have the neurosis and tensions of individualism, the diseased oyster that produces the pearl. At any rate, until the revolutionary 1940's, almost all the expression of Gold Coast writing was political journalism or law, from the pen of men like the politician Ephraim Casely Hayford, the lawyer John Mensah Sarbah, and Dr. Carl Reindorf, the Ga author of a history of the Gold Coast. In the 40's, one or two works marked a new course. Dr. J. B. Danquah, of the chief's family in Akim Abuakwa, produced the *Akan Theory of God*, and a play *The Third Woman* with a cosmic theme, set half in Heaven, and half in Tekyiman, the legendary home of the Akan race. In Anloga, on the seaboard across the Volta, the Rev. F. K. Fiawoo, a headmaster who belongs to an important Ewe family, with ramifications right through French Togoland, also published the translation of a play *The Fifth Landing Stage*, a picaresque story of the old slave days (the title refers to the stake where criminals were left to be drowned by the tide). Michael Dei-Anang, a distinguished civil servant, and the late Dr. R. E. G. Armattoe produced collections of original poetry. The scholar

J. H. Nketia has made a very interesting enquiry into *Funeral Dirges of the Akan*. But for description of life as it is lived, one has far to seek. So that, even if the literary quality of individual items in so crude a medium (from the literary point of view) as the radio may not always be as high as it should be from purely aesthetic standards, the mirror it holds up to life may prove of interest, not only inside, but also outside Ghana.

In the present collection, some manuscripts have been edited very slightly for syntax, and some for radio presentation, although most have been left exactly as they came in. Apart from the interest of a new people expressing itself, one hopes that the quality of I. K. Hoh, A. A. Opoku, and A. W. K. Mensah, to name only a few, will put their work beside the achievement of Ephraim Amu in music, Oku Ampofo in sculpture, and Kofi Antubam in painting. On the wider scale, one hopes that the living mirror of their world will assist the country to overcome the vast problems that face it in the years ahead.

Henry Swanzy
ACCRA, NOVEMBER 1957.

Ne eɖi be magbe mía denyigba
Si ƒe nu meɖu, si ƒe tsi meno
Hafi adze dzrovi bafowo ŋu la
Ʋua neyi mate afɔ.

Ne eɖi matsɔ miasi afia nye du
Kpe emeto siwo wɔ nu geɖe nam
Hafi egbe va zu alea, yome la
Ʋua neyi faa mato afɔ loo!

Should I ever be compelled to hate my Motherland
That fed and suckled me,
To please the common stranger—
Let the ship go, I follow on foot.

Should I ever be forced to use the left hand
To point to my town and compatriots,
Who did much for me in days of yore—
Let the ship go, I will follow on foot.

I. K. Hoh

The Countryside

The basic culture of Ghana is collective, its characteristic art-form, the dance at full moon.

In this section are grouped the main languages of the country —the Akan (Twi and Fante), the Ewe, the Ga-Adangme, the Dagbani and the Hausa, the six languages of Radio Ghana.

AKAN

Of these, the Akans are by far the most numerous, possibly three million people, speaking the various forms of Twi in the forest, and Fante on the coast. As may be seen, the language of the interior is less influenced by European modes than that used by the people of the seaboard, who have been in contact with white men for nearly 500 years.

The Poetry of Drums
By J. H. Nketia

The use of drums as "vehicles of language" is a widespread art in Africa. Drums, however, are not meant to compete with human speech in ordinary everyday life, but rather to supplement it in certain situations: to replace it in situations in which the human voice would be too feeble, or situations in which certain things are better drummed than spoken.

In Akan communities, the contexts of drum language are usually socially pre-determined. The husband does not talk to his wife in the home on the drums, but he may praise her in the dance arena on the drums. The drummer cannot say to the Chief: " You are not playing the game ", or threaten to stop playing the drum, but at the festival or the durbar, the drummer is privileged to do so on the drums. A Chief must always be addressed with the title " Nana ", but the drummer is privileged to call him on the drums without this. In Akan communities, the drummer is not a licensed beggar. He cannot go about drumming the praises of people for money. On social occasions, however, he is not prevented from receiving gifts of money and " drink " from dancers and those he praises on his drums. He is even allowed to ask for a drink.

Incidents in social life may be announced, though the choice of incidents that may be so announced varies from tribe to tribe. According to Carrington, the Lokele drum to announce births, deaths and marriages, but among the Akan this is not the case. Deaths of Chiefs may be announced on the drum sometimes long after the actual event, but deaths of ordinary people may not be announced on drums, as the Akan drum language is really chief-centred. On the other hand a state of emergency calls for drumming; for example, when there is outbreak of war, or fire, or when a person gets lost in the forest and a search party has to be organised.

The making of announcements, however, is only one of the functions of drums. There would be no hope for the drum language if that was its only function, in view of the radio, the telephone, the telegram, the newspaper and so on. Talking drums have a function to perform in dance situations—in giving directions to dancers, in using drum language as the basis of musical rhythms, expression of musical feeling and so on. They also have a function to perform on ritual and ceremonial occasions. Besides being used for making announcements, they are also important vehicles of traditional poetry—the unwritten literature of proverbs, personal poetry and what is sometimes described as " Drum history ".

The texts of Akan drum language may be grouped into four: First, there is the text of the drum prelude called **Anyaneanyane**, " the Awakening ".

Then there is the text of personal poetry and praises. Allusions to incidents of historical interests are common in this group.

Thirdly, there is the body of announcements and greetings. And lastly, there are the drum proverbs.

The texts of all these and the material for building up texts in new situations are traditional. The drummer, therefore, does not need to rely on his own resources, though he must have a good memory, fluency, knowledge of procedure and the knack for drumming the right thing at the right moment.

The full text of the " Awakening " may be played at about 4 a.m. on a day on which the **Adae** festival is to be celebrated, hence its title. The drummer plays it alone without an audience, though he knows that the Chief and other people will hear him and will be enjoying his poetry.

He begins with the signal **kon kon ken ken ken ken** which is interpreted as **Asamanfo, monko, monko** etc. **Akyeampon Tententen** (Spirits of the Departed, hence, hence . . . . Akyeampon the tall one . . . .). After that the drummer announces himself, and at the close he says either *I am learning, let me succeed* or *I am addressing you, and you will understand*. He then goes on to address various parts of the drum which are also " awakened " for the festival —the wood, the pegs, the skin, the string, the drum stick and the rattle on the drum and says to each one in turn: *I am learning, let me succeed.*

THE COUNTRYSIDE

He then proceeds to address the following, one by one: The Earth, God, the cock, the witch, the court crier, the executioner, all past drummers and lastly the god Tano.

Spirit of the departed,
  hence, hence, hence, hence.
Akyeampon, the tall one,
  very very tall.
Slowly and patiently I get on my feet.
Slowly and patiently I get on my feet.
Opoku the Fair one, I have bestirred myself.
I am about to play on the talking drums.
Talking drums, if you have been away,
I am calling you: they say come.
I am learning; let me succeed.

Wood of the drum, Tweneboa Akwa.
Wood of the drum, Tweneboa Kodua.
Wood of the drum, Kodua Tweneduro.
Cedar wood, if you have been away,
I am calling you; they say come.
I am learning; let me succeed.

Drum pegs knocked in by drummers,
Drum pegs, if you have been away,
I am calling you: they say come.
I am learning; let me succeed.

Elephant, Kotomirefi, that frees Kotoko,
Elephant of Kotoko that swallows other Elephants,
Elephant, if you have been away,
I am calling you; they say come.
He that saw your birth
Never apprehended your beginning.
He that knew of your formation
Never saw how you were born.
Shall we go forward? We shall find men fighting.
Shall we press on? We shall find men fleeing.

Let us go forward in great haste.
Treading the path beaten by the Elephant,
The Elephant that shatters the axe,
The monstrous one, unmindful of bullets,
Elephant, if you have been away,
I am calling you; they say come.
I am learning; let me succeed.

Ampasakyi, drum string of the bark of Obofunu,
Obofunu, the last born,
Drum string, if you have been away,
I am calling you: they say come.
I am learning; let me succeed.

The rivulet swallowed by its banks,
Yentemadu Akwakwa,
Cane, if you have been away,
I am calling you: they say come.
I am learning; let me succeed.

Drum stick of Ofema wood,
Curved drum stick,
Drum stick of Ofema wood,
If you have been away,
I am calling you: they say come.
I am learning; let me succeed.

Some iron rattles are drum snares.
Some iron snare-rattles are boisterous.
Snare-rattle, if you have been away,
I am calling you: they say come.
I am learning; let me succeed.

Earth, *Amponyinamoa,*
It is Ntikorakora that killed the defenceless one.
Earth when I am about to die, I depend on you.
When I am in life, I depend on you.
Earth that receives the body of the dead,
Good morning to you, Earth.   Good morning, Great One.
I am learning; let me succeed.

The Heavens are wide, exceedingly wide.
The earth is wide, very, very wide.
We have lifted it and taken it away.
We have lifted it and brought it back,
From time immemorial.
The dependable God bids us all
Abide by his injunctions.
Then shall we get whatever we want,
Be it white or red.
It is the God Creator, the Gracious one.
Good morning to you, God, Good morning.
I am learning, let me succeed.

When I was going to bed, I was not sleepy.
When I felt like sleeping, my eyes never closed.
All night he stood in his coop,
While children lay in bed asleep.
Early in the morning he was hailed:
" Good morning to you, Mr. Cock!"
The cock crows in the morning.
The cock rises to crow before the crack of dawn.
I am learning, let me succeed.

Condolences to you, plunderous witch.
Ampene Adu and Ampene Adu Oseewaa,
It was Ntikorakora that killed the defenceless one.
Do not kill me, sir. Do not kill me, madam,
That I may laud your name on the drums
   early in the morning.
Firampon, condolences!
         condolences!
         condolences!
I am learning, let me succeed.

Father Baa Antwi, the untiring court crier.
The chief crier, Baa Antwi, the untiring crier.
Court Crier, please come for your hat of monkey skin.
Good morning to you, Crier, Good morning.
I am learning, let me succeed.

When the Creator created the universe,
When the Manifold Creator created the world,
What did he create?
He created the Court Crier.
He created the State Drummer.
He created the Principal State Executioner.
If by chance the untiring Court Crier,
Baa Antwi, gives you meat in the night,
Be sure it is human flesh.
If the Principal State Executioner, wont to grasp,
Gives you meat in the night, do not eat it.
If he gives you meat in the night and you eat it,
Be sure you have eaten human flesh!
Principal State Executioner, wont to grasp,
Good morning to you; Good morning, fearful one.
I am learning, let me succeed.

Ɔpɔn Agyei Kyekyeku,
The drummer is drumming on the talking drums.
The Creator's drummer is playing on the talking drums.
Fair Opoku says he is about to play on the talking drums.
Let us go together. Let us return together,
And teach me the art of drumming.
Child of Dabɔ Kwasi Pepra, the drummer,
Fair Opoku says he is about to drum on the talking drums.
When he drums, let him drum smoothly and steadily, without faltering.
I am learning, let me succeed.

Duedu, the drummer,
Duedu Afari, Duedu the tall one,
Men-slayers in ambush in the dark primeval forest,
If you want to go anywhere, Man (whose natal day is Wednesday)
Wait for the light of the day.
Duedu, the drummer,
Duedu Afari, Duedu the tall one, is a warrior.
The drummer is drumming on the Talking Drums.
Opoku the fair one says he is kneeling before you.
He prays you, he is about to drum on the Talking Drums.
When I drum, let me drum smoothly and steadily, without faltering.
I am learning, let me succeed.

Ɔkwanin Akyem that fights over hills,
Ɔsekyere that snatches the powder pouch,
Ɔkwanin Akyem the noble one,
Child of Tweneboa Kodua, the noble one.
Fair Opoku says he is kneeling before you.
He prays you, he is about to drum on the Talking Drums.
When I drum, let it go smoothly and steadily;
Do not let me falter.
I am learning, let me succeed.

Adu Gyamfi Twere,
Bradu Adu Amafrako,
Adu Gyamfi Twere,
Adu, the unflinching one,
Child of Opoku the fair one,
Fair Opoku says he is kneeling before you.
When I drum, let it go smoothly and steadily;
Do not let me falter.
I am learning, let me succeed.

Chief spokesman of Adanse,
Kyei the noble one,
Chief spokesman of Adanse,
Ti Kyei of Dankyira,
The drummer is drumming on the Talking Drums.
Fair Opoku says he is kneeling before you.
He prays you, he is about to drum on the Talking Drums.
When I drum, let it go smoothly and steadily.
Do not let me falter.
I am learning, let me succeed.

Tweneboa Adu Akwasi,
Let us go to see the town of Menenkyem,
For noble Tweneboa Adu Akwasi,
You hail from Mmereyemu in Dankyira,
    where the sound of the drum never ceases.
Creator's drummer,
Fair Opoku says he is kneeling before you.
He prays you, he is about to drum on the Talking Drums.
When I drum, let it go smoothly and steadily.
Do not let me falter.
I am learning, let me succeed.

Kɔnkɔn Tanɔ, Birefi Tanɔ,
Asubirekete, the ubiquitous river,
River-god of the King of Ashanti,
Noble River, noble and gracious one,
When we are about to go to war,
We break the news to you.

Slowly and patiently I get on my feet.
Slowly and patiently I get on my feet.
Ta Kofi, noble one,
Firampɔn condolences!
        condolences!
        condolences!
Ta Kofi, noble one,
The drummer of the Talking Drums says
   he is kneeling before you.
He prays you, he is about to drum on the Talking Drums.
When he drums, let his drumming be smooth and steady.
Do not let him falter.
I am learning, let me succeed.

Across The Prah
By Andrew Amankwa Opoku
1. Departure

There is a popular saying: " When your neighbours are taking snuff and you do not join them, they say that your finger nails are dead ". In other words, whenever a new fashion comes in, everybody tries to indulge in it. When cocoa cultivation came, several people embraced it and migrated into the forest belt to make a start. But we Twi know that the starting of a new enterprise is not an easy thing, not the sort of meat an old woman's teeth can chew.

Kwame Antiri also made up his mind that he would go into the forest to try his hand at cocoa and see if he could succeed there. He had a small farm at Krabo, so he decided to wait till after the harvesting season. Besides, the year had not been a good one. His old cocoa trees had begun to die out. The farm had been seriously attacked by **akate** and swollen shoot. Concern about this alone had forced him to go and " eat " a fetish, in order that he might be protected from any possible enemies with the evil eye and who might be responsible for his troubles. Why, he had not realised that season even 50 loads from his farm! But the previous year his first plucking alone gave him over 400 loads.

One evening in December, Antiri called the head of his clan, his wife, children and other close relatives together, and told them about his plans. He made a long speech indeed. " Barima Ofori, listen and pass it on to Nana and the rest of the **abusua,** that if I call them together this evening, I do not do so for any evil purpose. The elders have said that if you sit in one place you sit upon your fortune; and because of that, the fortune-seeker does not fear travelling. I am sure you all know that this new cocoa industry had made travelling a fashion. I do not need to go far to find you an illustration. Not many days have passed by since our neighbour and friend Kofi Tuo and his family moved to Apragya (the other bank of the River Prah) to start cocoa farming. It is true that no one has followed them there, but it is also true that we have not had any ill reports about them. Perhaps in the words of the tortoise, they are saying, ' No one knows what we are doing in our shell.'

"Therefore, my Spokesman, listen and tell the old man and all my kinsmen that I too desire to go to the Prah-side, to take up a contract for one-third-share. If on arrival there I succeed in obtaining some of the land to buy outright, I shall buy it and settle there. If by the grace of **Tweaduampon,** the Almighty, we are so lucky as to find some benevolent person who will give us charge of his farm, and enable us to make a living, we shall hang on to that till we settle. But if it should happen that we should fail in our attempt, the saying has it, that ' when a trap relapses it comes back to its original position.' We shall come back to our old home and resume our ancient oil palm industry. That, I am sure, with your prayers, will never come to pass. Therefore we are met in parting. All that I am asking is, your blessing, with which you will usher me and my family forth, so that we shall not go and return as we went, but that we may rather set out and come back one day in fortune.

"Parting is hard, but what can we do about it ? Once we have been born men, our lot will for ever remain the bitter cup. You are yourselves witness that this half completed house is not large enough for us, we shall one day have to put up a little hut in addition to it. But ' Kwakye's thing is nice, it is money that did it, ' says the proverb. Again, when there is food in the house, we Twi do not say : ' Shut the door and let us go out to the bush to hunt for wild yam '. I have finished my talk to you."

So Antiri ended. Then followed Barima Ofori, who took up the word to the family, saying : " As the spokesman who does not know how to speak would say, ' Comrades, good speech for you '." The family responded, saying " Good speech is good."

It was then that the family head, Atomani, started to speak thus : " Is my nephew Ofori here ? Listen and say this to your elder brother and the rest of the family that in truth all the talk we have had today is true. Since I came to sit down here, if anyone has watched carefully, he would have noticed that a great cold has descended upon me. Today my nephew has recalled memories of sorrow for me. I am fairly advanced in age, and I have met many of our **nananom** alive. But what obtained in those days differs from present practices. Had it not been so, I would have said, ' A tree whose fruits Ananse has eaten and died of, is not one under whose shade his son Ntikuma should sit and doze.' For, permit my saying this, if there was anything to be gained from travel, I should not sit here today in this poor state in which you find me. But then the elders have said, ' The vulture's soul differs from that of the crow.' Therefore perhaps the very place where I went and met with woe may reward my child Kwame with weal. Tell him, that because I myself do not fit well into the pattern of threaded beads, I shall all the same refrain from stopping him. I give him permission to go: from the depths of my bowels, I say he may go.

One thing only do I beg him; when he goes away, he should never forget those behind, whether it ends well or ill for him, for permit me to repeat, when a trap relapses, it reverts to its original position."

Then the mother of the family, Aberewatia, also added her word and said: "We should take the matter as settled since the Elder has spoken. What is the saying? 'Water is finished in the house as soon as the elder has had his bath?' And besides, we know that 'when an elephant treads upon a trap, it relapses.' But I will add a few words because 'it is the mallet that splits the firewood.' You say you are going away to work, it is not a bad thing to do. It is a good idea.

"I hold up your arms for you. However, you are yourself aware that it is to a foreign place that you are proceeding. Take good care of yourself, so that no ill-wisher brings upon you any trouble or litigation to entangle your feet. When you go there, have no trouble with any one. Your only quarrel must be with money. Poor fellow that you are, Antiri, go and behave yourself modestly, like a simple person, and remember always what the vulture answered when his neighbours made fun of him because he fed like a fool on rubbish : 'I am using my stupidity to seek long life'. Never show off to make people hate you. Deny yourself and suffer, without complaining, in want and hunger, in order that people may not hear of you. Hunger is painful, but too much food is danger. Besides, ease after suffering is better than suffering after ease. Therefore when it comes to eating poor fare, have it so, rather than resort to display in public, which is followed by sorrowing at home in hiding. Let your wife and those who follow you in your train apply themselves to little undertakings, that will give them something to aid you; for, says the adage, 'If the male (bird) fails to weave the nest and the female does it, they both live in it.' You are setting out to labour, therefore root out any germs of vanity from your eyes. The duiker has not long to live in the forest to trouble about fat calves. You too are not going to stay long there, to be fastidious in your way of living.

"These are the few words with which I, Aberewatia, send you off. The spirits of your departed be your vanguard and rearguard. Those that have gone before flank you on your right and your left! Go out and make fortune and bring it home. I bless you again and again and again."

At this juncture, the **abusuapanyin** took rum and poured libation, and called upon the departed souls of the **Bretu** clan to follow their kinsman who was setting out on this adventure and to surround him with peace till he got to his destination, and in good time to guard him home without any mishap.

Everyone who was present and heard what the old man was saying felt a chill running over them. His words followed one another like water in a fall, and all praised his eloquence. All the while he was speaking, he was shaking like water carried in a brass pan. Some even thought he was possessed by some fetish or the souls of the departed. But as soon as he finished and was given speech-drink, he became quiet again. After this, all the kinsmen present drank some of the rum and dispersed. What was left now was packing of luggage.

Kwame Antiri made up his mind that on the very next Monday he would start. He paid a flying visit to Nsawam to purchase a few things that he would require in the forest. He bought cutlasses, axes, work dresses, gun powder and percussion caps, salt and some kerosene. When he had finished collecting all these, he said he would go into the valley beyond the Akwapim hills to take leave of his wife's people.

So he met all his relatives at their village and said goodbye to them. They in their turn blessed him and prayed for him to go and return with fortune. As the proverb says, " When the people of Nsuta eat their fill, then the people of Mampong have peace." His mother-in-law gave him seeds of the egg plant and gourds to give to his wife to take along with her, for who knows, none might exist where they were going. They followed him to the outskirts of the village, and stopped behind a stile as he went along the path. Dusk was approaching, when he got home, therefore he found some water for a bath and went to bed. The next day being Sunday, Antiri did not go anywhere; but the family made themselves a sumptuous meal and rested. After that, towards the evening, they went and bade goodbye to their near relatives, in order that none might have cause to blame them later on. Before going to bed, they carried their boxes, pots and pans and all other belongings they would not take along with them, and deposited them in the houses of their next door neighbours and relatives for safe keeping.

Early next morning, a mammy lorry came to stand behind their house and they loaded their luggage on to it. Relatives and friends came to see them off in proper fashion. They gave away the objects they no longer needed as parting gifts to friends and neighbours. These in their turn gave food for the road and other sendoff presents. The driver tooted his horn and pressed the starter. As soon as the lorry had started, all one could hear was shouts of " Don't be long! don't be long ! "

And now it was difficult to stand. Sorrow had descended on everyone. Several people had tears welling up in their eyes. It is true, they said, if you don't know what death feels like, you had better liken it to sleep, but travelling is more like death than anything else which men compare it to. A traveller is just like a dead person. As he is going, perhaps he is on his last journey. Perhaps he will not return to find those he is leaving behind, or even perhaps he himself may never return again. So most of the people who had gathered there began to shed tears. As for the children, they wailed aloud and it was some trouble stopping them. **Oseadeeyo,** the one who fulfils his promise, Kwame Antiri, had put into execution what he said in words. If the day dawned on him again, it would be in a strange land.

2. The Journey

If we were to narrate all that happened during the journey, we should be left with no leisure. Agya Kwame and his people started from Coaltar in the early morning and they arrived at Agona Swedru by mid-day. When they arrived there, they were famishing. So they asked the driver to permit them to go and find something to eat. They bought some bread and kenkey from the hawkers, and brought it to the lorry and ate it and drank water which they begged for.

But when they finished their meal and were expecting to continue their journey, the rain started unexpectedly to pour, and continued until nightfall. When it stopped, the driver informed them that the road was a bad one, and he would not be able to travel on it in the night. They were very much cast down by this news. Agya Kwame said finally that they would go and find shelter, under somebody's roof, somewhere. Even if they had to pay a sleeping fee they wouldn't mind—when day dawned they would start on their journey. True indeed, he said, it is as good to hasten as it is to delay. They were lucky, for their driver knew the house of someone from their own town, and he led them there himself, and they found suitable lodging. In short, their host and his wife showed them so much kindness that they realised that the proverb is true which says that when an Accra man goes to Kumase and meets **Nkramfoa** (a certain fish), he is delighted that he has seen his kinsman, because they both come from the sea.

At cock crow, the driver drove his lorry behind the room in which they were sleeping, and tooted his horn. The time was Harmattan season, therefore early rising was not an easy task at all; but, since one does not stop running before the pursuer gets tired, nor do travellers turn their battle against Osee into feasting on pork, they persevered, and came and boarded the lorry, after thanking their host and his benevolent wife, who had come to see them off.

The sun had risen when they reached Akim Oda. Here they hurried to the railway station, bought their tickets, and boarded the train just in time for Mokwaa country. Travel by railway was a new experience for Kwame Antiri and each member of his family, and from the start their hearts were not at ease. What gave them great trouble was the train guard who paraded up and down the train, asking awkward questions of the passengers. When he finally approached them, and told them to present their tickets for inspection, their ill luck was like that of fowls, who are always destined to perish at the end of the knife. The simple family had blundered into a compartment occupied by those who had paid double the fare they had paid. A lot of pleading had to be put on their behalf before they were hustled into their appropriate compartment.

As soon as they entered the correct class, they beheld a fellow-townsman occupying a seat there. Kwame Antiri accosted him with these words: " **Ohunkyɛree,** how do we meet ?" " We meet in peace. Nowadays I am in the Wasa country, working on a little project, but I had a message about a couple of weeks ago saying that a recent storm had blown off the roof of my house and I went to see it. I am now returning to my place in the forest once again, for it is the forest clearing season, and no labourer has leisure." They talked on for a long while, with their acquaintance who was called Kwaku Abebrese. He did not fear the train guards, because he had travelled this way so often that he had got to know them all very well. Because of that, the new-comers cheered up a bit. They had befriended the cub of the leopard: they no longer dreaded to be in the chase.

They chatted on until they reached the point where Kwame Antiri and his people were to detrain. Kwaku promised them that as soon as work slackened a bit he would come and look them up. Then the train started and they waved to their friend till the train was far out of sight.

Alone once more, the family asked for the road to their destination and found a lorry, and packed their luggage on to it. As they came from the town of the Adontenhene, in their own country, so they were going to stay in the town of the Adontenhene of the Mokwaa land, called Pewode, which lies on the banks of the Prah.

They arrived at mid-day, and asked for the house of the chief spokesman to the chief, for they hoped to lodge there. In less time than it takes to shut the eye and open it again, wind of their presence has gone round the entire town, and the news had reached those away in the fields, and even those fishing in the river Prah.

It was afternoon when the spokesman led them to the chief's house to salute the Adontenhene and his elders. They were given seats, and remained sitting for some time. It was not very long before the Adontenhene came out and sat down on the small dais in the open hall. Now the family rose and the spokesman led them to shake hands with the people assembled. When they had finished, they sat down again and the chief directed that they should be served with a bottle of rum as their " fatigue-drink ", the drink given to strangers on arrival. After this, they poured the dregs on to the ground, bowing to the chief and saying, "Thank you, sir." Then the Adontenhene asked Okyeame Paemuse to ask them their mission. The linguist stood up in the midst of the gathering, leaning upon his stick of office and said: " My father, this is what the Benevolent One says. He says it is all quiet here, but what brings you here this noontide ?"

As soon as he had finished speaking, Kwame Antiri rose up. Baring his chest, he went nearer to where the chief and his councillors were seated, and bowed low. He then began to tell his story, " Hear, O spokesman, and let it reach the Benevolent One that we do not come in evil. We are Akuapem people who come from yonder in the east. Our original dwelling place was at Coaltar on this side of the River Densu in the Abuakwa state. Our native town is Aburi which is the **adonten** or vanguard of the Akuapem state. We are cocoa farmers and it is on account of that we are here. We have heard very often about your state, that a vast virgin forest suitable for cocoa lies here. Hence, we said, we will come and see if, through Nana's kindness, he would be pleased to give us a little portion to squat on and work. I may say that some of our kinsmen have preceded us, and from what we have heard, you have received them very generously. If you were to show us the same generosity, we should be extremely grateful. In short, if we are here today, we wish to make it clear that we have come to stay. Permit me to say, we have come to man the forge, we have not come to buy a cutlass from the smith, and return."

As he finished, the spokesman thanked him, and spoke for **Ɔdeneho**, the Independent One, and for the entire state and said: " That is good tidings for you!" The gathering responded: " Good tidings is good !" Now the Adontenhene told them that they were welcome, and the spokesman and the elders came round and shook hands with them. After that, Paemuse, the spokesman, spoke again: " We meet you in peace here also. In fact some time has passed since we received word from your kinsmen of your coming. But with the arrival of your message, an evil wind blew over us, and we sent word to you to defer your coming for a short while. It is now that the storm has completely abated, that you have come, to find the state reviving once again to its former status. Indeed, there is a forest here, but a state is built with people and not with trees. That which made the Kumase state a big one was the cry, " add it on, add it on ". Therefore the Mighty One says that if indeed you have come to stay, then he receives you with outstretched arms. At present the shades have fallen, the journey cleared by your feet is long, therefore we shall disperse to allow you to go and wash, knowing that when day dawns tomorrow, the Fante nation will still be in existence."

After the linguist had finished, Odeneho, the Independent One, rose and the assembly dispersed. The strangers followed their host to the house, where he found them sleeping places, and a good bed for their leader.

3. The Farm Chosen

When day dawned, the chief and his elders assembled early in the morning and sent to inform Kwame and his two nephews who accompanied him that they were waiting to give them audience. When they arrived at the place they saluted them, and they were offered chairs to sit.

The spokesman stood up and once again enquired from them their mission. The Sannaahene (the Treasurer) who was now the patron of the strangers answered for them that they came to hear what reply Okyeame had for their demand of the previous day for some land to farm.

The spokesman asked them again to explain exactly what they wanted. Had they come to buy the land outright or would they hire the land and then give a third share of their cultivation to the owner of the land ? Or did they wish to take the land and plant the cocoa till it began to yield and have the farm split into two between themselves and the owner of the land ? Or finally would they rather prefer to hire farms ? Kwame replied that if they could have land which they could buy outright they would like that best. But if they could not, they would accept anything, since no one quarrels with his benefactor. When you have some corn in your mouth and you roast the rest, you are able to give it full time to boil.

After the assembly had given thought to the matter, the chief ordered that they should place the matter before the old women. The inner council of elders went into consultation and then informed them that the matter had been laid before the old women and they had given their consent. The strangers should be given some land to buy, for who knew, through them some prosperity might one day descend on the nation.

When it ended in this, the Sannaahene led them to thank the chief and the councillors for this favourable reply; and the young men were given three days in which to survey the entire forest, with a view to finding a suitable portion to sell to the strangers.

On the third day after this meeting, the strangers accompanied the elders to the forest, and there they were given a vast piece of land. On the north it measured 40 poles while the breadth was 45. The southern side which was bounded by the River Prah measured 38.

When they had surveyed the land they measured it up finally, and set up the boundaries, while the assistants asked for rum, a sheep and a delimitation feast. Then the party returned home to bargain for the price of the land. The Mmokwaa people explained that they wished to deal with the newcomers in a neighbourly manner so all they would ask would be for £200, a case of rum and a fat sheep. On the spot, Kwame and his family paid the cost to the last penny, and received a deed of purchase. They then repaired to the edge of the forest, and performed the **ġuaha** custom, or the customary act of conveyance.

This custom is a sign which provides evidence for future reference in a sale, exchange, or conveyance of property. It is done with a leaf, hence the name **ġuaha**, a leaf used in trade. This is how it is done: the seller and the buyer each put up a child to act in their stead. The children squat facing each other, and pass their right hands in between their thighs. Behind them are lined their sponsors. The elder supervising the sale then hands the two children the leaf of a plant called **kesenekesene**, or a strip of palm leaf. The seller's child holds the stalk end, the buyer's representative holds the tip, and each presses a cowrie under his right thumb on the leaf. Next the presiding elder orders the children to pull the leaf taut, till it snaps. When it snaps, each side takes away their bit of the leaf together with the cowrie, and keeps it somewhere for future reference. Should any litigation arise over the ownership of the land, the witnesses come forward and require either party to bring their **ġuaha** (torn leaf and cowrie) and they piece the two together, to see if they fit. The reason why children are employed in the performance of the **guaha** is that they will live longer than the grown-up witnesses.

At any rate, Kwame Antiri had his land by both rights. For the rest of the day, you should have been in the town of Pewodee to see for yourself. After the townspeople had divided the £200, they began to mourn it. The greater part, in fact, as the saying goes, slept on the backs of their mats.

4. The New Farm

Next morning Agya Kwame Antiri rose up early and roused all his people to accompany him to make a tour of the entire land to find a suitable spot where they could build their settlement. They had decided not to stay in the town, for out of sight, out of hatred. All day they covered, the ground, and finally they came upon a beautiful plateau. About two hundred yards below the plateau they saw large flat rocks frequented by flights of birds. From this they concluded that there should be water there. Sure enough, when they rushed to the spot, they discovered a spring which spouted into a box of rock. They drank some of this clean cool water to their satisfaction and named the spring **Oboadakasu** (stone-box-water).

They were too tired to do anything more that day, and, remembering further that the new moon does not emerge the same day and move across the town, they said they would just survey the site and mark it up with signs, and return the next morning to start the clearing. Then they returned home and informed their host and the women, and after they had something to eat, they went to bed.

At the first crow of the cock, on the third day, Kwame and his hosts set off again and since they have already made their tracks, it did not take them long to reach Oboadakasu. There they made their fire and began with the clearing. They continued in this manner till they had finally cleared the thorn from the bush. Soon Oseadeeyo and his children began to put up the framework of their buildings. The distance from the village to their new settlement compelled them to move into the bivouacs as soon as sufficient ground had been cleared around them.

You would admire them for their courage, when you hear the story of the early days at the settlement. But the Antiri family could not cry as they rightly should, because, they knew, one does not cry when one dresses one's own wounds.

The roofs and walls of the shelters were made of tree bark. When the wind blew, you could hear it whistling through the chinks. When you looked up at night, you could notice the stars piercing through the roofs into your eyes. When it rained, then you had to make sure that you were sleeping in the duiker's place, or else you would never sleep a wink. The black ants too were there to see to it that there was no peace at night. When these left for a bit, other disturbing insects took up their place, and said, " We don't agree." Had it not been for the fact that they slept every night with fires burning inside and around their rooms, they would have found life itself very difficult indeed, because they heard the cries of wild animals like the leopard almost every night. They even awoke in the morning some-times to find the marks of herds of wild cows, close behind their flimsy walls.

It was in the month of January, when the fruits of the **agyama** plant are ripe, that the family of Kwame Antiri went to live for the first time at the new settlement. When May came round and the corn was mature, they were a bit at ease, because their farms were beginning to yield and their livestocks was also increasing. Until then they had been living on wild yams and cassava, which they got from the forest and other people's deserted farms, or, in a crisis, on foodstuffs from other people.

You would have pitied them indeed in the months before May. You would agree that the meat of the animal poverty tastes bitter indeed. With the yam or corn, and their intestines to feed upon, the women and children made their way to Pewodee. As the proverb says, " If there is something in the house, no one will say ' shut the door and come with me to find wild yams '." So the women bent under the weight of the heavy loads, and the children were besmeared with clay, their little all-weather cloths hanging from their necks, their skin covered with sores which attracted a swarm of flies. The men, for their part, had gone to the forest with their guns.

At times the women and children only reached their settlement after nightfall from the market. When that happened, the children cried all the way till they reached home. Sometimes when they returned in good time, they would collect pawpaws all the way till they reached Oboadakasu. On other occasions when they were benighted, the children's wailing was accompanied by that of monkeys and other night criers. On reaching home, they found the hunters already returned, the animals quartered and made into hunters' soup, the men sitting in the shade of the trees switching their fly-switch and chatting away merrily. Behind them, their assistants would be smoking the venison, and others stretching the skins on the ground to dry.

When the women and children made their appearance, you would hear the " crock, crock " of the fowls, while their dogs would bark and run ahead to hover round the venison smoking on the fire. You would then hear welcoming shouts: " Here comes Enowaa, Here is Father, Hello Kwesi, Hello Afua, Afriyie, Safowa, Aku Sika."

As soon as the women arrive they join up their logs of fire. Some of them add fatigue to fatigue, and take their pots to go and fetch water. The eldest amongst them begin to peel the cocoyams. By now hunger has got the better of every one of them, and the whole settlement is quite quiet. But soon you hear the noise of the beating of fufu. Since there is plenty of venison, today's soup is going to be a very inviting one, and when the old woman puts in the soup ladle, the meat pops up in large quantities. She is all smiles, saying in her head:

Yes, is this not the way to beat the child of an Akan ?
If only I could have it like this always !

But on days when the hunters have failed, and only land crabs have been caught by the help of the children, the woman knits her brow in anger. The slightest puff of smoke sends tears welling up in her eyes. She turns the ladle with a jerk, and says thus in her head:

You take someone's child to treat her in this way,
If you don't eat, I will eat it myself.

5. " There is Knocking Where The Pioneer's Fire Burns "

At last the settlement was well established. They had made a few compounds of thatched houses, fenced around with bark of wood, because no palm fronds were to be found in the forest which could be used for fencing mats. Creepers and vines of the **ahum-kyim, nsurogya**, and **odumfee** trees were very scarce here, so that the only climber used was the thick one called **fra.** All their farms were blooming, and the plantains standing in full strength. If the forest were one that had been farmed before, there would have been no space because of the cocoyam shoots that would have sprung up. For the rains had been plentiful and all crops had made a good start. Cocoa, transplanted or sowed by seed, had all begun to grow branches. As for pineapples and sugar cane, they had even started selling some. If you had seen their fowls, turkeys, rabbits, goats and sheep, and especially the fatted ones, you would have thought that they had been at Oboadakasu quite a long time.

The Pewodee people were even coming to the settlers to buy strange new foodcrops like cocoyams, Chinese potatoes, **borobe,** garden eggs, pumpkins, spinach, citrus and other fruits.

One afternoon when Kwame had returned home to find something to eat, he heard someone say, **"Agoo."** It was his own kinsman Atweri of Mpakadan who had arrived with his family. When he had given them water to drink, he asked them the reason for their coming to Oboadakasu. Atweri replied that they had not come on any evil purpose, for he would ask permission to say that what obtains in Raintown obtains in Suntown. In other words, the same misfortunes that had befallen Kwame Antiri had befallen him too. The Swollen Shoot disease has attacked his farm, and as a result the Agriculture Department had sent labourers to cut out the trees completely. This he considered and said he would not sit down in despair, for, permit the saying, if you sit in one place, you sit upon your fortune, therefore he would move further afield to make a new start and see if that would not be best. After they had talked awhile, they went and had some raffia palm-wine, and sat down to talk over it. Meanwhile one of the lads had brought home a fat black antelope. The women prepared a nice meal with it for the visitors and then they had their baths. When night came, they talked about home a little and retired to bed.

Next day, Kwame Antiri and his guests rose early, and went to Pewodee and placed his case before the Adontenhene and his elders. He in turn promised them that he had heard what they had said, he would consult with his elders and give them his reply the next day. By then he would have time to discuss the matter with Kurontiri and Akwamu, Gyase and Adonten and have their opinion. Next day they waited till late in the afternoon before they went. When the spokesman heard of them, he assembled all the hosts. Then Kwame Antiri informed the assembly that his kinsman who had arrived did not bring any evil errand—he came in peace. He had come to find land to take on a one-third share basis to grow cocoa. He begged therefore that the owner of the forest and his elders might look at his face and give him a favourable consideration. The Chief sent the elders out into consultation. When they returned they informed the gathering that they had consulted with **Aberewatia** (the Old Woman) and she said she agreed from the depths of her bowels that the strangers should be offered any measure of land on a one-third share basis as they had applied for. The gathering applauded the decision. Then the strangers appealed further that since families group together, they would wish their portion of land to be continuous with Kwame's so as to be near them always, and so that if need be they might be able to build their settlement together. When they had settled all details, they thanked the chiefs and went back to Antiri's village late with the moon.

When the appointed day came, the chief sent his elders to demarcate the land as promised, for Atweri. In this case, since he did not buy the land outright, they did not mark it out with **ntome** trees, but they merely used natural landmarks and trees to mark off his portion, asking for one sheep and a pot of palm wine. After that, they came to an agreement on the following terms. With the exception of food crops, any other cash crops or saleable commodity that the land yielded, such as cocoa, coffee, rice, oranges etc. must be divided into three, and a third share given to the owner of the land. Every year when the annual festival came round, the family of Atweri would be expected to come before the chief to pay their homage. They would bring a panful of foodcrops, a live sheep and a bottle of rum, with which the chief could pray for them. When they had finished with all these details, they gave some presents to the chief's representatives and they left, greatly satisfied.

Later on, Odekuro Kwame Antiri also charged them a latecomer's fee, and gave them a place to put their houses. The little village of Oboadakasu was growing. Labourers and strangers, traders and hunters, soon followed the settlers and filled the village to the fullest capacity. In fact they did not lie when they said, " Settlers' fire, there is ' **agoo** ' following after it."

Little by little, the two families began to increase in numbers. The lads and lasses who went out with Kwame Antiri had reached maturity. He had bought guns for his sons Kwame Fianko and Kofi Sakyi. Even Amua Okae who was a mere toddler at the time they arrived, had grown into a young woman and had had her initiation ceremony performed for her. " Her mouth had been touched with mashed yam and eggs." And again," close trees rub against each other "—love soon began to show its head. Kofi Sakyi spoke with Akua Korewaa, the niece of Atweri, and she responded favourably. After they had concealed this for a while, Kofi Sakyi broached the news to his father. At first it was a little hard for his father Kwame, for his first born Kwame Fianko was also a bachelor. How could he as a father ask for a wife for the younger son first ? But the only young woman at the settlement who could be a possible partner for Fianko was a bit light, and he would throw off his cloth against anyone who attempted to make him marry. One does not out of shyness marry a friend's crooked legged sister.

At last Kwame Antiri went and offered head rum. The 40th day arrived soon enough, and the cock did not crow before all the young people in the neighbourhood began to pour into Oboadakasu. By midday the little street was packed full. The bandsmen set up a grand **Ositi** dance under the shade tree. Come and hear how the drums were echoing in the forest, and see the young men waving their handkerchiefs and sprinkling lavender upon the dancing maids. See the housewives moving from house to house, stewards carrying pots of wine along the only street. You would be bound to say: " Something will happen today."

Indeed, Pewodee girls are all out to impress. Yaa Boatemaa says she will give a good account of herself. She wears her hair very bushy and well trimmed at the back of her neck. In fact, when you look at her black hair brushed and sparkling, you mistake it for a hat made out of the hair of the black monkey. Her eyebrows have been painted black, her face is slightly powdered. When she enters the ring to dance, the chief drummer himself takes up the drumming, as Yaa begins to spin round like a marble. Then follows a storm of presents which rain upon her in the circle. Some throw actual cash, others shea butter and handkerchiefs. Presently, who should enter the ring but Kofi Fianko ? He dances round and round Yaa Boatemaa, till he finally embraces her, putting a gold sovereign on her forehead to congratulate her. I have finished telling you !

Oh Love, come put your hand round my neck.
Oh Love, come touch my heart with your hand.

When the bride and the bridegroom reached Kwame Antiri's house, they were offered seats and then he brought rum. His eyes were extremely red, he had stepped on palm leaves ! It was to-day that he had seen that he had become a real adult. True it is that he had his masters back at home, yet here in the jungle, he was his own **abusuapanyin**. Though a heathen, he knew that no one avoids the thumb to tie the knot, no one avoids Tweaduampon in any undertaking. Because of this he prays for the newly married couples, saying:

Nana Nyakopon drink for you,
Mother Earth drink for you,
Departed Souls of the Bretus receive drink.
Departed Souls of the Asonas receive drink.

Okumahemfo river receive drink.
Minta river receive drink.
God, host of Akuapem, behold here is your drink.
I do not call you for any evil purpose.
Today, thanks to your providence,
We are joining family with family
We are linking our children in marriage.
We pray you to descend upon them with posterity and safe delivery.
You old women that have proceeded thither
So sweep children to them,
That they bring forth at short intervals,
Delivering twins and triplets
*Let them bring forth Badu (the Tenth Child),
   and have a round little hut in addition.*
*Let them eat the sheep of the Tenth Child
   and sleep upon the Tenth Child's mat.*

The Tale Of Ananse And Twala The Thief
By T. C. Aninfeng

Some years ago Ananse left his town of Inyati on a journey, having with him a boy who carried his small leather bag. Soon they came to a certain town, where Ananse was buying something in the market, when a thief of Twala fell on Ananse and his bag, saying, " This is my leather bag, and all that is in it is mine."

Then Ananse cried out loudly for help, " Ho, people, one and all, please help me and save me from the hand of this worst of men". But the spectators said, " Come, both of you, before the Judge." So they took Ananse and Twala before the Judge. The Judge asked them the reason for their fighting and quarrelling. Said Ananse, " We have a difference, and we seek your judgement." Then the Judge said, " Which of you is it that complains of the other ? " At once Twala came forward, and said, " Judge, this white bag is my bag, and all that in it is mine. It was lost, and I found it with this worst man Kwaku Ananse and his son Ntikuma." Said the Judge, " When did you lose it ? " " Only yesterday " said Twala, " and I have had a sleepless night because of its loss ."

Then the Judge told Twala that if the bag was his he must tell him what was in it. Twala began: " Some water-bottles, a she cat, two chairs, a cow with two calves and a lion and two lionesses. Also it contains a kitchen with two doors, and the town of Takoradi, and the railway line from Luanda to Malanje, and the airport of Accra, and the island of Madagascar, and the house of your Honour, and the Map of the New World, and the River Volta, and the House of Broadcasting which will broadcast this news, and the land between the Gold Coast and Dahomey, and four Gold Coast girls, four beggars, two ships and thousands of people who are watching the football match between the Gold Coast and Nigeria. And the bench of Zulu magistrates, and a number of Bamangwato, my country-men, who will assure you, that the bag is my bag."

Then the Judge turned to Kwaku Ananse and said, " You, Ananse, what do you say ? " And Kwaku was filled with anger, because Twala had told such lies about what was in the bag. So Ananse came forward and said, " May our God give the Judge wisdom. I had in my little blue bag the town of Cape Coast, and the river Mississippi, and the Hanging Garden of Babylon, and the Rain-maker, and the Boys who are spending new Christmas, and the White City, London, and the Kingdom of Solomon, and two Sky-scrapers, and the Moon, and the man who carries the world's evil, and a thousand Executioners who will kill you, Judge, if you judge that the bag is not my bag."

After that, the Judge rose and said, " Never did tongue say, or ear hear, anything more wonderful than what you tell. Never was heard anything like what you tell. Is this bag the bottomless Sea or the Last Day, to collect so many things in it ? Open the bag." So they opened the bag and in it was a small dry fish.

Then Ananse and his son Ntikuma ran and ran and ran as fast as their legs could carry them to their home town. But the men of law caught Twala and killed him.

Ananse's Punishment
By J. K. O. Lindsay

There was a terrible famine in the little town where Ananse lived, and he, like the other inhabitants, found it very difficult to obtain food for his family.

One day, gazing despairingly at a pool of water near their farm, he saw a very wonderful thing happening: a little island on which a palm tree was growing was slowly emerging from the midst of the pool. On the palm tree were many palm nuts. On seeing the fruits on the palm tree, Ananse determined to reach this wonderful island and try to pluck some of the palm fruits to send home for food. But how he was to reach this island was his immediate difficulty.

He searched round the bush forest near the pool and soon found a little old boat which did not seem fit to bear his weight on the water. He managed to row away to the island. He had enough rest under the palm tree before he started to climb it. He aimed at dropping the palm fruits which he plucked into the boat he had left under the tree; but each time he did that he missed his target and the fruit rolled into the pool. To his annoyance, the last fruit also missed the boat and rolled into the water. As soon as Ananse climbed down the tree he plunged into the pool to recover some of the fruits. To his horror he found himself in front of a small, beautiful cottage. From this cottage came a grand old man who asked Ananse what he wanted. Nervously, Ananse told him how he had arrived there. The old man expressed his sympathies and promised to be of help to him.

The old man went into his cottage and brought out a queer-shaped cooking pot. He gave it to Ananse and added that he and his family would never be hungry again because from then onwards all food for them would be provided by the magic pot. Ananse was given instructions on how the pot could be invoked to serve food whenever it was needed. Before Ananse left the old man he tried to see how the pot worked; he invoked it to provide his first meal. He thanked the old man and told him how grateful he was for getting such a help from him for his family.

When Ananse reached home, the wicked, greedy and selfish part of him prompted him to hide the pot and say nothing about it to his wife and children who had grown weak and thin. He pretended that he was very hungry and tired because he had been out for a very long time in search of food.

After several weeks Ananse's family and many of his friends in the town noticed that unlike them, Ananse was growing robust and plump, while they were getting thinner and weaker. His activities and movements became very suspicious. He was therefore tailed and shadowed wherever he went. His eldest son, Kweku Tsin, a split personality, one day turned into a house-fly, and followed his father into his bedroom where he had hidden the magic pot. It was Ananse's mealtime and so he brought the pot out from where it has been hidden. He started invoking it to do what it always did for its master. Immediately, food was served and Ananse had his usual, secret, hearty meal. After this he went out in search of food for his family.

When Ananse left the house his son who had witnessed how the magic pot worked, went to bring it out from the hiding place. He invited his brothers and sisters and his mother to have an enjoyable meal.

Ananse's wife in her indignation wanted to make her husband ashamed and so decided to invite many of her friends to come and enjoy the excellent meal provided by the magic pot. Those who were invited were greatly disappointed because the magic pot in trying to provide enough food for the great number of visitors present overworked itself and melted.

Ananse returned very late in the evening, from the farm with very little food. When he was ready to have his meal he went into his bedroom as usual, but the magic pot was not there to serve him any food. He knew how wicked and selfish he had been so he dared not ask for the whereabouts of the pot. He went to bed without any food.

The next day Ananse went to the little island in the pool. He climbed the palm tree and started to pluck the few fruits on it. This time the fruits did not roll into the water. He descended the tree very quickly, picked up all the fruits, threw them into the water and plunged into the pool after them. Again he found himself in front of the small, beautiful cottage; the old man was sitting there ready to listen to what news Ananse had to tell him.

This time the old man gave Ananse a stick which he told him would help him to solve all his difficulties. The old man instructed him on how to invoke the magic stick to act. Ananse thanked him and left.

Ananse was too eager to know what the stick would do to help him. He therefore began his invocation, saying, " Stick, stick, I would like you to do to me what you always did to your master when he was in difficulties ". The stick immediately gave him a thorough thrashing before Ananse realised that he had to jump into the water and save himself from punishment.

Ohia And The Thieving Deer
By J. V. Mensah

There once lived upon the earth a poor man called Ohia, whose wife was named Awirehu. This unfortunate couple had suffered one trouble after another. No matter what they took in hand misfortune seemed to lie in wait for them. Nothing they did met with success. They became so poor that at last they could scarcely obtain a cloth with which to cover themselves. Finally, Ohia thought of a plan which many of his neighbours had tried and found successful. He went to a wealthy farmer who lived near, and offered to hew down several of his palm-trees. He would then collect their sap to make palm wine. When this should be ready for the market, his wife would carry it there and sell it. The proceeds would then be divided equally between the farmer, Ohia, and Awirehu. This proposal having been laid before the farmer, he proved quite willing to agree to it. Not only so, he granted Ohia a supply of earthen pots in which to collect the sap, as the miserable man was far too poor to buy any.

In great delight Ohia and his wife set to work. They cut down the trees and prepared them—setting the pots underneath to catch the sap. Before cock-crow on market-day, Ohia set off, with a lighted torch, to collect the wine and prepare it for his wife to take into the town. She was almost ready to follow.

To his great distress, on arriving at the first tree instead of finding his earthen pot filled with the sweet sap, he saw it lying in pieces on the ground—the wine all gone. He went on to the second and third trees—but there, and at all the others, too, the same thing had happened.

His wife, in high spirits and ready for market, joined him at this moment. She saw at once by his face that some misfortune had again befallen them. Sorrowfully, they examined the mischief, and agreed that some wicked person had stolen the wine and then broken the pots to hide the theft. Awirehu returned home in despair, but Ohia set to work once more. He fetched a second supply of pots and placed them ready to catch the sap.

On his return next morning, he found that the same behaviour had been repeated. All his wine was again stolen and his pots in fragments. He had no resource but to go to the farmer and tell him of these misfortunes. The farmer proved to be very kind and generous and gave orders that Ohia might have as many pots as he should require.

Once more the poor fellow returned to the palm-trees, and set his pots ready. This third attempt, however, met with no better results than the two previous ones. Ohia went home in despair. His wife was of the opinion that they should give up trying to overcome their evil fortunes. It was quite evident that they could never attain success. The husband, however, determined that, at least, he would find and punish the culprit, if that were possible. Accordingly he bravely set his pots in order for the last time. When night came, he remained on guard among the trees. Midnight passed and nothing had happened, but toward two o'clock in the morning a dark form glided past him to the nearest palm-tree. A moment after he heard the sound of a breaking pot. He stole up to the form. On approaching it he found that the thief was a bush-deer, carrying on its head a large jar, into which it was pouring the wine from Ohia's pots. As it emptied them, it threw them carelessly on the ground, breaking them in pieces.

Ohia ventured a little nearer, intending to seize the culprit. The latter, however, was too quick for him and escaped, dropping his great pot on the ground as he ran. The deer was very fleet, but Ohia had fully determined to catch him—so he followed. The chase continued over miles until mid-day arrived, at which time they had reached the bottom of a high hill. The deer immediately began to climb, and Ohia though almost tired out, still followed. Finally, the summit of the hill was reached, and there Ohia found himself in the midst of a great gathering of quadrupeds. The deer, panting, threw himself on the ground before King Tiger usually known in West African stories as a leopard. His Majesty commanded that Ohia should be brought before him to be punished for this intrusion into such a serious meeting. Ohia begged for a hearing before they condemned him. He wished to explain fully his presence there. King Tiger, after consulting with some of the other animals, agreed to listen to his tale. Thereupon Ohia began the story of his unfortunate life. He told how one trial after another had failed, and how finally he had thought of the palm wine. He described his feelings on discovering the first theft—after all his labour. He related his second, third, and fourth attempts, with the result of each. He then went on to tell of his chase after the thief, and thus explained his presence at their conference.

The quadrupeds listened very attentively to the recital of Ohia's troubles. At the conclusion they unanimously agreed that the deer was the culprit and the man blameless. The former was accordingly sentenced to punishment, while the latter received an apology in the name of the entire conference. King Tiger, it appeared, had each morning given Deer a large sum of money wherewith to purchase palm wine for the whole assembly. The deer had stolen wine and kept the money. To make up to Ohia for his losses, King Tiger offered him, as a gift, the power of understanding the conversation of all animals. This, he said, would speedily make Ohia a rich man. But he attached one condition to the gift. Ohia must never—on pain of instant death— tell any one about his wonderful power. The poor man, much delighted, set off for home. When it was reached, he lost no time in setting to work at his palm-trees again. From that day his troubles seemed over. His wine was never interfered with and he and Awirehu became more and more prosperous and happy.

One morning, while he was bathing in a pool quite close to his house, he heard a hen and a chicken tell Mother Hen about three jars of gold buried in Ohia's garden. The hen bade the chicken be careful, lest her master should see her scraping near the gold, and so discover it. Ohia pretended to take no notice of what they were saying, and went away. Presently, when Mother Hen and her brood had gone, he came back and commenced digging in that part of the garden. To his great joy, he soon found three jars of gold. They contained enough money to keep him in comfort all his life. He was careful, however, not to mention his treasure to anyone but to his wife. He hid it safely inside his house.

Soon he and Awirehu had become one of the richest couples in the neighbourhood, and owned quite a large amount of property. Ohia thought he could afford now to keep a second wife, so he married again. Unfortunately, the new wife was of a very jealous and selfish disposition. In addition to this she was lame, and continually imagined that people were making fun of her defect. She took the idea into her head that Ohia and Awirehu—when together—were in the habit of laughing at her. Nothing was further from their thoughts, but she refused to believe them. Whenever she saw them together, she would stand and listen outside to hear what they were saying. Of course, she never succeeded in hearing anything about herself.

At last, one evening, Ohia and Awirehu had gone to bed. The latter was fast asleep when Ohia heard a conversation which amused him very much. A couple of mice in one corner of the room were arranging to go to the larder to get some food, as soon as their master who was watching them was asleep. Ohia thinking it was a good joke, laughed outright. His lame wife heard him, and rushed him into the room. She thereupon accused him of making fun of her again to Awirehu. The astonished husband, of course denied this, but to no purpose. The jealous woman insisted that, if he were laughing at an innocent joke, he would at once tell her. This Ohia could not do, without breaking his promise to King Tiger. His refusal fully confirmed the lame woman's suspicions and she did not rest till she had laid the whole matter before the chief. He, being an intimate friend of Ohia, tried to persuade him to reveal the joke and set the matter at rest. Ohia naturally was most unwilling to do anything of the sort. The persistent woman gave the chief no peace till she summoned her husband to answer her charge before the assembly. Finding no way of escape from the difficulty, Ohia prepared to die. He called all his friends and relatives to a great feast, and bade them farewell. Then he put his affairs in order—bequeathed all his gold to the faithful Awirehu, and his property to his son and servants. When he had finished, he went to the Assembly Place where the people of the neighbourhood were gathered together. He first took leave of the chief, and then commenced his tale. He related the story of his misfortunes—of his adventure with the deer, and of his promise to King Tiger. Finally he explained the cause of his laughter which had annoyed his wife. In so speaking he fell dead, as King Tiger had warned him. He was buried amid great mourning, for everyone had liked and respected him. The jealous woman who had caused her husband's death was seized and burnt as a witch. Her ashes were then scattered to the four winds of heaven, and it is owing to this unfortunate fact that jealousy and selfishness are so widespread through the world, where before they scarcely existed.

"The Iron Bar"
The Honourable Nana Kwasi Akuffo, Omanhene of Akropong-Akwapim, Born At Akropong, 21st June, 1863
By C. V. Hutchinson

The consecration of a Chief.
Was a solemn state of function
That was brought down from old Egypt
By the clans of the Akans.

With your cousins the Ashantis and Fantis,
With your cousins the Akims,
You have observed the ceremonies
Which justify the pride of an old race.

Nana, the spiritual exponent of an ancient dynasty,
You have been twice ritualized;
You have been twice washed in the Nile of the Mountains;
Your person and mind are sacred with blessings from ancestral throne rooms.
In the grove of departed Kings,
In sincerity and strength,
You have made declarations
To uphold your country's rights.
Though faith has juggled with you,
None can injure you, a priest of the soul,
When your "centre" is on guard.
Your country adores your tenacity.
You are the great " IRON BAR " of our parable:
" Where the iron bar is laid, it is there laid for reason ".
The iron bar is the King builder,
The girder that strengthens walls.
Your strength is as great as that of the iron bar.
Time has annealed your mind
To weld great walls together—
The great walls of your enlightened face.

Adonten, Nifa, Benkum, Kyidom and Gyase,
All are brimful of intelligence.
Only a Solomon can govern Solomons
And bring unity and progress unto them.

Nana, while you and your processors have been occupied in State affairs, for the welfare of your people,

Your subjects have proved themselves industrious,
By fostering the cocoa tree.
One cocoa-pod from abroad in the hands of your intelligent farmers,
Has raised the millions of trees and the thousands of men to affluence
    and respect.
Glancing at your nation, we find it replete with civility;
With a language compatible to its good manners;
One that can read and write in its own tongue;
A Christian nation, indeed, an adorable nation.
With such material in your hands,
A written propaganda on useful industrial topics
Could reach most for digestion
And ensure desirable ends.
We must not forget your women.
With cultivated habits,
They are graceful in their movements and speech,
And most of them are also educated.
Comely and faithful, with a knowledge of moral vows.
They are great mothers of a great country.
All that your women do meets with approbation,
Even to their soft voice.
Their civility and courtesy
Have often called reflection.
Of the good work of the Basel Mission.
The country wishes as much success to the new mission.
Nana,
There is the pleasure of recording the bravery of your ancestors.
They distinguished themselves at the battle of Katamansu
And took spoils that are much prized among your regalia.
On the mountains of health and oxygen, things are done in excelsis.
Your state was the first to grasp the Christian religion from Basel.
In hospitality and in state functions,
You emulate your ancestors.
The Iron Bar!
There is reason for our epitome;
May your wisdom assist you in raising your intelligent men still
    higher,
As patterns for their kinsmen.
Strength comes from security;
Wisdom from experience;
Prosperity from the muscles;
The country compliments you and your nation.

Drum Proverbs
By J. H. Nketia

Nearly every Twi proverb quoted in ordinary speech can be reproduced on drums. Many resourceful master drummers, therefore, often interlard their drum calls and praises with suitable proverbs of encouragement, incitement and so on.

There is, however, a set of proverbs which are specially constructed for use on drums, among them the proverbs of the Akantam dance played by the Fontomfrom orchestra. The proverbs of Akantam have regular metrical form, in which sound, and absence of sound or pause, have definite temporal relations. Repetitions of words, phrases or even sentences are made for metrical or special musical effect.

The Akantam, then is a cycle of proverbs. Each piece containing at least two proverbs, is preceded by certain introductory rhythms. The proverbs are then played rhythmically in unison by all the heavy drums, the small drums providing the musical " ground ". The piece is then concluded with musical rhythms merging into the introduction of the next piece. One of the proverbs quoted in each piece serves as a refrain and occurs with other proverbs in the cycle.

It is the drummer of the talking drums that indicates which proverb is to be played next in the cycle. The introductory and concluding rhythms are, therefore, meant to give him time to think while the dancers in the ring are kept busy.

> The Path has crossed the River.
> The River has crossed the Path,
> Which is the elder ?
> The Path has crossed the River,
> The River has crossed the Path,
> Which is the elder ?
> We made the Path and found the River.
> We made the Path and found the River.
> The River is from long ago.
> Truly the River is from
> The Creator of the Universe.
>
> *Akyereko Kwagyan,*
> *He crosses the Nwabe River and gets to Ohwim.*
>
> Red Ant, you are clinging to the bunch of kola nuts.
> Red Ant, you are clinging to the bunch of kola nuts.
> You are not going to pluck it, either to eat or to sell.
> What is the Red Ant going to do with the bunch of kola nuts ?

Duiker Adawurampon Kwamena,
Who told the Duiker to get hold of his sword?
The tail of the Duiker is short,
But he is able to brush himself with it.

Tree-bear, condolences to you.
He strolls high up, double bent.
Tree-bear, condolences to you.
He strolls high up, double bent.
Tree-bear, Kwaduampon Kyerefo,
I dwell in my house of thicket.
When I speak, men hear me.
And what do they say to me?
Tree-bear, condolences to you.

Duiker Adawurampon Kwamena,
Who told the Duiker to get hold of his sword?
The tail of the Duiker is short,
But he is able to brush himself with it.

The hunter that kills the elephant
   may eat the wood-mouse.
The hunter that kills the elephant
   may eat the wood-mouse.

Duiker Adawurampon Kwamena,
Who told the Duiker to get hold of his sword?
The tail of the Duiker is short,
But he is able to brush himself with it.

What of yours do we take,
What of yours do we take?
Squinted eye will kill me.
Squinted eye will kill me.
Looking awry is from long ago.
This squint is from the time of creation.

Duiker Adawurampon Kwamena,
Who told the Duiker to get hold of his sword?
The tail of the Duiker is short,
But he is able to brush himself with it.

Rustling noise by the wayside
Means what creature?
The wood-pigeon, the wood-pigeon!
Wood-pigeon, Seniampon,
He goes along the path
   eating grains of millet.
Condolences, Wood-pigeon!

Duiker Adawurampon Kwamena,
Who told the Duiker to get hold of his sword?
The tail of the Duiker is short,
But he is able to brush himself with it.
Koroboa Apatupere Kuruwa,
When it plucks pepper, it swallows it
   with a gulp.
It is using the pepper as medicine for its chest.
Duiker Adawurampon Kwamena,
Who told the Duiker to get hold of his sword?
The tail of the Duiker is short,
But he is able to brush himself with it.
" I am bearing fruit ", says Pot-herb.
" I am bearing fruit ", says Garden egg.
Logs of firewood are lying on the farm.
But it is the faggot that makes the fire flare.
Duiker Adawurampon Kwamena,
Who told the Duiker to get hold of his sword?
The tail of the Duiker is short,
But he is able to brush himself with it.
If the Odum tree claims to be a deity, he deserves death.
If the Odan tree says he is a deity, he tells a lie.
With what do we carve out drums?
We carve drums with Cedar wood.
Condolences to you, Tweneboa Gyan Nkansa.
Duiker Adawurampon Kwamena,
Who told the Duiker to get hold of his sword?
The tail of the Duiker is short,
But he is able to brush himself with it.
The great Toucan,
I have bestired myself.
Let little ones lie low.
Duiker Adawurampon Kwamena,
Who told the Duiker to get hold of his sword?
The tail of the Duiker is short,
But he is able to brush himself with it.
Kurotwamansa, the Leopard, lies in the thicket.
The thicket shakes and trembles in the dark forest.
Duiker Adawurampon Kwamena,
Who told the Duiker to get hold of his sword?
The tail of the Duiker is short,
But he is able to brush himself with it,

The antelope lies in its thicket-lair,
The hunter lures him with his call.
The hunter deserves to die,
For he will not answer him.

Duiker Adawurampon Kwamena,
Who told the Duiker to get hold of his sword ?
The tail of the Duiker is short,
But he is able to brush himself with it.

Wild Bear, Akuampɔn,
How did it happen that the water buck
   got tied up in cords ?
It is because he could not hold his tongue.

Duiker Adawurampon Kwamena,
Who told the Duiker to get hold of his sword ?
The tail of the Duiker is short,
But he is able to brush himself with it.

The tall forest palm tree is bent low.
The tall forest palm tree is bent low.
Whether it will fall or not,
The jealous one is mighty anxious,
   over-anxious, over-anxious;
The jealous one is deeply anxious,
   over anxious, over-anxious.

Duiker Adawurampon Kwamena,
Who told the Duiker to get hold of his sword ?
The tail of the Duiker is short,
But he is able to brush himself with it.

We were fifty thousand when we started.
We were thirty thousand when we returned.
All of them were left behind around the river,
Led by the Clock-bird, foremost of all.
Condolences to you, Drummer, veteran of war.

Akyereko Kwagyan,
He crosses the Nwabe River and gets to Ohwim.

Let us all go on the journey.
Let us all go together.
The multitudes that went have not yet returned.
Let us all go on the journey.

Akyereko Kwagyan,
He crosses the Nwabe river and gets to Ohwim.

Something of a bitch of Creation,
Something of a bitch.
My mates and I went to the river.
When they got hold of me,
I thought they were going to carry me across the river.
But they threw me plump into the river.
If I could not swim, I would have got drowned.

Akyereko Kwagyan,
He crosses the Nwabe river and gets to Ohwim.

Ever since the Creator created things,
Ever since the Manifold Creator created things,
The drummer is treated gently and kindly.
A person becomes a drummer
    that he might get something to eat.

Duiker Adawurampon Kwamena,
Who told the Duiker to get hold of his sword?
The tail of the Duiker is short,
But he is able to brush himself with it.

The Wild Bear has gone mad.
What shall we do with him?
What shall we do with him?
The Wild Bear has gone mad,
What shall we do with him?
We shall leave him on the path of the armadillo.

Duiker Adawurampon Kwamena,
Who told the Duiker to get hold of his sword?
The tail of the Duiker is short,
But he is able to brush himself with it.

Real fowls are pecking grains of millet.
Ruffle-feathered fowl, are you one of them?
Real fowls are pecking grains of millet.
Ruffle-feathered fowl, are you one of them?

Duiker Adawurampon Kwamena,
Who told the Duiker to get hold of his sword?
The tail of the Duiker is short,
But he is able to brush himself with it.

Akyereko Kwagyan,
He crosses the Nwabe river and gets to Ohwim.

Afram

By Andrew Amankwa Opoku

Asuo meresen
Asuɔkɔɔ a me ti da mmepom
Mede m'ani makyerɛ pom
Mifi Tete Kwaforoamoa
Ɔdomankoma Bɔrebɔre bere so
Misii mu nyɛ nnɛ
Menam kwan so ara
Asuo meresen.

Asuo meresen
Asukɔkɔɔ a ɔnam afaben mu
Menam aboɔ so
Menam anwea so
Mapere kwantenten
Mapompono apompono
Biribi ntumi nsianka me
Asuo meresen.

Asuo meresen
Meresen nhema
Owia befie na menam kwan so
Owigyinae de akwantemfo
Bɛba abegu nsunoa
Asutwafo pata me a,
Merennyina mma wɔnnsen
Asuo meresen.

Asuo meresen
Menam nnuhini mu
Menam bunu so
Mise enhuru a, na ehuru
Wugye kyim de wo nan susu a,
Mɛwɛre wo adi m'anim.
Kwan-nua na mepɛ
Asuo meresen.

Asuo meresen.
Mede me mma retwam
Wusi adwokuo o,
Woto darewa o,
Ebiara nyɛ me ahuro
Otidie na ɔrekorɔ no
Adwene na watu atene no
Asuo meresen.

Afram
By Andrew Amankwa Opoku

River, I am passing
Red River whose head lies in the mountains
I have pointed my face to the sea
I am from **Kwaforoamoa** of old
Ɔdomankoma the Creator's time
I started not today
I walk on the way still
River, I am passing.

River, I am passing
Red River that flows through red earth
I go over stones
I go over sand
I have traversed a long way
I have meandered and meandered
Nothing can stop me
River, I am passing.

River, I am passing
I am passing at dawn
By sunrise I shall be on the way
Noon will bring travellers
To crowd my fords
When the rowers plead with me
I shall not stop to make them pass
River, I am passing.

River, I am passing
I go over roots
I go over the depths
I bid it foam up before it foams
If you dare me and measure with your foot
I shall make you slip and go before me
A wayfarer companion is what I want
River, I am passing.

River, I am passing
I am passing with my children
Set a basket trap
Or string in hooks
Neither of these to me is foam
There goes the **Otidie** fish
The mudfish sallies forth
River, I am passing.

Asuo meresen
Merebu mafa wo tintimman so
Ɔdom ne mmɔnkɔ
Nti na wode atena atware me a,
Ɛnde kɔda gye w'ahome
Ɔkɔtɔ ne abebeɛ
Na wɔyɛ mmɔborɔ
Asuo meresen.

Asuo meresen
Meresen na mfuomfoɔ nso mmɛsen
Asuogya na kwaeɛ da
Wusuro a, w'afuo da saguan so
Mede m'abɔmma ne nwankɔ rekwati wo
Woankɔ Asuogya a, agye atwa
Mewe a, na worehweɛ, nso
Asuo meresen.

Asuo meresen
Ogyamma abere ma akuafo resisi haban
Mmɔforobɔfoɔ akoduru dupire
Ɔpatweri a esi asukɔn so frɛfrɛ me
Oduahyɛn akogyina ntɛntɛnoa akohu nea ɛreba
Ɔkɔre Brasiam ataa kyikyi ahu akyirikyiri
Ɔpɔw ne ahude apinkyim mmusuo reba, nso
Asuo meresen.

Asuo meresen
Da bi na wɔde kyinii
Na egye me taataa
Adum ne adupɔn ne abako
Na ɛtɔ nwini gu me nsuo so
Ma ɛsono ne oburum ne ɛkoɔ
Bɛnom dwudwo wɔn ho
Asuo meresen.

Asuo meresen
Nnɛ de menam mfua ne nkyerekyerewa so
Tɛtɛ Kwasi adaworoma
Wakɔfa sikadua kookoo ne amammum
Abɛto ɔman mu, ama
Abusua ngu nkuruwa bio
Obiara rehwete kɔ nea sika wɔ
Asuo meresen.

River, I am passing
I am overflowing your dams
If it is for **Odom** and lobsters
That you dam me up
You had better go home and rest,
Only the crab and the river snail
Deserve to be pitied
River, I am passing.

River, I am passing
Ogyamma fruits are ripe, calling upon farmers to mark out their farms
New settlers have gone to start new farmsteads
The palm fronded shed on the bank calls me
The monkey has espied from the tree tops what is approaching
The eagle has seen afar through the telescope,
Civilisation and inventions ushering in calamity, but
River, I am passing.

River, I am passing
Let farm-goers pass on too
The forest is on yonder bank
If you fear the crossing, your farm will be in the grassland
I am diverting my tributaries and lagoons from you
If you do not cross, you have nothing but roots
You can drain my waters to catch the fish only when I dry up but
River, I am passing.

River, I am passing
Once my course was canopied
And my steps were timed to the flutter of the leaves
Adum and mahogany and **abako**
Cover my waters with shade
For the elephant, the buffalo and bush cow
To drink and regale themselves
River, I am passing.

River, I am passing
Today I go through wastes and arid savanah
Thanks to Tete Quashie
He has brought the tree of wealth and national upheaval
Into the country
And clans no longer group together
But each individual scratches towards where money is
River, I am passing.

Asuo meresen
Meresen akoģye m'ahome
Misii kwan so mmɛn ha
Daa menenam aboɔ ntam
Mede nnɔnnɔ ne nhaha rekɔ
Ɔtwe a ɔda adukurom na ɔtentɛn yi
Mayiri makɔfa aģyanka asi dufunu so
Asuo meresen.

Asuo meresen
Nnomaa bɛba abeģuare
Na Asunoma abenu
Kyɛadeɛ nnyina nnye aseda
Ayeyi nim ne wura
Nso ɛmfom kwan da
Ebedi m'akyi abɛto me enti
Asuo meresen.

Asuo meresen
Meresen abasam o,
Batafo nunu bɛka me a,
Mede serew senkɔ ara
Obi mfa Ɔsɛeko nyɛ mprakowe
Afe kwan wɔ hɔ yi,
Ɔnammɔn biako na efi ase
Asuo meresen.

Asuo meresen
Meresen no sɛn nie
Kurotwiamansa anomeɛ wɔ me
Ɔdɛnkyɛm ahomeģyebrɛ minim
Ɔpantene awoeɛ a obi nhu
Ɛhyɛ me kwankyɛn pɛɛ
Me na misuw ɔkyekye nkesua
Asuo meresen.

Asuo meresen
Mede sikafuturo rekɔ
Meso abohemmaa
Metaforo dwetɛ sɛ dufua
Minim dadeɛ fibrɛ, nso mintu nkomena
Wodɔ me mu asukɔ a, siadeɛ
Nso merekɔ pom akɔpɛ ahode
Asuo meresen.

River, I am passing
I set out on the road a long while ago
Daily I pass between rocks
I am bearing all and sundry away
The duiker that sleeps in the hollow of the buttress is afloat
My flood waters have caught the orphan that floats on the wet log
River, I am passing.

River, I am passing
Those returning from farms will come to bathe
And the fisherfolk will dip nets for fish
The benevolent one stops to receive thanks
Praise knows its owner
Therefore it never misses the way, it is never lost
It will follow and overtake me, therefore
River, I am passing.

River, I am passing
I am passing by yards
When the wild pig ploughs right up to me
With laughter I flow on
No one engaged in battle with Osei tarries to feast on pork
A year's journey we know
Begins with a single step.
River, I am passing.

River, I am passing
I am passing how?
The leopard's watering place belongs to me
The crocodile's lair is known to me
The hatching place of the python
Is hidden near my bed
I spoil the lizard's eggs
River, I am passing.

River, I am passing
I am carrying gold dust away
I carry precious stones
I lick silver, like pastules
I know the source of ore yet I dig no mine
When you dive into me, prosperity
Yet I am going into the sea to seek wealth
River, I am passing.

Asuo meresen.
Afram asubosom menam ntɛmso
Asiemmire Bɔfoɔ se
Ogye kwan akɔ asuogya
Ɔdomankoma bɔfoɔ
Ma me kesua ansa
Obi nkwati me nkɔ srɛso
Asuo meresen.

Asuo meresen
Mede asɛm na ɛrekɔ
Nsunoa asɛm a mpanyin aka
Ɛno na sunsuan apra abrɛ me yi
Miyiri trɛw kɔka he ara a,
Ampaniampa ne ampampara wɔ hɔyi
Ɛtentɛn ani ara afebɔɔ
Asuo meresen.

Asuo meresen
Nnan rebɛyɛ kuro
Na mewɔ hɔ
Kurow rebenyin ayɛ ɔman mihui
Mpanyin rehyehyɛ amammuo na menam ha
Ɔman ne man hyeɛ ne me ara
M'adanseɛ ho nni akyinnyeɛ
Asuo meresen.

Asuo meresen
Mebɛtoo nananom, mahu mmanana
Tete a atetew yi
M'anim ara na wɔbɛpompam
Nea ɛmmaa da wɔ m'anim
Da a Ataara se ɔrekɔhye po
Me na mede no kɔeɛ
Asuo meresen.

Asuo meresen
Ataara renoa sa akɔtow abenetuo,
Watwa abo ayam atuduro
Kodiabɛfoɔ adeɛ wɔ ɔne ne dɔm
Ɔbɔfoɔ kum ɛkoɔ a,
Minni ne nam
Ɛkoɔ kum bɔfoɔ a, menkɔ n'ayie, enti,
Asuo meresen.

River, I am passing
Afram, the sacred river, I move fast
Asiemire the Hunter says
He wants a chance to cross to the other side
Odomankoma the Creator's Hunter
First give me an egg because
No one goes to the plains without crossing me,
River, I am passing.

River, I am passing
I bear a great tale
Decisions of great moment taken yonder by the elders
Have been swept to me by the drain waters
However wide I spread my floods,
So long as truth remains truth
It will continue to float for ever
River, I am passing.

River, I am passing
Before the hunting camp grew into a town
I was present,
When the town was going to become a state, I saw it.
When the elders were making the constitution I was passing this way.
I am the very boundary between nations
My testimony is beyond doubt.
River, I am passing.

River, I am passing
I met the grandsires, I have seen the grandchildren
This decaying past
In my presence would be repaired
The unknown lies ahead of me yonder
The day when Ataara set out to set the sea on fire
I bore him thither
River, I am passing.

River, I am passing
Ataara is preparing to go and fire the war-declaring shot
He has made his bullets and ground his gunpowder
He claims whatever belongs to the Kodiabe people.
When the hunter kills the buffalo
I don't partake of the meat,
When the buffalo kills the hunter, I don't go to his funeral, therefore
River, I am passing.

Asuo meresen
Ɔkoforoboɔ di nkonim a,
Ɔbɛte ne ntoa abedware me nsuo
Odi nkoġu a, me mu na ɔhohoro ne nisuo
Ɔsa no anyɛ asabi a,
Ɔde ne sadwa bɛba me nsunoa
Wɔhye pra so a, me na mɛkyerɛ wɔn amanfo
Asuo meresen.

Asuo meresen
Adu Bɔfoɔ de Ɔsɛe dɔm rekɔ Krepi
Me na mitwaa no asuo
Ɔde Akwasi Buroni dommum resan aba
Mekyɛɛ no adwene ne brɛsuo
Anyankonsɛm beduru Ɔsɛekurom a,
M'adaworoma na Ramesa retwa akorɔ
Asuo meresen.

Asuo meresen
Buruku si do afura nwera abɔ hyire
Ɔtɛteaamforo mma yɛnkɔ a,
Ose dabi ; osi asɛm so
Abantenten a obi amfa nsa anto
Osuo aboro boɔ
Esi dea esie ara, me deɛ,
Asuo meresen.

Asuo meresen
Merekɔ ama nkyirimma aba
Mpanyin nyin kyɛ a,
Mmofra tɔ ape
Mnɛɛmmafoɔ a ɛnom me
Anyi me ayɛ nakamfo me po a,
Akyikafoɔ a ɛbɛba abɛto suġyenee bɛka
Asuo meresen.

Asuo meresen
Nso mitie asukɔn so asɛm
Aġoru asɔ wɔ hɔ sɛ biribi
Aheṅgoru ne atɛntɛ ġu so dennen
Dwomfrɛfo afrɛ dwom abɔ m'abɔdin
Gofomma de wɔn asaw asian abehyia me
Mmabaa hi wɔn ho sɛ ntɛw wɔ pa so nanso
Asuo meresen.

River, I am passing
When **Ɔkoforoboɔ** (Victor of the Heights) wins victory
He will cast off his ammunition bag to bathe in my waters
When he suffers defeat he washes his tears in my waters
If the battle fails to be staged,
He holds his drinking parties on my banks,
If they become annihilated I will show their ruins
River, I am passing.

River, I am passing
When Adu Bɔfoɔ was marshalling Ɔsee's hosts to Krepi,
I ferried him across
When he returned bringing the European captive
I gave him gifts of mudfish and drink of welcome
If Christianity will reach Ɔseekurom (Kumase)
It was through my help that Ramseyer crossed over
River, I am passing.

River, I am passing
Buruku stands yonder clad in white cloth and besmeared with white clay
'Ant-never-climbs' has refused to accompany me
He will not, he stands there for a cause.
High tower that was not built by any hand,
Rain drenched stone,
It remains where it is but as for me, I am
River, I am passing.

River, I am passing
I am going to make way for the generations that follow
When adults live too long
Children become stunted
If the present generation who drink my waters
Do not praise and extol me
The latecomers who come to find clean water will speak.
River, I am passing.

River, I am passing
Yet I listen to what goes on on the banks
A grand play is in full swing there
State drumming and horn blowing continue in earnest.
The precentors have called me by my appellations
The dancers have descended to invite me with their dance
The damsels spin themselves like marbles upon the table.
River, I am passing.

Asuo meresen
Momfa atumpan nye me akurum
Mamame hommere so
Mommɔ me adawuro mu
Me ara na merekorɔ yi
Me ara na mereba yi
Mego mu brɛbrɛ saa ara de akɔ
Asuo meresen.

Asuo meresen
Merekɔ me nkyi
Afiri huan a, ɛkɔ ne nkyi
Towia agyigye gonn agu borɔ akyi
Aka kakraa na ɔsram ama ne ho so
Aturukuku ne aburuburo repɛ birebuo
Ɔbrɛfoɔ nso amee rebutu ne nkukuo
Asuo meresen.

Asuo meresen
Sa ara na ɔdesani nso resen
Asukɛse meresen na asuwa ɛ ?
Ɔbirɛmpɔn resen na awurakwaa resen
Biribi nsianka me na asianka wo bi
Yɛto ɔbotan a, yɛabu afa so
Ɔwew ne mayɛ bere mu nyinaa
Asuo meresen.

Asuo meresen
Meresen akɔbɔ asukɛseɛ mu
Asuo Firaw abegye me adɔm
Wasi ntɔkwanan te Dodi retwɛn
Mede akɔntɔnkɔntɔn yi ara
Ɔkwantiaa yɛ amane
Ɔkwantenten akwaaba
Asuo meresen.

Asuo meresen
Me nso mɛkɔ dea mifire
Odwotwafoɔ mmɔ akɔkoraa wiram
Minya miduru Firaw mu a,
Na me brɛ ano atwa apirefie
Ɔno ara de me bɛkɔ akɔma
Nana Bosonopo, akɔto adikanfoɔ
Asuo meresen.

River, I am passing
Salute me with **Atumpan** drums
I have risen in majesty
Sound the gongs in my praise
I who go forth
Am the same that returns
River, I am passing.

River, I am passing
I am going yonder to my origins.
When a trap relapses it reverts to its original position.
The setting sun is ablaze behind the horizon
In a few moments the moon will be up
The pigeons and doves seek their nests
The tired one has fed to repletion and is turning his pots
River, I am passing.

River, I am passing
In the same way man is passing too.
Big river I am passing and what of the rivulet ?
The royal lord is passing and the servant is passing
Nothing stops me and so nothing stops you too
When we come across the rock we flow over it
During the dry season and the floods alike
River, I am passing.

River, I am passing
I am passing to join a bigger river
River Volta has invited me to be her ally
She is standing in readiness at Dodi waiting
I continue meandering thus, for
Short route is trouble
Long route deserves welcome
River, I am passing.

River, I am passing
I too shall go whence I proceeded
The highwayman never grows into an oldman in the bush
Soon as I reach the Volta
My toils shall have come suddenly to an end
She herself will bear me to
Nana Bosonopo to meet those that have gone before
River, I am passing.

Written at Mankrong on the Afram—14–9–55

A Fisherman's Day

By Samuel K. Otoo

I am a Fanti fisherman. My work is fishing. It is an interesting and absorbing occupation, nevertheless, it is hard and dangerous as you will find later on. Two things make me like being a fisherman: one is to provide myself and my family with the daily means of livelihood; the other is to work, so that I may be useful and helpful to the community in which I live, that is, to be a good citizen. Other than these two reasons, I am proud to add that my work provides jobs for other people such as lorry drivers who distribute fish inland, fishwomen who dress or cure the fish for the markets, canoe makers who make my canoe from big trees, and for many other people. I live, generally speaking, on the coast close to the sea, but I can carry on my work also in the interior in big rivers like the Volta, the Pra and the Tano as well as in big lagoons like the Keta Lagoon, or in lakes like Bosomtwe in Ashanti.

My working tools are expensive, the two most expensive being the canoe and the net. I use different sizes of canoes to suit the different kinds of nets and traps, as well as different sizes of meshes to suit the different kinds of fish I catch. Due to the rapidly changing economic conditions, canoes like the **Semahen** which used to sell for 7s. or 8s. two decades ago now cost anything between £10 and £14. Nets have also grown in size and cost and so has the cost of other fishing tools such as oars, paddles, calabash, sailcloth, and fishing yarns and cords. Correspondingly the price of fish has also gone up.

Fishing is hazardous, all-weather work. I have always to war against one or the other of the elements as winds, weather, waves, currents and time. Sometimes the sea becomes rough, often unexpectedly so, and I am in danger of losing either my tools or my life or both. Unfavourable winds may send my canoe drifting to places far away from my home and make me face death by starvation. I am equally at the mercy of strong eastward or westward currents, while mist may hide all landmarks—my principal guide for coming back to land after fishing at sea—and force me to cast anchor even though I may be only a few hundred yards away from my own native beach. There is another risk from mists. Sometimes they are so thick that the net I have set and my craft cannot be seen by a passing steamer, and so I may lose my craft and my life. To avoid this danger I sometimes carry whistles and these I blow to attract the attention of an advancing steamer, or I may flash torchlight or scratch matches to show the whereabouts of my net and canoe. At other times too I have to race against time and manage to land my fish fresh, otherwise I may be forced to dispose of them rather cheaply because red-eyed herrings, my principal daily catch, do not sell for much. I have no power craft at present to help me win my race for time, and I do not carry a time piece either; I have to rely wholly and solely on my skill to use the oar and the reading of the positions of some principal stars at night and of the sun by day. I have no compasses to help me find my whereabouts, but I rely on some familiar landmarks as forests, tall trees and prominent buildings to help me come ashore when I fish far away out at sea.

Let me describe to you a typical day's work with the **Adii** (ali) net, the most important net used by fishermen in Ghana. The net can be used, tanned or plain white, throughout the week save on Tuesdays—the day of the Sea God according to some fishermen, but to me, just a day of rest. My canoe seats nine people; in the early days of this net a crew of three could fish effectively, but not today. The herrings, they say, have become so wide awake that a small **Adii** net cannot cope with them successfully. In the early days just a packet of the net measuring 400 yards in length was used to advantage, but today anything less than two packets cannot be regarded as good enough.

Now for the preparation. All the crew of the canoe should be told in advance to prepare, that is, they should get in readiness such articles as **kenkey** or **garri** (farina), charcoal for kindling fire, and water. In the early days water for the crew was carried in three or four beer or gin bottles lashed together by cords, but with increased crew this water holder has become inadequate, and water has to be carried in kerosene tins. More recently it is carried in an American four-gallon petrol can, as it has a lid which can be screwed on tightly to avoid wastage and it can also stand rough use.

We are going on a night fishing. When any member of the crew wakes up at night, he first looks up in the sky and reads the positions of some principal stars. If it is too early he may go back to sleep, but fear of oversleeping keeps him awake, and so he may go to the beach to ascertain the tide. (Fishermen usually prefer to put to sea when the tide is high as this means less labour when pulling the canoe to the surf. Also fish is more easily caught when the tide begins to flow out or in). When conditions are favourable both as regards time and tide, he returns home quickly and wakes up the rest of the crew. The necessary materials are rushed to the beach and the canoe dragged or lifted on the shoulders to the shore. With everything in its right place in the canoe, we push off and out into the sea. If the wind is favourable we crowd on sail, otherwise we reach the herring area by using our oars only—a very tedious affair.

To be able to know that we have reached a good area we do a number of things. First we stop rowing and keep as perfectly still as possible and then take soundings, that is, find the depth of the sea, by using our depth-finder—a long string to which a lead weight is attached. The depth-finder will not only tell us how deep the area is but will also tell whether the area is free of submerged rocks by a peculiar feel on the string. The depth is measured in fathoms. After the soundings one or more of the crew would stand on the seats. What for? To find out whether there are shoals of herrings in the area. You see, when we stand on the seats we are thus able to see further and deeper. When no signs of herrings are seen, they sit down and we begin to use our oars again. We keep on taking soundings and looking for herrings until we are successful.

The net is not cast at random. We first get nearer to be sure that the fish seen are herrings. After this we also find out the direction to which the fish are moving. If they are moving to the west, for example, we start casting the net towards the west, about 30 or 40 yards away, race with the shoal, get past them and close the net in behind them in the form of a ring. The " buttons " (pieces of string about six or eight inches long each fixed at two yards intervals on one edge of the net) are " closed ". The fish find themselves in captivity, but not without struggle to win back their freedom. When they find that their forward advance is arrested by the net, they turn back and make for the rear only to find that the way there is also closed. They then move helter-skelter in the net trying to find a way of escape. When the area the net has been set in is deep beyond the width of the net, the fish may succeed in passing out from under the net if the lead weights used in the net are not heavy enough to keep the net stretched down to the bottom, or they may run away over the corkwood floats if the lead weights overbalance the floats. The number of corkwood floats and lead weights of an **adii** net, therefore, keep changing in quantity to suit the area where the herrings are found.

When, however, the herrings are successfully trapped, this is generally what follows: some of the crews in the canoe jump into the ring and swim helter-skelter to frighten the fish and drive them into the net, or, when cold, stamp their feet in the canoe to obtain the same effects. Thus frightened, the fish make for the net and are caught, save those which are too small or too big for the meshes. The net is later drawn into the canoe, and the fish caught removed from the meshes. The net is later drawn to the canoe and the fish caught removed from the meshes. The net is washed. If a good catch has been made, those on land can determine it when they see the helmsman using the long oar when the canoe is not under sail. You see, with a good quantity of fish in the canoe the helmsman finds difficulty in using the ordinary oar to steer. A good day's catch may fetch £20, £40, £80 or more, according as fish is scarce or not.

A means of catching fish inshore is by the use of the drag-net. This net can be used at any shore which is free of rocks. It consists of two arms each about 100 to 200 yards long with a bag at the centre. The net is cast in a semi-circle, and each is pulled ashore by ropes measuring about one mile or more. The arms guide any fish thus enclosed ultimately into the bag of the net. It is used extensively by colonies of Ewe people scattered all along the coastal strip of the Country.

Another means of catching fish is by hook traps. Each trap may consist of between 200 and 500 hooks arranged on a line. Suitable baits made generally of herrings, fresh or salted, are used, but in the absence of herrings small river or lagoon shrimps serve the purpose very well. This kind of traps suffers from periodic scarcity of baits and calls for the provision of artificial baits at present unknown in this country. Local initiative, however, has discovered the use as baits of a special kind of the sisal plant which is prepared and used when herrings cannot be got for trapping such fish as the jack mackerel (**Opaa**) and the kingfish (**Safor**). Hook trappers use small canoes which seat two or three people. Other useful nets are woven locally for various fishes.

Every experienced fisherman must know the names and movements of some principal stars, the names of winds, the fisherman's S.O.S. signal, must be able to read and interpret the weather particularly with regard to storms, and the fisherman's fish-finding instrument. Truly, every skilled fisherman boasts of his knowledge of star-lore. The fisherman's S.O.S. signal is simply one of raising up an oar by the canoe in distress. When the signal is seen every canoe in the vicinity speeds up to the rescue of the distressed canoe irrespective of whether its crew are strangers or not. If the sign is seen from on land, food and water are rushed to the inmates of the canoe, and if the distressed crew want to come ashore their helmsman is replaced by one of the rescue crew or a native one who happens to know these waters well. Those who fail to observe this rule are severely punished by the **Apofohen**, the chief fisherman, because for such emergencies strangers sojourning in the village pay a beach rum (footing fee) of 10/- or more to the **Apofohen** for distribution among the fishing community.

The fish-finding instrument is an interesting device. Every experienced fisherman, should be able to identify certain common fishes, for example, herrings, both by sight and ear. When surface-feeding fish come to the immediate surface of the sea in shoals, their bluish-black backs make the area of the sea black, and this discloses their presence in the neighbourhood in daytime. At night their scales appear as flashes of small electric lights and they can be seen several hundred yards away. When the herrings cannot be seen on the surface, the fisherman uses his fish-finding apparatus. The apparatus consists of an oar and the right or left hand according to which of his two ears is more sensitive. He pushes the blade of his oar into the sea and grasps the end of its handle with his fourth finger and lower part of his palm. The other fingers close and the thumb also bends either to meet the tip of the first finger or is placed over it. The fisherman then listens through the hollow thus made. He just can know what is going on beneath him, as for example, the presence of rocks (if the area is not too deep) and the ' cries ' of every surface-feeding fish present. Fish constantly cry for food, for their mates, and also when they are caught in a net. In the last instance the cry attracts its kind to the area, and in their mad rush to be of some assistance to their fellows, are themselves caught by a net. An experienced fisherman can distinguish the cry of many common fish.

Yet another important device used by fishermen is the buoy or wooden floats for locating the ends and somtimes the middle part of nets and hook traps. (It is made generally from the **Dwumba** tree). In the case of the **adii** net as with other nets, it warns late-comers of the presence of the net or trap and acts as distinguishing mark. A recent sailing device introduced by the late Sir Arnold Hodson, a former Governor of the Gold Coast, is the ' lampool ' (the lee-board) which checks drifting when a canoe is under sail. The apparatus is a piece of board, 4" long by 1" or $\frac{1}{2}$" wide; it is pushed into the sea on the side of the sail and tied with ropes to the seats.

There is other important fishing gear such as the spear or the calabash, but I feel special mention should be made of the common match stick. To many people its importance begins and ends in lighting the lamp or fire or pipe, but to the fisherman it renders a very useful and important service besides this, for it is the match stick which enables him to buy or place orders for **adii** nets with the suitable meshes he requires. A mistake with regard to its length will affect him badly; if its lighting end is made too big or too small it also will upset him, because he does not know and cannot recognise the figures $1\frac{3}{4}$, $1\frac{7}{8}$ (inches) and the rest used by manufacturers to show sizes of meshes, but with the match-stick in his hand he can choose or place orders for suitable nets. The match-box itself also serves as a pouch for his tobacco as well as a purse for his odd coins.

The Ghana African is a great music lover, but there is none more a lover of music than the fisherman. I, in common with my comrades, sing whenever I can. The oars used for propelling the canoe are applied simultaneously to keep the balance of the canoe, and to secure this as well as to wear away fatigue, the crew of a canoe sing. We sing when dragging our canoe to or from the beach; we sing while mending our net as well as when we are at play. A recent local invention to aid singing during our playtime or to help us to relax is the 'Piano', a hollow wooden box with a slit across which are fastened four or five pieces of thin steel or bamboo of varying weights and sizes. This, with vocal accompaniment, provides ample music for an evening's pastime.

Komenda Hill
By Bossman Laryea

O Komenda Hill, in war a bastion,
In peace a forum, I've seen your glories,
And, O, am yours and all for now and aye.
Far and wide you dominate land and sea
Whose breezes salute you, and consecrate.
Your dome the sun scans, your vales the rains deepen,
But, indomitable, you stand serene.
O sacred hill, I hail your large welcome:
To the student knowledge distilled, the sick
Wine, the traveller beauty, the care-worn peace.
But it's your surrounds I adore, and keep:
Their morning greens dew-pearled, and fresh, and pure;
Their farms well-patterned, varied, and tended
To raise a royal palm, to milk-fill the
Coconut, to sugar the cane, to feed the grain.
Then night, which hides your wounds and brings perfumes,
Invokes the moon's light or a harbour's eyes
To jewel your sea, its rocks and its sands.
Live on, O noble hill, live on, to shelter
Your soft-eyed student, to guard your secrets,
To protect your peasantry, and to change
My doubts to faith, my heart's darkness to light.

Ahanamanta
By Joseph Ghartey (Kobena Gyata Akwa)

Yaw mframa no aba ha bio,
  Mframa a otwa sukwadwom !
Ɔama ndua mpo rutwa ewuo,
  Abɔdze nyina hwer ahom,
    Nhataw wusuu
      Apo egu.
Ndɛ ndua nyina dzi adagyaw,
Hɔn asɛm ayɛ yayaayaw.

Mframa dzesɛɛfo bɛn nye yi !
  Ɔaporow nhyiren nyina egu,
Nhyiren haanhaan fɛfɛɛfɛw pii,
  Hwɛ, ndɛ hɔn huam nyina etu,
    Ndowa rigyam,
      Woeku hɔn tam.
Nhyiren na wɔdan hɔn tsena,
Na afei wɔbɛdan woana ?

Ndzɛmba nyina ayeyɛ mbɔmbɔmm,
  Wonnya beebi nngyina koraa,
Nsu pa na ɔma hɔn win fɔmm
  Ma wonya egyinanan pa
    Nna ɔawew yi,
      Ntsi wonnsi pi,
Ahanamanta ! Na dabɛn
Na ɔbɔkɔ ma dɛw aabɛn ?

Ampa, awerɛhosɛm a,
  Dɛ sɛɛ na yaw esisi dɛm,
Naaso 'hanamanta repra
  Wiadze ama enyigyesɛm,
    Ama nsutɔ
      Na ahotɔ,
Ɛhɛɛ, orisiesie wiadze
Ama prɔmprɔmyɛ, ama mee.

Dɛm na bra biara mu so tse.
  Ɔyɛ a na 'hanamanta
Esi m' ma tsir abrɛ adze,
  Ɔyɛ a na ɔato nyinsuwa,
    Aber yi mu,
      Mma nnkyi nyinsu
Na ɔpɛ dze twa esusuow,
Aber awiadze serew bio.

Harmattan

Sad the wind is here again,
The wind lamenting,
Even the trees are wailing,
All nature losing strength;
The leaves have
Deserted the trees,
Leaving all of them bare;
What a sad state they are in!

O what a killing wind!
It has blown off all the flowers,
Many were the flowers in lovely bloom,
Today all their sweetness is gone.
The bees are mourning,
The wind has spelt their doom,
On flowers their life depends,
On what now will they live!

Sadness has descended upon everything,
All nature is bewildered.
It is water that gives them life
And the wind has taken all away;
The drought
Has made them weak.
Harmattan! When will it depart
And leave the world to happiness?

Yes, it is sad
That decay and sorrow so encompass us
Yet Harmattan is clearing
The world for good tidings,
Is clearing the world
For rain and happiness,
Yes, it is preparing the world
For plenty, contentment.

And so it is with every life,
Sometimes Harmattan sweeps through it,
Then heads are bowed with sorrow,
Sometimes inevitable seems weeping.
At such times
Do not weep,
For rains surely follow drought
When the world smiles again.

Mami Takyiwa's Misfortune
By Albert Kayper Mensah

O you who think the deed more worth than thought,
Consider the misfortune of Takyiwa.
Her fisher-husband kept her, but loved her not,
And had with her a fair but ailing daughter.

Each day except Tuesday Takyiwa would sit
In rain or sunshine at the market place
Doing all she could to eke a profit
From the carefully priced fish her husband brought.

She did not care how scanty was her cloth,
Though she was never seen in dirty rags.
Her care was how to send her daughter forth
Into the cruel world she knew too well.

Without some trade or training she was doomed;
But nothing she could do would make her father
Think of stopping habits that consumed
The needed cash to spend on training her.

He carefully calculated every penny,
Insisting that Takyiwa had to give
A satisfactory estimate of any
Expenditure or sales she daily made.

He would not scruple to invade the kitchen
To count the peppers one by one and check
And would up-braid Takyiwa for an itching
Palm, if he felt unsatisfied.

He did all this to get sufficient money
To spend on private pleasures—and the church.
For of the pastor's flock there wasn't any
Who gave so much at harvest or to charity.

The pastor asked him once about his wife,
And why she went to market every Sunday
Instead of thinking of eternal life
By joining him to church and Leaders' Meeting.

He told the pastor he had done his best
To help the wife to quit her heathen ways,
But she would treat his efforts as a jest,
And do her worst to set his daughter against him.

On one occasion he donated money
To the happy pastor, asking public prayer
For the quick conversion of his wife and only
Daughter, to the ways of thrift and piety.

At last the daughter grew, and took a lover,
And it was clear she was to have a baby . . .
And O what fury did the man uncover
From every hidden corner of his being.

He promptly told the pastor and his flock
Of the horrid scandal of his only daughter;
And he moved high heaven with unholy talk
To force his daughter's man to pay a fortune.

He felt the money his, by right of custom,
And even wouldn't tell the wife how much;
But he bought a new canoe, as was the custom,
And lent it to some fisher-friends for profit.

And when at last the daughter had to leave
To make a home as best she could with him
Who, for her sake, had made his parents grieve,
Her father gave her nothing but his prayers.

This wickedness so tore the other's soul,
That she was taken ill and died.
And ugly rumour that she stole,
Made her passing little known or mourned.

To give the widower spiritual relief
The pastor went to see him day and night.
He praised his cheerful calmness under grief,
And put it down to strength and depth of faith.

At last his time too came. He had to die,
And could not ask his daughter to his side;
But before he breathed his last and tedious sigh
He sent for the pastor and his elder flock.

They felt the end of a great soul was near,
And asked that he might speak some spiritual word
To cheer the congregation who would hear
The pastor's carefully worded funeral speech.

Then, in a grave but feeble voice, he said . . .
"The thing that all my life I've loved and sought
Was fame . . . no matter how it came to me.
I thought the deed more worthy than the thought.
But now I know the reason is the thing ".

He begged the silent pastor to forgive
The wicked life of lies he'd fooled him with,
And try to get his daughter to forgive
Him too, for killing the unhappy Takyiwa.

This said, he died; but on his face was such
A tragic look that made the pastor weep;
And looking round, he knew *that* life was not worth much
To God; because in his own room

He saw a mighty idol on a stool;
And along his pillow was a row of talismans,
While a smelly juju formed a mouldy pool
Around which empty raw gin bottles lay.

New Life At Kyerefaso
By Efua Theodora Sutherland

Shall we say
Shall we put it this way
Shall we say that the maid of Kyerefaso,
Foruwa, daughter of the Queen-mother was
as a young deer, graceful in limb. Such she
was, with head held high, eyes soft and
wide with wonder. And she was light of foot,
light in all her moving.

Stepping springily along the water-path, like a
deer that had strayed from the thicket
springily stepping along the water-path, she
was a picture to give the eye a feast. And
nobody passed her by but turned to look
at her again.

Those of her village said that her voice,
in speech, was like the murmur
of a river quietly flowing beneath
showers of bamboo leaves. They said her
smile would sometimes blossom like a lily on
her lips and sometimes rise like sunrise.

The butterflies do not fly away
from the flowers, they draw near. Foruwa was
the flower of her village.

So shall we say,
Shall we put it this way, that
all the village butterflies, the men, tried to
draw near her at every turn, crossed and
crossed her path, and said of her,
' She shall be my wife, and mine, and
mine, and mine '.

But, suns rose and set,
moons silvered and died, and as the days
passed Foruwa grew more lovesome, yet she
became no-one's wife. She smiled at the
butterflies, and waved her hand lightly to
greet them as she went swiftly about
her daily work,
' Morning, Kweku
Morning, Kwesi
Morning, Kodwo ', that was all.

And so they said, even while
their hearts thumped for her,
" Proud !
Foruwa is proud . . . and very strange. "

And so the men when they
gathered would say
'There goes a strange girl. She is not just
stiff-in-the-neck-proud, not just breasts-
stuck-out-I-am-the-only-girl-in-the-village
proud. What kind of pride is hers ?'

The end of the year came round again, bringing a season of festivals. For the gathering in of corn, yams and cocoa, there were harvest celebrations. There were bride-meetings too. And it came to the time when the Asafo companies should hold their festival. The village was full of manly sounds, loud musketry and swelling choruses.

The path-finding, path-clearing ceremony came to an end. The Asafo marched on towards the Queen-mother's house, the women fussing round them, prancing round them, spreading their cloths in their way.

    Osee ! rang the cry,
    Osee to the manly men of old !
    They crouched like leopards upon the branches.
        Before the drums beat
        Before the danger drum beat, 'Beware !'
        Before the horns moaned
        Before the wailing horns moaned, 'Beware !'
They were upright, they sprang
They sprang
They sprang upon the enemy.
    But now, blood no more !
    No more thunder-shot on thunder-shot.

But, still we are the leopards on the branches
We are those who roar and cannot be answered back
Beware, we are they who cannot be answered back.

There was excitement outside the Queen-mother's courtyard gate.

'Gently, gently', warned the Asafo leader.
' Here comes the mother-queen.
　　Spread skins of the gentle sheep in her way.
　　Lightly, lightly walks our mother-queen.
　　Shower her with silver
　　Shower her with silver for she is Peace '.
And the Queen-mother stood there, tall,
beautiful before the men, and there was silence.

　　' What news, what news do you bring ?'
　　she quietly asked.

　　' We come with dusty brows from our path-finding, mother.
　　We come with tired, thorn-pricked feet.
　　We come to bathe in the coolness of your peaceful stream.
　　We come to offer our manliness to new life.'

　　The Queen-mother stood there, tall
and beautiful and quiet.　Her fan-bearers
stood by her, and all the women clustered near.

　　One by one the men laid their guns before her feet, and then
she said,
　　' It is well.　The gun is laid aside.
The gun's rage is silenced in the stream.
Then let your weapons from now on be your minds and your hands'
toil.
　　Come maidens, women all, join the men in dance for they
offer themselves to new life.'

There was one girl who did not dance.

　　' What, Foruwa !' urged the Queen-mother.　' Will you not
dance.　The men are tired of parading in the ashes of their grandfather's glorious deeds.　That should make you smile.　They are
tired of the empty croak, We are men, we are men.
They are tired of sitting like vultures upon the rubbish heaps they
have piled upon the half built walls of their grandfathers.　Smile
then, Foruwa, smile.

　　Their brows shall now indeed be dusty, their feet indeed thorn-
pricked, and ' I love my land ', shall cease to be the empty croaking
of a vulture upon the rubbish heap.
Dance.　Foruwa, dance !'

Foruwa opened her lips and this was all she said:—

'Mother, I do not find him here.'

'Who? Who do you not find here?'

'He with whom this new life shall be built. He is not here mother. These men's faces are empty, there is nothing in them, nothing at all.'

'Alas, Foruwa! alas, alas! what will become of you, my daughter?'

'The day I find him, mother, the day I find the man, I shall come running to you, and your worries will come to an end.'

'But Foruwa, Foruwa,' argued the Queen-mother although in her heart she understood her daughter. 'Five years ago your rites were fulfilled. Where is the child of your womb? Your friend Maanam married. Your friend Esi married, both had their rites with you.'

'Yes mother, they married, and see how their steps once lively, now drag in the dust. The sparkle has died out of their eyes. Their husbands drink palm-wine the day long under the mango trees, drink palm-wine and push counters across the draughts board all the day, and are they not already looking for other wives? Mother, the man I say is not here.'

This conversation had been overheard by one of the men, and soon the other heard what Foruwa had said. That evening a new song was heard in the village.

> There was a woman long ago,
> Tell that maid, tell that maid,
> There was a woman long ago,
> She would not marry Kwesi
> She would not marry Kwaw,
> She would not, would not, would not.

One day she came home with hurrying feet, I've found the man, the man, the man.

> Tell that maid, tell that maid,
> Her man looked like a chief
> Most splendid to see
> But he turned into a python
> He turned into a python
> And swallowed her up.

From that time onwards there were some in the village who turned their backs on Foruwa when she passed.

Shall we say

Shall we put it this way

Shall we say that a day came when Foruwa with hurrying feet, came running to her mother. She burst through the courtyard gate and there she stood in the courtyard, joy all over.

And a stranger walked in after her and stood in the courtyard beside her, stood tall and strong as a pillar. Foruwa said to the astonished Queen-mother.

" Here he is, mother, here is the man ". The Queen-mother took a slow look at the stranger standing there strong as a forest tree, and she said,

" You carry the light of wisdom on your face, my son. Greeting, you are welcome. But who are you, my son ? ".

" Greeting, mother ", replied the stranger quietly, " I am a worker. My hands are all I have to offer to your daughter, for they are my riches. I have travelled to see how men work in other lands. I have that knowledge and my strength. That is all my story ".

Shall we say

Shall we put it this way, strange as the story is, that Foruwa was given in marriage to the stranger.

There was a rage in the village and many openly mocked saying, " Now the proud ones eat the dust ",

Yet shall we say

Shall we put it this way that soon, quite soon, the people of Kyerefaso began to take notice of the stranger in quite a different way.

" Who ", some said, " is this who has come among us ? He who mingled sweat and song, he for whom toil is joy and life is full and abundant ? "

" See ", said others, " what a harvest the land yields under his ceaseless care ! "

" He has taken the earth and moulded it into bricks—See what a home he has built, how it graces the village where it stands ".

" Look at the craft of his fingers, basket or kente, stool or mat, the man makes them all ".

" And our children swarm about him, gazing at him with wonder and delight ".

Then it did not satisfy them any more to sit all day at their draughts under the mango trees. " See what Foruwa's husband has done," they declared. " Shall the sons of the land not do the same ? "

And soon they began to seek out the stranger to talk with him. Soon they too were toiling, their fields began to yield as never before, and the women laboured joyfully to carry in the harvest.

A new spirit stirred the village. As the carelessly built houses disappeared one by one, and new homes built after the fashion of the stranger's grew up in their places, it seemed as if the village of Kyerefaso had been born afresh.

The people themselves became more alive and a new pride possessed them. They were no longer just grabbing from the land what they desired for their stomach's present hunger, and for their present comfort. They were looking at the land with new eyes, feeling it in their blood, and thoughtfully building up into a permanent and beautiful place for themselves and their children.

" Osee " ! It was festival time again.
" Osee " ! blood no more.
Our fathers found for us the paths,
We are the road-makers.
They bought for us the land with their blood,
We shall build it with our strength
We shall create it with our minds ".

Following the men were the women and children. On their heads they carried every kind of produce that the land had yielded and crafts that their fingers had created—Green plantains and yellow bananas were carried by the bunch in large white wooden trays. Garden eggs, tomatoes, red oil palm nuts warmed by the sun were piled high in black earthen vessels. Oranges, yams, maize filled shining brass trays and golden calabashes—Here and there were children proudly carrying colourful mats, baskets and toys which they themselves had made.

The Queen-mother watched the procession gathering on the new village playground now richly green with recent rains. She watched the people palpitating in a massive dance towards her where she stood with her fan-bearers outside the royal house. She caught sight of Foruwa. Her load of charcoal in a large brass tray which she had adorned with red hibiscus danced with her body. Happiness filled the Queen-mother when she saw her daughter thus.

Then she caught sight of Foruwa's husband. He was carrying a white lamb in his arms, and he was singing happily with the men.

She looked on him with a pride that cannot easily be described.

    The procession had approached the royal house.
    " See!" rang the cry of the Asafo leader.
    " See how the best in all the land stands,
    See how she stands waiting,
    Waiting to wash the dust from our brow
    In the coolness of her peaceful stream.
    Spread skins of the gentle sheep in her way,
    Gently, gently,
    Spread the yield of the land before her
    Spread the craft of your hands before her,
    Gently, gently,
    Lightly, lightly walks our mother-queen for she is peace."

No Ten Without Nine
By Lionel Idan

Deep in the jungle Africa,—
Please, worry not your maps—
Where sun and rain show off their strength,
And heat men's energy saps,
Where leaves are green throughout the year,
And fruits big monkeys claim,
There stood a hut owned by a man,
Kweku Ananse by name.

A running stream below a hill
Did boast of a precious store,
For, all along its marshy banks
Were crabs ne'er seen before.
These crabs Kweku had claim on them
For, the marsh was his by birth;
And anyone who dared intrude,
Did so at risk of death.

Old age had stamped its mark on him
When last I saw his face;
It was the day he made new traps
His old ones to replace.
Next day he took his palm-leaf sack
And snailing down the hill,
He sudd'ly heard the shouts of boys
Which made him keep quite still.

They were three tough, delinquent boys
In search of rats not crabs.
They hadn't seen nor were they near
Those crabs now caught in the traps.
But if old Kweku picked a crab,
That would show them the way;
For, they would leave no stone unturned
To see them gained the day.

The sun climbed up, the stream rolled by,
Still Kweku did not stir;
The matter was so grave that he
Must handle it with care.
At last he called to mind a plan
On which his fame did thrive;
He had evolved this plan from his
Philosophy of life.

" Hei, you, my little bonny boys !"
Kweku called out to them.
" Why waste your time hunting for rats
Which sane men do condemn ?
My traps have caught big golden crabs
Among all crabs the best;
Take as much as can fill your palms
And help me pick the rest."

" Thank you, old man," replied the boys,
Who reached there in a flash;
" But we can see you are too old
To plod along this marsh.
Old man, do please enjoy a rest
And leave all in our care;
We'll set your traps and bring your crabs
Before we get our share ".

So saying they all rushed away,
Ere long they all came back;
They'd set the traps, and brought the crabs
In Kweku's palm-leaf sack.
Each had as much as filled both palms;
In fact, each had just two.
They thanked Kweku and left the place
With smiles of gratitude.

" Well, such is life; " old Kweku said.
" It's got a lot of fun;
He who would want more than his share
Without resort to the gun,
Must learn from this philosophy
Which suits all types of men:
If you allow your friend his nine,
You'll get more than your ten."

EWE

The Ewes are a people living east of the River Volta, with a language linked more closely to Dahomey and Yoruba than to the Akans. They have two main centres—the long coastal spit, sometimes not more than a hundred yards wide, that runs for over forty miles from Aflao to the Volta, past Keta, Anloga, and a dozen other villages and towns. The other centre (in Ghana) is in the mountains of Togoland round Ho and Hohoe, spreading into the lowlands of Kpandu. The larger part of this vigorous people lie, of course, over the frontier, in French Togoland.

Ewe Poetry
By Israel Kafu Hoh

Pedants and purists scornfully denounce the existence of anything like African Poetry, still less, anything like Ewe, Twi or Ga Poetry; but like Louis Pasteur in science, one can say "Poetry is of no country". Whoever can speak, whoever can sing, whoever can dance, has the art of poetry. The fact that European poetry is established and advanced, is no guarantee that no other nation can write and publish her own; but there is one thing which must be avoided: the slavish imitation of European poetry and the mechanical translation of it into an African language. Though the idea and pathos can be fairly closely represented, the metre and the rhythm can never be exactly copied. Here are beautiful verses from Gray's *Elegy*:—

> Full many a gem of purest ray serene
> The dark unfathomed caves of ocean bear:
> Full many a flower is born to blush unseen.
> And waste its sweetness on the desert air.

These have been rendered in an Ewe setting:

> **Sika kple adzagba geɖee ta**
> **Ði gbɔ ɖe atsiaƒu gɔme.**
> **Seƒoƒo nyuiewo ke ɖe dzogbe**
> **Eye woƒe atsyɔ kple vévẽ tsi gbe si.**

But this has not the same weight and grandeur as the English original of Thomas Gray, though the thought and feeling are almost identical. No, these Ewe translations of English poetry are not what we call Ewe Poetry. But this is in lines directly written or spoken by Ewe bards, men, women, and children, to agree with an Ewe metre and an Ewe rhythm. Listen to this lullaby:

> Tu, tu ġbɔvi ; tu, tu ġbɔvi,
> Dada me' afea me o,
> Papa mel' afea me o,
> Meka nafa 'via na
> Ɖevi, d̦evi dzudzɔ ' via kpoo !

Away, away, little goat!
Mother is not in the house,
Father is not in the house,
For whom will you cry?
Little child do not sigh.

No one can deny the genuineness of this Ewe poem and the magic spell it casts upon the worried child who sleeps calmly after a few rounds of its repetition. That is the effect of a true poem. It must excite a responsive feeling commensurate with the weight of its words, rhythm and metre.

Listen to these shanties:—

> Yiwoe, yiwoe xexee míele,
> Yigãa ġbea ku, xexee míele.
> Kɔkɔlikɔlikɔhɔe,
> Ŋɔliwoe léa 'bayaxa d̦e ta, Ŋɔliwoe.

Hey ho, we are in the open;
The sword is unsheathed,
We are in the open.
Cock-a-doodle doo,
Ghosts are carrying brooms, Ghosts.

Follow the activity of the rhythm, the lightness of their expressions, the vivacity of their metre, and you are moved to short, quick, strenuous movements.

The same rhythm is characteristic of the Ewe madrigals often used on moonlit nights by children who play in the streets in jocund revelry. The faster ones excite youthful activities, the slower ones soothe the instincts of pity and admiration. Here are two examples:

'Mad̦e xɔ nɔvi srɔ̃ 'lanyo na wòa ?
Aye ! aye ! 'lanyo na woa ?
Tɔvi xɔ tɔvi srɔ̃ 'lanyo na wòa ?
Ganya menya ġblɔna o. Ed̦o 'ġblɔ fe.

> Some one covets a neighbour's wife
> Will it please you?
> Hey ho! Will it please you?

> Should a brother covet a brother's wife,
> Will it please you?
> It is not easy to talk of money.
> It is now time for it.

These are the more simple forms of Ewe Poetry, commonly used by children, men and women under various conditions. There is a more serious form of poetry in which the rhythm is more slow, and more irregular, and the effect of admiration or pity deeper and stronger.

Atia ḑe manɔ ġaġlãġbe
Xevi suea ḑe nawɔ dɔfe ḑe 'dzia,
Dzoġbetia ḑe manɔ ġaġlãġbe
Xevi suea ḑe nawɔ dɔfe ḑe 'dzia?

> Would there be a tree in the open
> To nestle a little bird?
> Would there be a desert plant in the open
> To nestle a little bird?

Tua neġblẽ mayia 'ʃe matu bu
Tue nye ame l' abɔ
'Meaḑe ġbe hã 'mea ḑe 'lɔ
Aʋa la ġblẽ nye Gasu ġake
Meġado ġaliġo d' aʋa me.
Tua neġblẽ mayia 'ʃe matu bu.

> Damage the gun, I'll go home for new.
> The gun is the steward at hand.
> When one is unwilling, the other will not.
> Though the odds be against me, Gasu,
> Yet shall I persist steadfast in battle.
> Damage the guns. I'll go home for new!

Lɔnyelawo ku vɔ keŋ, monye dzaka.
Ekpɔtɔ nye ḑeka ḑe futɔwo dome:
Kpɔ̃ kpl' aġbaliwoe va tɔ si ġe
Aye dzi, aye dzie woano
Esia tae medo le dua me ḑo.
E, nyaa ḑewo wɔa nublanui—
Yemele 'ġbe no ġe o, eyata manya zɔzɔ
Ne menye tsyɔvi la manya 'fɔḑoʃe
Lɔnyelawo ku vɔ ke, monye dzaka.
Ekpɔtɔ nye ḑeka ḑe futɔwo dome.

My lovers have died, I'm forlorn.
I am alone among enemies,
The leopard and the antelope
Have come to the brook.
They must take precautions.
It was for this that I went out of town.
Yes, some talk is full of pity—
Before my father died, he said
He was not going to live. I should be careful
When I was made an orphan, I must step aright.
My lovers have died, I'm forlorn.
I am alone among enemies.

There is yet another class of Ewe poems of this type, but in the lighter vein. It is generally of quick tempo and most popularly used by our bards.

Duho be ye' hatsoviawo
Amewo le Kpalime
Amewo le Kadzabi
Midzɔa 'bɔnu 'bɔnu
Ne miafa akaya lae.
Akaya la gbe hotsui nyui
Be kavegevi sɔŋ miefa gee
Akaya lee ʋua gblẽm
Eyata ʋua 'hã metsɔ 'fɔ nyuie o.

Duho says his choristers,
Those at Kpalime and those at Kadzebi
Should collect their tithes
For the repair of the rattle
The rattle refused to be adorned with cowries
And wished to be fringed with threepenny bits.
It is the rattle that spoiled the drum,
So that the music of it went bad.

Meto hagbe me yɔ Toti kple Vɔsã
Blewu dzie nyea mele
Ganaa ɖe nexlɔ̃, nexlɔ̃ koto,
Avutsua ɖe hã neblu tegbee.
Hadzisee nye segbe na Ahɔ̃suglo
So-kple-So be aʋa dzɔa
Atsyɔ̃e yewoaɖo.
Nu le do na mi loo, hasinɔwo
Maatsi ku o, maatsi dɔ o.

Gbe lé dzo ketowo ƒe
Ahɔ̃su be yeakpɔ Dahumetɔwo ƒe fia Kundo
Tuġutuġu meléa ahlihã o
Ahɔ̃su zu nyaġlama dze wo dzi.

> I called Toti and Vosa in poetry,
> I make no haste.
> Dare any hyena laugh, let him laugh
> And let the bitch bark ceaselessly.
> To sing is Ahosuglo's destiny.
> Sokpleso says they would dress at war time.
> With apology to you, bards,
> With no intention of death,
> With no intention of illness,
>
> There is strife in the camp of the enemy,
> And Ahosuglo will go to the chief Kundo of Dahume.
> The centipede is not caught with rioting,
> Ahosu is a problem for them.

The newest class of Ewe poems belongs to the class of hymns and vernacular music composed for schools, in which the famous Ephraim Amu was the precursor. Some are real songs and others are mere poems written or spoken to Ewe rhythm.

Miade nyiġba lɔ̃lɔ la
Enu wónye woaƒo asia ?
Mia tɔgbiwo tsɔ woƒe aġbe
Gblé ɖe eta xɔe na mí,
Eɖo nye kple wó sia nu
Be míawɔ míatɔ sinu
Nuvevie nyanya, ɖi ɖoɖo
Kple ameɖokuitɔdidi
Blu mía zɔli heġblé
Mía denyiġba lɔlɔ̃a ale ġbeġbe !
Denyiġba, wò nyonyo, denyiġba, wo ġbeġblẽ
Alesi míele ko, siġbe ko wòanɔ hã.

Aġbale-nunya ƒuƒlu, alo hotsui kpɔkpɔ fũ
Kple aġbe yaka nɔnɔ
Meyina kple anyiġba lɔ̃lɔ̃ o.
Tabɔbɔ kple amedoame
Nyuiedidina na amesiame
Kple lãdodo ameɖokui
Na xɔ̃lɔ̃vi ƒe nyonyo ko
Woawo mee tomefafa
Kple ngɔyiyi nyuiewo dzɔ tso.

THE COUNTRYSIDE

Our beloved native land
Is it a thing to meddle with?
Our ancestors sacrificed their lives
To gain it for us.
It is now the turn of you and me,
To do what we can.
Fastidiousness, shirking
And selfishness interfere
With our advancement and spoil
Our native land horribly.

Not pedantry, the multitude of riches
Nor riotous living can
Go with the love of our native land.
Humility and respect
Good will to all men and
Self sacrifice for the good of others.
These are the promoters of peace and advancement.

You will realise and appreciate that these modern Ewe poems are those only that are sometimes written in more than one stanza, short or long. There are also comic poems in Ewe:

Tsixeŋ! tsixeŋ! tsixeŋ!
Wɔɖi vloea ɖe ƒoyem
Amea ɖee kpɔ asrã feta ɖeka
Mado ne wòakpɔ eteʃe.

Chihen! chihen! chihen!
I have a bad catarrh.
Would that I could get a little snuff
To snuffle for my relief.

Wee! wee! wee!
Vuvɔ vloea ɖe wɔyem
Amea ɖee kpɔ tsi dzodzoea ɖe
Maƒo zã, zã, zã.

Wee! wee! wee!
I have a bad cold
Would that I had some hot water
To bathe with vigour.

Alele ! alele ! alele !
Nye dɔme le ɡbe ɖem
Amea ɖee kpɔ akatsa tre ɖeka
Mahatsɔ lé avui ɡbɔ.

> Oh! Oh! Oh!
> My stomach is noisy
> Would that I had a gourd or *kasa*
> To make it less noisy.

Oho ! oho ! oho !
Fifia vloea ɖe wɔyem
Amea ɖee kpɔ tɔ fafaa ɖe
Mahadze eme doo.

> Oho! Oho! Oho!
> I feel very warm
> Would that there were a cold stream
> Where to take a plunge.

Nane le asinye
Amea ɖeke menyae o ;
Ke nusi wònye la
Nye ɖeka koe nyae.

Haɡbea ɖe le asinye
Haɡbe ɖeka pe ko ;
Gake ne medazi la
Mesea nya ɡeɖe le eme.

Avɔa ɖe le asinye
Olombo dɔʋua ɖe ;
Esi ne metae la
Meɖoa ŋu ɡbaɖeɡbe.

Awua ɖe le asinye
Ablotsi wu vavãa ɖe ;
Gbesiɡbe medoe la
Nu etɔ̃e dzɔna.

Ŋkɔa ɖe le asinye
Ahanoŋkɔ leɡbea ɖe ;
Ne amea ɖe ƒoe ɖo nam la,
Nye lame fiena yii.

Dzesia ɖe le asinye
Mí kple amea ɖe tɔe ;
Gbesiɡbe míewɔe la,
Míekoa nu ɖea tsitsi.

I have something
No one knows what
But what it is
Is known to me alone.

I have a poem
Only a single verse
But when I sing it ever,
I gather from it.

I have a cloth
A very beautiful *Olombo*,
Which when I put it on,
Reminds me of days gone by.

I have a suit
A beautiful European suit
The day I put it on,
There is something of significance.

I have a sign
It belongs to somebody and me.
The day we make it
We rejoice and make merry.

With these few examples I have tried to explore hurriedly the whole gamut of Ewe Poetry, past and present. What then are our capabilities and our future possibilities? Heaven forbid that we look with contempt on the only record of the thoughts and feelings of our forefathers as they are shown in our poems, and refrain from emulating and improving upon them.

Akoli The Rich
By L. K. Safo (Translated by Roland Agodzo)

Once there lived a man by name Akoli. He was a cotton spinner and weaver, but was so poor that I don't think his type of poverty exists today in any part of our country. To worsen his situation, he had a wife and three children, with whom he lived in a wretched little cottage near the banks of a river.

It so happened one day that two rich friends, who were passing through the neighbourhood of this poor man, incidentally began to discuss poverty. One of them, Akpalu, said he strongly believed that if all people could get some financial help to establish their businesses, poverty could be eradicated from the lives of men. Agbenyega, his friend, interrupted him at once and said " I don't agree with you for a moment. It is God's plan for the world that all men shall not be equal. To some He has given wealth and general prosperity, but others He has destined to be poor and face all the suffering and privations of this world. No amount of financial help can therefore change the status of a man whom God has destined to be poor ".

Akoli was busy at his loom when the two friends came to him. " This is a hard working man, though he is poor ", said Akpalu to Agbenyega, " and I am prepared to demonstrate to you that with some help he could just be as rich as any of us ", he continued. " Do you think that if you had a loan of one hundred pounds to put into your business, you could prosper ? " Akpalu asked Akoli. " One hundred pounds ?" exclaimed Akoli, " that's too much." " I can assure you that if I had twenty pounds today, I would be a man," he added. No sooner had he completed his answer than Akpalu thrust his hand into the inner pocket of his coat and pulled out a sum of one hundred pounds in currency notes. " Take this and make a change in your life ", he said to Akoli. Before the latter could ask what rate of interest he was to pay on the loan, the two friends had left and were out of earshot.

Immediately they were out of sight, Akoli packed his tools into an old basket and closed for the day. On his way home, the thought of where he could keep the money in his cottage worried him. He had no box and moreover there was no door to the hut in which he lived, a mat made of palm leaves was all the door to it. When he got home he was greatly relieved when he found that his wife was not there to know where he was going to keep the money, and so after taking one pound out of it, he placed the remaining £99 in an old pot and covered it up with a large quantity of the chaff produced out of corn. With the one pound, he went to the market and bought cotton for his work. He also bought a piece of calico as headgear.

But it was not long before Akoli returned from his workshop to receive the biggest shock in his life. To his horror he found that the old pot in which he had kept the £99 was not there. He called loudly to his wife and said, " Where is that old pot in which you kept corn chaff ? " His wife replied, " This morning I had no money to buy soap for my washing, and so when the soap seller was passing, I begged her to give me three penny worth of soap in exchange for the pot, if she could find any use for it. She kindly consented, and so I took the soap and she in turn took away the pot ". " Good heavens !" Akoli exclaimed " Why should a grown up woman of your age behave so foolishly ? At least you ought to have had the common sense to empty the pot to make sure there was nothing precious in it. Look, you've now ruined me. I kept 99 currency notes amongst the chaff ". " And why should a grown up man of your age behave so much like a child? You ought to have told me that you were keeping some money there ", retorted the wife.

For nearly one hour Akoli and his wife quarrelled before it occurred to them to go after the soap seller, but then it was too late; she was nowhere to be found. The next morning Akoli went to his workshop greatly worried, but most of all he dreaded the next interview with the two rich friends who had given him the money. He determined to run away at the slightest sign of their approach and to avoid meeting them at all costs.

For the first fortnight Akoli kept watch and very strictly too, but as time went by he slackened, and got absorbed more and more into his work.

One cool afternoon, while he sat in his workshop weaving, he sang this song softly to himself " God the creator sent people into the world, each man according to His own destiny," and before he came to the end of the song he heard footsteps behind him. He suddenly looked back, and there were the two rich friends on him again; too late to run away. Akpalu said, " My good friend Akoli, why still in these ragged clothes ? Or is it because you don't want to use the money I gave you ?" Akoli had no reply to give, other than the story of his misfortune with Akpalu's money which nearly made Agbenyega split his sides with laughter. " I told you so," said Agbenyega to Akpalu, " that no one can change God's plans for us in this world. He intended this man to be poor, and you can't make him a rich man ". Akpalu on the other hand was determined to prove Agbenyega wrong, and so for the second time he thrust his hand into his pocket and gave Akoli another sum of one hundred pounds. "Be careful this time, and let me see some improvement in you the next time I call," he concluded. As soon as the friends had left, Akoli wrapped the money securely in his headgear and went home. When the wife asked him why he had closed so early, he told her he wanted to go to the town and buy some materials for his work. He went, and after having bought some thread he also bought a shilling's worth of beef, because for over a year his family had not tasted any meat.

He was safely on his way back to the cottage when he saw a hawk hovering in the sky, apparently in search of materials to make a nest. In no time it swooped, and snatched away from Akoli's head the headgear in which he had wrapped the remaining sum of £99. In his anguish he conjured all the supernatural powers at his command to stop the hawk; he even threw the beef he had bought at the hawk, but that did not help him either. The hawk flew away.

Akoli's feelings at the loss of his money for the second time can be better imagined than described. He became very sorrowful but once again tried to find consolation in the song that "God the creator sent people into the world, each man according to His own destiny." He kept to himself this second gift of a hundred pounds and the way he lost it. He could not bear to meet Akpalu and Agbenyega again and so he thought of removing his workshop, but because he couldn't find any other suitable site, he had to leave it there and hope he would be so watchful this time that the friends might not take him by surprise as they did the first time. But again his watchfulness lasted just for some weeks, after which he forgot about himself, and the two rich friends came upon him again, to hear the story of the loss of this second sum of money.

" I am afraid I can't continue to give you any further help, lest I also become as poor as you are," said Akpalu to Akoli, and with this statement the two friends left. A few yards away from the workshop, Agbenyega stumbled over a piece of lead and picking it up, he threw it to Akoli and derisively said, " Look, you had two hundred pounds and failed to put it to good use, take this piece of lead and see if you can make anything out of it ". Akoli knew this was a taunt, but he took the piece of lead and said a hearty thank you.

That evening a fisherman knocked at Akoli's door and said that he had been fishing, but one of the pieces of lead attached to his net was missing and so he had come to try if he could have any from him. Akoli gave him the piece of lead he had that afternoon from Agbenyega. The fisherman was so pleased that he promised to reward Akoli with part of his catch. Early the following morning in fact he brought a very big fish to Akoli's wife, and when she cut it open, she found in it a small shiny substance like a piece of stone, which she gave to her children to play with. It was later on found out that this piece of stone could shine in the dark and give light just like a lamp. Before long, nearly every body in the neighbourhood knew that Akoli's family was in possession of a miraculous piece of stone, and so one day a jeweller came to Akoli and asked if he would like to sell the stone, and for how much. The jeweller seemed so anxious to have the stone that Akoli realized it must be something really precious. " I am prepared to part with it if you'll pay me a thousand pounds, " was Akoli's reply to the jeweller. All efforts to make him reduce the price of the stone failed and the jeweller knowing very well that it was worth more than that, gave Akoli a cheque for a thousand pounds and took the diamond away.

The same week, Akoli left his humble cottage and bought a big house in a town not far from where he lived. He also brought all the weavers in the district together and succeeded in making himself their marketing agent, through which he enlarged his fortune immensely. Beside this, he had farms which brought him a handsome and regular income so that within a few years he was obviously the richest man in his district, and had many servants to do his bidding.

He naturally tried to find the two friends who had given him the money and the piece of lead, but they had gone abroad. Many years later, Akpalu and Agbenyega again visited the place where Akoli had his workshop in the days of his poverty, " But you don't expect to find Akoli the rich working here, do you ?" said a man standing by. They were very surprised, and enquired the way to the town where Akoli was living. He recognised them with pleasure, and entertained them lavishly. They talked much about his history, and Agbenyega had to admit that Akpalu was right when he said that the poor, if given an opportunity, could make good. On the other hand, Agbenyega pointed out that it was necessary for the opportunity to be within the understanding of the poor. £200 had been too much—Akoli could not do much with it. But a simple lead weight for a fisherman's net had been the foundation of his fortune.

Poems Of Eweland
By Israel Kafu Hoh
The Lagoon (Afubaka)

Glide on steadily that we reach home early,
Good marketing and fishing vessels.
In the twilight is the setting sun.
The winds are cold and my pores are sealed.
Little gulls and big lagoon birds
That fly in and out the sails,
Driving to catch your prey,
What will you do to aid us reach home early?
Push the boat steadily to reach home;
It is getting dark, the ripples are breaking.
The common lagoon fishes that jumped
Into the vessel have long since died.
Ye winds, push the barge steadily homewards;
Ye market women, blow air into the sails,
Let the stick and the paddle get to work.
Let the hand and the feet get work.
It is getting dark, that we reach home early.

Be still and calm, gentle Lagoon,
Guide us safely, mother Gbele,
Till we reach our destination.
Let your flood which comes from underground
Bring us delicious fishes of all kinds,
That famine, poverty and illness pass by.
Let your dryness that smiles to show
The white teeth that bring us wealth
Come without obstruction, dear Afubaka.

Sing Unto Me

Sing unto me, beautiful damsel,
You, thin-voiced minstrel, sing unto me.
I know that it is difficult
To sing on being asked;
But let me hear the echo of your voice,
Which only soothes my pining heart.

Dance unto me, beautiful damsel,
You slender necked maid, dance unto me.
I know that the drummers
Have not yet started playing;
Step off, and the sight of that alone,
Shall give me the strength I need.

The Bar (Aziza)

When the Volta is in flood, the bar is fearful—
Fishing boats rest over the sands,
River boats ply along the sides.
The banks are nearly lost.
Crocodiles raise their heads above the water.
The mangroves grow new leaves and branches,
Big fish come ashore and food is enjoyed.
But the boat that goes astray
And meets the tide where the sea and the river meet
Tumbles and pours its contents ashore.
Dead creatures, fineries, treasures
Line up along the coast.
A smaller boat is broken in pieces
Providing fuel for dwellers along the river.
Truly, it is the boat that would break
That crosses the river at the bar.

Clouds (Alilikpo)

The King's white curtains, tremble ye in the breeze,
Or move ye in the invisible hands
Of your fashionable stewards into place?
There is joy at home, a case is won.
We have also hoisted up our white flags of joy
To frolic here, below with you.

The King's mourning robes, your reddish brightness
Makes me wild with rage and reminds me
Of death and patriots long deceased,
This evening with great fear.
We, here below, are also clad in mourning,
Looking serious with our lives.

The King's ceremonial robes, your bluish hue
Is a definite sign of love.
We are also dressed in our lovely blue,
Moving here and there on earth below,
That friendly visits make us sociable
Now, on earth, and later on in heaven.

The King's funeral robes, your blackness
Bespeaks pain and sorrow at heart;
And I hear the fall of tears
From the eyes of your worthy stewards.
We are dressed in our funeral robes,
Bemoaning the death of our beloved ones.

Full-Moon (Dze-ave-dzi)

Full-moon, the white, round face of the moon,
Like the broad white face of an old man,
   smiling gleefully to his children—
You are always willing to listen to the grief
Of every lunatic and to comfort him.
Full-moon, O full-moon, we long to see your face.

Full-moon, O full-moon,
When the old recline with their chins in hand,
Puffing smoke into your smiling face,
Counting their silent troubles,
What a relief do they not find in you?
Your single finger through the prison bars
Affords boundless comfort to the troubled soul.

Full-moon, O full-moon,
We love you for the coolness of your rays.
Children run and travellers march;
Tales and riddles are told in your light,
Without much fatigue or sleep.
You are the joy of every child,
Full-moon, O full-moon, we long to see your face.

Moon, that makes water shine like silver,
And the shells twinkle on the shore,
The dew that falls on the grass and the roof
Reflects light like a mirror in the sun.
Full-moon, O full-moon, we long to see your face.

Full-moon, O full-moon, we long to sing our madrigals;
The vellums of our drums have long been muffled.
Full-moon, come and let us stretch our limbs,
At hiding, walking and **Ampe**,
And drive away our idleness and age;
Loved ones to unite, life to enjoy.
Full-moon, O full-moon, we long to see your face.

The Sky (Dzifo Le Fie)

The sky at night is like a big city
Where beasts and men abound,
But never once has anyone
Killed a fowl or a goat,
And no bear has ever caught a prey.
There are no accidents; there are no losses.
Everything knows its way.

The Sun (Xe)

Where are your children, sun ?
Where are your children ?
As you have eaten all your own
Why do you chase the Moon,
To take her children for your own ?
You can never succeed, good Sun,
Go and look for your own,
Everyone must care for his own.

Ama Had A Child (Ama Dzi Vi)

Ama had a child in Porto Novo last month.
Its eyes were white, perfectly white,
The brows were high, the hair black and straight,
The cheeks were high and lips were thin,
The wrists were thick and marked.
There were rings on its neck,
And its stomach stood in folds
Its back was wide and its calf was thick,
The toes and fingers were short;
Its cry was like the music of the angels at Christmas.
Ama had a child in Porto Novo, last month.

Baby (Vidzi)

A baby is a European,
He does not eat our food;
He drinks from his own water pot.

A baby is a European,
He does not speak our tongue;
He is cross when the mother understands him not.

A baby is a European,
He cares very little for others;
He forces his will upon its parents.

A baby is a European,
He is always very sensitive;
The slightest scratch on its skin results in an ulcer.

Two Ewe Hills
1. Adakluko

Art thou initiated into the **Youe** cult?
Art thou part of the oracle?
Or, art thou newly baptised?
Why art thou clad in white,
And shaven clean on the head?
I pity thee profoundly.
Hadst thou invited us by word or gift,
To keep thee joyful company, we would
Dance with thee at the ceremony.
But because thou hatest social strife,
Thou hast chosen to stay alone,
Far away from the crowds of men, Adakluko hill.

2. Gemi

Gemi, the cockpit of our warriors,
The castle of the Bayas,
The Oven of the Amedzofes,
Let thy massive, grey, projecting stones,
Which thy children in days of yore
Threw at foes to keep them from off thy gates,
Dazzle still more brightly;
Like a flash-light into the night,
That innocent children far away,
May point at Gemi and repeat
" Gemi, Gemi, Thank you very much ".

Prayer (Gbedododa)

I passed by the village of the potter
And he made a sacrifice for sunshine.
When I reached the farmer's hut,
He was praying hard for rain.
The boatmen were crying for the wind,
But the mosquito asked for quiet.
Both our benefactors and malefactors,
Do pray to God for success:
But which prayer does God hear?

The Thrushes (Atsutsruewo)

There are old thrushes on the tree.
Trotting, trot, trot, trot.
There are young thrushes on the tree
Crying tchui, tchui, tchui.
They are hungry, they are cold;
They need their mother badly.
Kofi did it, Kwadzo did it.
They removed their nests with a stick
To be used for a toy.
Ama came with hurried steps
And sang without a pause:
" A ringworm-head is a stone ".
Kofi got angry, they were sad.
They wept bitter tears.
They climbed up very gently
And took them back to their mother.
The birds were mute, the boys were mute.
There was joy, there was laughter.

The Vulture (Akaga)

I am a lean bird, and sinewy.
My neck is long, my head is bald.
My wings are large and long,
But I fly with patience,
For speed quickly ends in destruction.
My legs are long, but I hasten slowly,
For no man ever lies full length.
I hated men before they hated me.
I hate reckoned grains and dirty water,
Subservience and intimidation,
Living in secluded enclosure
And hearing dirty talk.
Here, on my high baobab tree,
I see what goes on in many homes—
And my children and I
Laugh to scorn the folly of men.
Every stream is mine,
I drink and bathe freely in every one.
Every farm, market and dunghill
Is mine and I always eat my fill.
There is no chief before or after me,
Whom I may revere to work against my will.
I am proud to be a Vulture,
And a king in my small village.

In The Valley (Balime)

Chalanchoes stood by the roadside,
And the pigweeds were in bloom.
I heard the distant rumbling of many waters,
And bent over the sensitive plants,
That spread over the thorny hodges,
And played at touching them to shrink.
A little onward yet, the sweet music of birds
Gave way to the racing and squeaking of squirrels,
And the noise of the streams grew louder yet.
But just a little farther, was profound silence,
Where the entangling branches of the tall trees
Cast a gloomy shade over the valley below.
There, the red flowers of the big tall trees
Adorned the mushrooms and forms with such colour
As if fairies in their jubilation
Were revelling in the camp.
The silence in the skies above,
The streams that ran below,
And the beauty of the foliage around,
Held me in thrall.
I forded to get behind the stream.
I passed and went away.
But the voice of the distant waters
Still lingered in my ears,
And the beauty of that experience
Still haunts me in my mind.

The World (Xexeeame)

The world, some said,
Is like the shade of a chameleon;
It is now this hue, now that.
But I heard Goakli say one day,
" The world is such a spacious place,
Yet how narrow is our room
It's so close that, when you rise too high,
You might break your neck against the clouds;
When you spread your self too far,
You might dash your arms against its sides;
And when you tread too heavily,
The earth might break under you,
And make you sink into the ground ".

Down Below The Volta River
By Adolph Agbadja

Many years ago, a young man and his father were carrying some gallons of palm oil, from Eweland, to Dodowa for sale. In their journey, they eventually reached the Senchi Ferry, and were put on the ferry-boat.

The young man, together with his friends, on board, went to the edge of the boat, and were looking at the smooth gliding of the water, when all of a sudden, he tumbled into the River.

He became so frightened that his high screams from the surface of water kept ringing in the ears of the people outside, for several minutes, as he struggled to swim ashore. But it was a desperate attempt; he sank into the deep River.

In fact, he never expected to live any more; never hoped to see any better thing with his eyes again; never believed, that he could ever come out of this deep water and see human life. His only thought was that sooner or later, he would be swallowed by a big hippopotamus, or be wedged between the saw-teeth of a cruel crocodile.

But it was rather astonishing to him, that none of these mishaps overtook him in the water. Breathing slowly through his nostrils, with his mouth tightly closed, he was just gradually and straightly descending, as if by means of a parachute, until at last to his utter amazement, he landed on a smooth and sparkling flat ground —a vast limitless floor.

Here at once, he began to see a big market of all sorts of pleasurable and delightful things; all sorts of valuable merchandise for human interest, including high-scented perfumes and aloes, precious stones, silver, and gold. The whole ground was overspread with florins, florins, nothing but florins, so beaming that his eyes could not rest on them for a minute.

But something awe-struck him about the whole place. The area looked desolate and remained quiet. There were no signs of human beings or animals living there. Not a shrill of birds, not a buzz of a bee, nor the tone of a human voice, could be heard by him. There were no halls, no rooms, in short, no shelter of any description. Also no vegetation what-ever could be found there. According to him, the thunders of rain which seasonally pour over us here, did not reach there at all. However, the rays of the hot sun which make us perspire on earth, gave light to the whole area.

In the centre of this valley lay a large table, well stuffed with all kinds of lively commodities for human taste. There were rows of whisky, gin, brandy; numerous tins of cigarettes, packets of matches, bottles of lavenders and lotions; trays of tasty juices, beverages, sweet-cakes, lofty loaves of bread, and crackers of biscuits. Again, there was something remarkably queer about the whole show. The young man failed to see, in reality, the people for whom these different kinds of food and varieties of articles were provided. For there was nobody beside the richly-laid table. In his wonder he kept looking round, if he could see any person at all, to talk to, but he failed to see any immediately. Although he was very hungry, yet he feared to approach the rich table, in order to enjoy some of the food. So he still stood at the very spot he landed, turning round his head from side to side.

Within a short interval, there appeared at the table, a slender tall beautiful woman, with a smooth brownish skin, having a clear-cut face, very captivating to behold.

Standing afar, and casting his youthful eyes on the mysterious figure, the young man at once became nonplussed, tongue-tied, and immovable. A complete fear came over him. He preferred vanishing at once from there. He wished he had wings to fly with, but he had none. He looked round the whole lifeless estate, but he did not find any place of social activities, which he could run to join. And there he stood as a stump in the field, not knowing what to do.

Soon, he noticed that the clear-cut, alluring face turned towards him, and calling: " Handsome young man, come to me; I am the Queen of Riches—you are at home; I will give you your heart's desire; I will make you rich—come now! come now!"

The young man kept mute; he could not move his ankle a bit forward. His fear increased and he wanted the aid of a magic hand to snatch him away from this incredible arena, but no such aid came to him. The whole affair was too marvellous to him, too wonderful to his senses, so much so that he became terrified! He dreaded what might befall him, at that table with this woman alone sitting at it. He hesitated.

And there, one could see a gazing competition taking place between two strangers.

Soon again the soft voice rang: "Handsome young man, come to me, O come to me. I am the Queen of Riches, and I will give you riches upon riches. My heart is willing to receive you; my hands are ready to serve you, and my mouth is ready to kiss you—come please, please come ".

At hearing these pleasing sentences, from the Fair Woman, his heart was stirred, his soul vivified, and his entire body was magnetised. All forms of fear then left him. He felt happy, because of the attractive, inviting and kind address that pierced his heart, from this enchanting woman. Very soon, he found himself clasped in the slim, but warm arms of the beautiful woman, with words of lovely reception: "Welcome to you. I am the Queen of this Horizon, having at my command, all these abundant riches, and I have power to give them to whomsoever I will. Gather therefore, as much as you can. Eat and satisfy your soul; drink and quench your thirst".

The young man thanked her with a cheerful heart and a smiling face, and ended by saying: " And madam, how can I go home, since it was by accident I came here ? As I sit before you now, I know nothing again of my home town; the way is lost to me. All my senses have changed; I can't know my way back home. "

" I shall lead you safely home, after you have made your selection of these valuable wares. Just look on the floor and you can at once notice the heap of money, which men labour day and night for, in your poor land. Now turn your sharp eyes to yonder place, and there you see so many pleasurable and delightful things, which you bother yourself to get in your home. Well, on this table, you have victuals to fill your hollow stomach. All these, plus the rest, too many to mention, are at your disposal."

The young man spent a considerable time with the Queen of Riches, gathering a heavy wealth, which he packed into bags made from crocodile skin. In fact, he had a nice time with the Queen.

Early one morning, he informed the Queen about his departure. The Queen put him into a boat, with his massive treasure, and entered the boat herself. In a minute's flight, they were on the surface of the Volta River. Then she began rowing the canoe, till they reached the shore, from where, the young man could easily get a transport to carry him home. At this end she vanished from him with the boat, leaving the young man with his treasure.

About ten that morning, he got a lorry which brought him home safely to his family. All of them, who never hoped to see him again in life, rushed with a great astonishment to meet him, as he appeared to their sight. In the house he was received with showers of cheers, and measureless affection. He was carried shoulder high throughout the house for minutes upon minutes. There took place a great feast that day. The whole house was filled with shouts of joy from everybody who entered into it. All were happy, all were pleased, all rejoiced with the young man, and congratulated him highly for bringing this bulk of treasure home.

GA-ADANGME

The Ga-Adangme people have given their name to Accra. Their society has links with the East rather than the West, although it has borrowed from both. It is influenced mostly by its priests. Its myths of origin are among the most poetical in the whole of Africa, and its main cultural possession is the astonishing song cycle, the **Klama**, which consists of upwards of 60,000 stanzas, kept by heart for over four hundred years, and sung, in part, at every festival. But its modern expression is somewhat limited, perhaps because of the impact of the national capital—and, in this collection, for the purely local reason that it does not have a relay station in its two main states of Yilo Krobo and Manya Krobo.

August Fish
By E. K. Martey

Shrilly the chilly air bites my pores.
That makes me feel August is near.
Soon I shall bid my nose be shut
Against the retchful smell of August fish.

Were I a gull, I would take wing
Down the ocean to find my prey,
I would neither labour nor toil
To provide me with tomorrow's meal.

Were I a cat, I would not mew
Nor follow those tiny creatures round
The home in merry-go-round
In vain attempt to meet a day's meal.

Were I a school boy with no funds,
I would be more than glad.
A load from the shore to the house
Would earn me much to buy some tart.

Were I a mother, I would not chide
My child who screams for fish.
I would but give him due comfort—
For a month more and there will be fish.

Were I a fisherman, I would but mend
And dry in sun my fishing net.
I would much comfort take in this—
A month more and there will be fish.

A Hawker's Day
By Richard Bentil

The little village lying south of the Achimota School is called Anumle, " the bell is heard ". In one of the nicely lined up and two-roomed quarters, a woman lived with her husband, a workman in the local workshops, and their daughter of just over eighteen years.

The time of the day was a very cold and chilly morning, with the fog almost obscuring any object barely fifty yards on. The roosters in the vicinity sounded their second shrill clarion on the approach of daylight. Just over there, in front of Mami Yaa's husband's quarters, Ama lighted up the hearth's fire to prepare the day's hawking meal of pap, otherwise known as **koe-koe.** Within the next hour, the large earthenware black pot was fuming furiously away with the heat of the carefully prepared breakfast. At the chime of the school clock tower for 6.30 a.m., the first announcement for a ready breakfast came with Mami Yaa's first hawking song of the day **koe-koe.** And Ama quickly responded with **anuor-tea-ei-blodo-oo!** the usual invitation to the customers to buy the loaf of bread as well as the pap, as they came with their pans for their two-penny, or three-penny scoop of **koe-koe.** With almost all the nearby buyers' tail finished, Ama folded up her soft rag pad to carry away the whole pot of pap. A young girl friend followed her with a wooden plateful of bread. At the first stop, at Mr. Adjei's quarters, she extended the old invitation—**koe-koe**—and scooping out his two-penny's worth, Mr. Adjei helped her away on to the next door.

Immediately Ama had left, Mami Yaa prepared for her the mixture for the morning's fry of tart. When she returned with a cloth knot of coppers, threepences, sixpences and shillings from the morning's hawking of **koe-koe,** she dropped down her empty pot to get ready the hot palm oil for the day's frying. With the first six tarts nicely done, she continued the day's second hawking song, **ashie-ei-tatale-oo! ashie-ei-tatale-oo! Namo, baaye tatale-oo!**—a very amiable invitation to the local residents, which sent the " kiddies " weeping after their mammies for the coppers, and flocking off for a very enjoyable sweet. So Ama fried almost till after midday and sang away her joy of the sales with **ashie-ei-tatale-oo!**

Almost at 4 p.m. Mami Yaa got ready her large enamel bowl and a large empty toffee tin, to stand on top of a large mount of **garri.** Ama's hawking song was changed to **e-fuor-ei-ǵaali,** meaning the swelling constituents of her **garri,** when soaked in water. The grand invitation was brought to the local workmen as they spread out their handkerchiefs for their sixpenny's worth—a real handsome meal for the next day's hard labour.

Ama's large white enamel-plated bowl was now empty of its heavy load, but she had one of the heaviest knots tied at her cloth's end—£1 5s. of an afternoon's sales that had brought in very good dividends. As she entered the house singing her last lines of **e-fuor-ei-ġaali!** Mami Yaa greeted her with the happiest laughter ever to be caught on her cheeks.

Yet there was still something left for the day's hawking. The evening call of dusk, with the thrush's farewell songs echoing in the nearby thickets, summoned Ama to get ready her large frying saucepan, very well ripened plantains and firewood, to the street corner nearest her quarters. Barely before 7 p.m. she started frying out what seemed to be one of the finest sweets for the table of even the rich. **Ashie-ei-kele-oo,** she exhorted and the plates streamed up in a long queue. The pennies, twopences and threepences dropped as she measured out the triangles, rectangles and squares of carefully sliced ripened plantains. **Ashie-ei-kele-oo,** and yet more of the customers streamed in to buy and cool down their taste with this delicious dish. At the end of the day, at 11 o'clock in the late evening, Ama had yet another £1 5s. to her chest of sales and hawking.

And so the story continues, day in, day out, with Ama hawking away the best of her youth, to get for herself the costliest of cloths, headkerchiefs, gold ear-rings and bangles, beads, oh! the loveliest of ornaments that she can find for the great day—the great moment of her life—her wedding.

DAGOMBA

The open lands north of Ashanti have no common language, although Dagbani, the language of Dagbon around Tamale and Yendi, is understood, if not spoken, by Dagomba, Mamprusi, Moshi, and indeed all the Northern tribes apart from the Lobis. A collection of its stories was made by A. W. Cardinall, and published as **Tales told in Togoland**, in 1931.

Kamyana Ka Ti Balim Tingbɔŋ
By A. B. Derimanu

Ŋun lee ġari o kpee ni suhu peli
Ninvuɣuso Ŋun kpe moɣu n-tumdi paa tuma
Bee Ŋun zi o tinkpaŋa
Ndiri wahala ka balinda tingbɔŋ.

Yɛlmaŋli ti Ma Tingbɔŋ yɛlya
Ni ŋum kam balimi o ni suhuyini
On' tʃɛ ka o nya o kuli anfaani
Ka lahi too ġbinliriġa ni suhupeilli.

" Di lan binġula zuɣu n-puli ni
N mali mɔri, taɣma, tʃi, ka n-mali
N-yɛn ti ŋun kam mali suhiyini
N balindi ma ni yɛlmaŋli.

Tumtumda ġbi n-vibġi n-puli
N-zuri n-bi yura bɛn nnyɛ
Salma, lului, kursabli ni Anzunfa
Ka n-puuni bɛr di zuɣu.

Dinzuɣu tumtumda sanyoo nyɛla
Wahala, dzelinsi, wɔlġu din ka nyɔri ni kum
Fasee O tʃe n-bi yura maa nahimbu
Ka labna n-ti naan balim man tingbɔŋ.

Kamyana yi ban doli yɛlmaŊli sɔli
N-ti balimdi ma ni suhi yini
Kan naai tin ya bindira pam
Ka yi zaa suhu naan palġi.

Tee-miya yi yaanima Zemana sa
Salma au Anzinfa bɛ daa bɛ mili
Be daa balindima mi, ni suhu pelli
Ka bɛ zemana maa nyaɣsim ka zaŋbuɣsi."

Dinzuġu sokam labmina n-ti balim tingbɔŋ
Ka niŋ kuli yi simdi
Tʃɛliya ka ti balim ka dzɛm ti Ma tingbɔŋ
Ka ti tingbɔŋ ŋɔ bindira niŋ bayana.

Come Back To The Land
By A. B. Derimanu

Who is the happier man
Is he the wandering labourer
Or the man who stays in his cottage
Delving or nursing mother earth ?

Sure mother Earth promises the honest man,
Who will faithfully serve her,
Plenty of yield as daily bread
And make him the happier man.

" For his livestock, plenty to eat.
In pod I have reserved
Hay, fodder, maize I hold
For the honest man who serves me.

The labourer digs deep
With the aim of stealing my precious ores
Gold, diamond, bauxite, iron, silver—
Making my belly to ache.

For his reward I promise
Labour, toil, vain-sweat and want
Until my precious ones are left unmolested
And he learns to come back to the land.

Come, all ye honest people
To learn to serve me
And I will give you plenty
To make you happy men.

Remember your ancestors of yore
Gold and Silver they knew none
But served me diligently with cherished heart
And their happiness knew no bounds."

So come on, all hands back to the land
To make the hoe our friend
Let us nurse and serve mother earth,
Make our dear land self sufficient.

Each For a Purpose
By A. B. Derimanu

" Moo, moo," said the cow to the donkey,
" You are a queer hornless beast.
Selfish man needs only your labour for money
"Cause your right place you have missed."

" Oh obstinate specimen of the mule,
Your place is with the monkey,
And not to stay with men of rule,
There to rest with the bee that makes honey."

The donkey stirred himself so high,
And lifted up his stupendous head to the sky,
As if to lodge a personal complaint
To his Maker against Man the sly.

A moment of calmness ran through his nerve,
And he to his companion said "For a purpose each is created.
Mine is to exert energy and to serve,
Yours to be loved and elevated."

" Whatever my lot is, I am content
For I choose to have my finger in no one's pudding.
In my Maker, I am confident,
My labour shall have an ending."

" Remember, the slaughter house is your final place of torture
And your carcass to man is meat.
But mine belongs only to the vulture.
And each has to serve under man's feet."

HAUSA

This brief sample of Ghana traditions would not be complete without the wandering Hausas, who have been coming for trade since the early 1800's, and who now live in large Zongos, especially in Kumasi and Accra.

The Hausa Trader
By J. H. Sackey

Beneath the trees along the highway
From the morn and through the whole day,
Squats the hard and bearded seller,
Tall and slim Hausa trader.
With his robes about his shoulder
Does he try to get a buyer,
Often calling passers-by,
Calling them to come and buy.

> "Master, master,
> Look at this
> It's a lovely Kano cloth,
> It has travelled very far,
> Over thousand, sandy miles;
> From the plains and dust of Kano,
> Over hills and through Dahomey.
> Through the great Ashanti forests
> To this green and pleasant coastland.
> And the price is very cheap,
> Eighty shillings won't be bad
> For a many-patterned cloth
> From the northern plains of Kano!"

"Stay, O stay,
O master, stay!
What about this curious bag?
It is made from crocodile,
And it's very, very rare!
I am sure your wife will like it,
She'll be glad to carry one;
And since I wish to be your friend
I will take a hundred shillings!"

> And at this the pretty woman
> Bent and fingered long the bag,
> Feeling long the creature's scales
> That were clearly on the bag.

A cry of triumph issued out
From the tall and bearded trader;
And taking now his cotton fez
He stroked his shaven head with feeling.
" Ah! she likes it! " beams the trader,
" It will fit her very well;
All the nice and sporting ladies
Wish to carry crocodiles! "
And as he spoke he hung it up,
Hung it on her flattered arm.

  Embarrassed by the cunning man,
  The husband thought and thought again;
  And as he looked down at his wife
  He could see her longing eyes.
  Fingering something in his pocket,
  Now uncertain what to do;
  But after weighing, reckoning, thinking,
  Thinking hard with pouted lips,
  Spoke the man, he spoke with courage,
   " I will give you sixty shillings! "
" Master, master,
I will lose;
Even ninety will be bad;
But since I wish to be your friend
I will take your ninety shillings! "
" Bearded man, I have no ninety,
Sixty-five or not at all;
I have not your time to argue,
I have not your time to bargain."
" Then make me glad with seventy,
It's special price for you;
Here's the bag, and bring your money,
Bring the money, gentle master! "

  The bargain now
  Is made and finished
  And the couple turn to go;
  But " master, stay! "
  He shouts again,
  Shouts again the eager vendor.
  " What about the little rattles,
  They are cheap, the little rattles;
  Little master in the house
  Will love to play with sounding rattles.

Half-a-crown will give me pleasure,
Only give me half-a-crown."

In the end he squeezed a florin
From the good and smiling lady,
And with a grin and cheery manner
Bade them come again tomorrow.

    His various wares spread on the pavement
    Thus he piles his little business;
    Hard and keen in all his dealings,
    Thrifty, dogged, avid vendor.
    A cotton fez adorns his forehead;
    Whitish robes hang from his shoulders;
    And he can shift at second's notice
    And find another vantage station.
    Everywhere that people gather,
    There you'll surely find him wander;
    He's a suave and cunning seller—
    Bearded, tall, Hausa trader.

Wakan Sule

By Malam Bello Osman

Bida tai ka sa tafiya wadansu su bar ǵida,
Ya na fidda bera har budurwa ta bar ǵida,
Bida tai ka sa ma maza da mata su zam kuda,
Da kumya da addini su zam babu ko daya,
Ana ya da loko cikin kasashe bidan sule.

Ana kashe wasu cikin dawa, wasu ko cikin ǵida,
Ana mai da wasu diya a bautadda su ǵida,
Ana mai da wasu da a harba su bar ǵida,
Farilla da sunna ba su neman su san ǵuda,
Ana tattukad ma'anan jihadin bidan sule.

Ku duba sabo da sule ǵidan yari ya cika,
Ku duba sabo da sule barayi ka bincika,
Ku duba sabo da sule masunta ka hallaka,
Majema karofi, 'yan farauta da 'yan baka,
Barayi da masu fashi bida yau bidan sule.

A Song For A Shilling
By Malam Bello Osman

Let us get up, men and women to chase a shilling.
Let us get up, men and women to work for a shilling,
Let us get up, men and women to work hard,
Let us get up, men and women to work hard for our daily bread.
How are we going to get our daily bread?
We get our bread with a shilling.

Let us look into the field today, and see what a shilling has done.
A shilling has placed others to be Heads of States,
Others to be big above their friends, others to possess big houses,
Others, fine clothes, others sweet foods, and others degrees in Education.
Others become engineers, others doctors and others economists.

So brothers and sisters, let us get up and work hard for a shilling.
See! today, a shilling has sent others to prison,
Women to run away from their husbands,
Children to run away from their parents,
Fathers to run away from their children,
Just in need of a shilling.

The poem continues for many more verses.

The Tragedy Of Nana Kwame Dziratuo II, Omanhene Of Kokoroko State
By Bidi Setsoafia

Booming of talking drums, summoning people home for a state meeting.

Afua Dokua:	Ah! papa, what means this frequent state drumming, daily summoning people at work from their farms again and again? So the Chief Linguist Okyeame Kuma and the elders mean to depose the Omanhene by all means.
Okyeame Kakraba:	Hold your tongue! One bad trait in you modern youth is this damnable act of poking your inexperienced noses in serious matters of state. Who put it into your silly head that the Chief Linguist is bent on destooling the Omanhene? These affairs are more serious and far above your age.
Afua Dokua:	Why, papa, I am now 20 years old! I am a member of the Kokoroko Women's Association. You know Dora Mansah is our leader, and I know too that Okyeame Kuma is the leader of the elders against the chief.
Kakraba:	Yes, this second world war has put these insolent traits—this empty show of bravado into modern youth. Because your brothers are mobilizing and returning home from East Africa, you speak freely anywhere of serious heavy matters of state. I won't blame you. It's the chief's fault. He gives occasion to some elders of the state to urge you on. I have always held my own philosophical views about these affairs. Hum, this small little Kokoroko State so tormented with petty rival factions! The Omanhene refuses to learn reason, rushing rashly in passion, and insulting men in the street, and giving us, the elders, no peace!

Drums boom again

Afua:	Papa, the drum still calls the people.
Kakraba:	I am not deaf, Afua. It's barely two hours since I arrived in this farm. I have done

	practically no work, but I am now to rush home to discuss the ill behaviour of a chief, a proud tyrant. Oh God help us! But who is that running down the hill?
Adjei, the herald:	Okyeame Kakraba, the Chief Linguist desires your presence immediately. Aren't you hearing the drum? The people have almost assembled.
Kakraba:	Clear away, you babbling liar! You said so yesterday, but I found only a handful of men at the meeting, after I rushed down in hurried haste. Get going. I'll follow.
Afua:	Adjei, the great herald, are you drunk again?
Adjei:	No! Afua, be careful!
Kakraba:	Afua, pack up and lead on.
Afua:	Thank you, papa.
Kakraba:	(*walking, soliloquizing*) When men who have never known suffering; who have not been sympathised with, and, therefore, never known the precious gem in sympathy for men, are placed in such high, honourable positions of trust to govern men, they feel their only duty is to rule and rule hard, and not to serve and sympathise.
	What! can this be true? The babbling Adjei is right. The market place is indeed packed full!

Hustle and bustle, drumming

Okyeame Kuma:	Okyeame Kakraba, we've long been waiting for you. Join us at once now, now. The crowd is impatient.
Kakraba:	Not to lay aside my dirty farm attire? Are we at war?
Kuma:	More than at war, my friend. Look at me! Just down here in these dirty clothes.

Drums resound again

Adjei:	Silence! the meeting starts! *Muntie! Tioo!* Listen.
Kuma:	Listen, chiefs, elders, linguists, men and women of this noble Kokoroko State!
Adjei:	Silence! *Muntie! Muntie! Tioo, Tioo!*

Kuma:	The purpose of this meeting is well known to you all. After our meeting yesterday, the bragging chief with his parasite, that Okyeame Manu, went to the stool farm at Kwantamansi. They took along with them one Mensa Nyame, that rich trader, with the damnable autocratic purpose of selling part of the stool farm to him. When I heard the news of this boastful, bad drunkard chief—
Nsiah:	(*from behind the crowd*) You are also bad, a traitor. You are aiming at the stool yourself. *Kwasea!* You fool!
Kuma:	Who is that drunkard counteracting my words outside? Who is that?
Nsiah:	(*louder*) Your enemy, Kwaku Nsiah! I say you are aiming at the stool: A traitor! Worse than that name!
Kuma:	Corporal Bonsu, arrest him at once. He is of the Omanhene's group. These fools are the parasites of the state who eat and drink freely from the state coffers, living fat on state properties.
Corporal Bonsu:	We've caught him long time!
Amoah:	Bind him!
Nsiah:	Ah! Corporal Bonsu, you break my collar bone. Stop stamping your feet at my back bone!
Corporal Bonsu:	Shut up, you fool! You were a go-between when the chief was after my wife, while I was away fighting in Abyssinia. You assisted him to marry her. I have a good mind to cut your throat at once!
Adjei:	Silence! *Muntie! Tioo!* Silence!
Kuma:	I'll ask the State Secretary to read the charges against the chief—the charges we drew yesterday, and which we submitted to His Excellency the Governor through the District Commissioner, Mr. George Birdbath, here.
State Secretary:	The charges are twelve. First and foremost, as you all know, there is his autocratic character, not only a hard hearted tyrant, but a dis-

THE COUNTRYSIDE 121

	respectful, proud bully, respecting not even the stool fathers. He abused his elders in the streets and called them profligates, fools, cats and dogs! Contrary to native custom.
	Second. He held oldman Akufo's throat in public, because he tried to advise him. He held him, shook him hard and threw him flat on the ground. The old man's cloth was at the mercy of the wind.
Corporal Bonsu:	Yes, it was madam Dora Mansa, the leader of the Kokoroko Women's Association, who by chance came to the scene, and assisted the poor old man.
State Secretary:	Third. He brought a jujuman from a French Territory far North, and one Okramo, a devilish medicine-man also from the North, to kill the Chief Linguist Kuma, the Odikro Sampeni, and the Linguist Kakraba. These people drank, danced and sang their devilish songs, turning the place into a brothel or a den of hooligans, rather than a home of a Christian chief.
	Fourth. Contrary to the laws of this honourable Kokoroko State, he sold stool properties freely, as if they were his personal properties. He being the chief custodian of these properties, I mean the man who should see to their preservation and safety.
	Fifth. Marrying freely the wives of his subjects who were His Majesty's soldiers at war in Abyssinia fighting for our country. The noted example is Christie Asantewa, former wife of lance corporal Bonsu.
Adjei:	He should be murdered.
Amoah:	He should be drowned in the Black Volta and his body quartered.
Adjei:	Silence! *Muntie! Tioo!* Listen!
State Secretary:	Sixth. He wreaked vengeance on the corpse of his dead enemy. I mean he went secretly to the bath—bathing place as we commonly call it—where the corpse of the old Okyeame was placed, and slapped the dead man hard

seven times, spat in his face, shouting, " You bad Linguist Appiah, you could not escape my vengeance to hell, you rogue, take these to hell." These are serious charges against the customary laws of the Kokoroko State. " None shall beat, flog, slap, kick nor spit at a dead man."

Amoah: He should be hanged at Ussher Fort.

Adjei: Deposed quick !

Amoah: Deposition too mild for him. I say again, let's drown him in the Black Volta.

Adjei: Silence ! Listen to our Secretary !

State Secretary: Seventh. He is a voracious drunkard, drinking hard in public, leading to petty disgraceful acts.

Yaa Mansah: More so in these days.

State Secretary: Eighth. On the 8th August, 1940, three years ago, he got drunk at Akwasidae Festival in the midst of a great crowd of people, and was talking hard while the Chief Priest was praying, against native custom. When asked to slaughter a sheep, he rebuked the elders saying that they were trying to take his money by force, and abused them in bad temper.

Ninth. Contrary to the laws of the Kokoroko State, he quarrelled with his palanquin carriers while carried in state with distinguished chiefs of other states. He charged the palanquin bearers that they were running too fast with him, and ordered them to stop, while he stood firm and slapped hard the two carriers at the front.

Amoah: Yes, by slapping them they nearly threw him down, had not the Chief Linguist Kuma begged and implored them pardon.

State Secretary: Tenth. He joins freely and sings obscene songs freely with hooligans, contrary to custom at any time he invites these drummers to the palace.

Eleventh. Contrary to the Laws of this honourable Kokoroko State, he nearly had a hand to

	hand fight with Lance Corporal Bonsu at the gates of the palace last New Year Eve. Twelfth. He quarrelled openly with the District Commissioner, Mr. George Birdbath, two years ago, and pushed him and dared him to a fight.
Yaa Mansah:	He thus disgraced our State which for many years had won high praise and commendation from many District Commissioners.
Amoah:	Let's rush to the palace and strangle him to death.
Adjei:	Depose him and dynamite him.
Amoah:	Bomb him.
Adjei:	Silence!
Kuma:	Okyeame Kakraba, let it be known to the elders of this honourable State that we shall select some people right now to go and tell the chief plainly in the face that we are tired of his autocracy and misrule, and we are therefore appealing to the Governor to accept our resolution and leave that he should now be deposed. The former Governor has kept the report of the commission that enquired into his bad actions ten years ago. We have now again sent our petition to the present Governor. We have impressed it on His Excellency that the matter claims immediate action.
Kakraba:	According to our plan, three elders of the State, two women of the Kokoroko Women's Association, guarded by Lance Corporal Bonsu and his five ex-servicemen, will go to the chief's palace now and inform him, of our plan.
Kuma:	Adjei.
Adjei:	Yes, Sir!
Kuma:	Take the lead and get the chief informed that we are coming now to see him, as I have intimated to him.
Adjei:	I'll haste on and get him informed.
Kuma:	My friends, let's move on.
Kakraba:	(*Soliloquizing.*) Wisdom in fact is a rare fast bird.

Hardly caught and owned by very few.
Nature indeed is always frugal this wisdom to share.
But true and never changing the old saying still stands.
" Fools tread where angels fear to tread."

  Our great chief Nana Dziratuo II vehemently disagreed with the Governor, and worse still, he quarrelled with the District Commissioner, Mr. George Birdbath, under whose very able guidance this state moves. He forgets Mr. Birdbath is the representative of the Governor here.

They reach the chief's palace with drumming.

Adjei: Okyeame Kuma, I have given word to the guard at the palace gate, and he has informed the chief accordingly. The chief himself is coming down to meet you.

Nana Dziratuo: Look here, you usurping Chief Linguist Kuma, may I know the reason of your coming down to the palace with these profligates, damnable, hopeless ex-servicemen, and women who never hesitate to insult my honourable wives in the market? Why! I say why! I hate to see this Corporal Bonsu in my house.

Corporal Bonsu: This palace is not your house! It is the property of the whole Kokoroko State, and I have the right to come here as anybody else. You hate to see me here, because you seduced and married my wife Christie Asantewa when I was away fighting in East Africa.

Nana Dziratuo: You were not supporting her. You refused her the privilege of enjoying your gratuity or allowance behind, and she was demanding assistance from me. What do you want me to do?

Christie Asantewa: You were determined to starve me—you wicked, hard hearted husband. By the way, all your friends have left again for Burma. You and these your hooligan friends refused to return to Burma, though the war is still on.

	You choose to be here, tormenting me with your abuses, after you starved me for a year.
Corporal Bonsu:	I ordered that you should no more be paid my allowance, because I learned that you were living a bad life behind my back.
Christie Asantewa:	What evidence have you to support that accusation ?
Corporal Bonsu:	The evidence is that you are now the wife of the chief. Do I need any other evidence stronger than this ?
Nana Dziratuo:	I must stop you from insulting my wife like that. It's against native custom for a common man like you to speak to a chief's wife in such an insulting manner.
Corporal Bonsu:	I wonder if that custom permits a chief of the Kokoroko State to marry his subjects' wives during their absence fighting for our country ?
Kuma:	Enough, Corporal Bonsu. I must beg leave to interrupt, Nana—
Nana Dziratuo:	What ! Beg leave of me ! Have you obtained my leave as the paramount chief of this state before you were holding illegal meetings against me all about ? These are steps to usurpation, damnable, cruel, wicked, and treacherous ! And I must tell you plainly, Okyeame **Kuma**, that with all these illegal arrogant steps, you can't step into my shoes as the paramount chief of this Kokoroko State. Never ! You can only be a Linguist, holding long heavy Linguist staffs before me, the crowned Omanhene of this state. Even if I am thrown away from the stool, as you were plotting to do, you, this Okyeame Kuma, you cannot, I say you cannot, sit on this stool. What royal blood have you in those your tiny arms ? Those small arms will continue to hold long heavy Linguist staffs, till the gods of this state dash you to hasty death, for these your usurping tricks.
Kuma:	I won't answer these frantic utterances.
Nana Dziratuo:	Neither do I expect you to answer.

Kuma:	Okyeame Kakraba, inform Nana that we have come to inform him that the elders of the Kokoroko state have now again formally submitted their present dispute between them and him, Nana Dziratuo II, to the Governor for His Excellency's final decision. In fact let it be known to him in unmistakable terms, that the elders of this Kokoroko State are tired of his flagrant disrespect for the customs of the state. Our fetish priests and oracles are annoyed, and the god of the Black Volta cries daily in the night, disturbing our crops with poor harvests, because he, Nana, the head of this state, refuses to honour them.
Antwi, the Chief Priest	And I, the chief priest of the state, have been blamed by the people, as if I were not performing my duties to the gods.
Kuma:	And to add to all these—
Nana Dziratuo:	And to add to what? I must now stop this arrogant fool in the person of a Chief Linguist from aggravating my anger any longer.
Kuma:	I, an arrogant fool?
Nana Dziratuo:	Yes, you! What right have you to address me so insolently? Now, Linguist Manu, my only faithful linguist, have you sent my urgent note to that showy District Commissioner, Mr. George Birdbath, that I want to see him very urgently this hour! These are the result of some of *his* actions.
Okyeame Manu:	Yes, I did, Nana, and he sent a reply that he would be coming.
Nana Dziratuo:	Look here, Linguist Kuma, I must inform you, that the position of a chief is a sacred, honourable one, far above the low status of a Linguist in a state! I wish you usurping Linguists and elders of this state, even common soldiers who call themselves His Majesty's Lance Corporals, know this very well, no less the women who call themselves leaders of the Kokoroko Women's Association—I wish these common women who have no royal blood in their veins

	have these my words well smoked into their common heads.
Dora Mansa:	Look here, Nana Dziratuo, your royal blood does not permit you to insult the elected leaders of this state, persons who were elected not by their nonsensical gullible hereditary royal blood, but by merit of their good character, excellent service and wisdom.
Nana Dziratuo:	Dora Mansa, that is what some of you think. But you are grossly mistaken. Let not your leadership of the Kokoroko Women's Association blindfold you to think that chiefs are elected only by hereditary right! You can be born in a royal family, but let your character be questionable, dirty, treacherous and plotting —like this philosophical linguist Kakraba here —you never can be elected a chief.

Car approaching

Manu:	The District Commissioner is here, Nana.
Nana Dziratuo:	Good morning, Mr. Birdbath. Do you know why these men are here, wild in their speech and action?
Birdbath:	How can I?
Nana Dziratuo:	You should know, because you are in league with them against me, the elected royal blooded paramount chief of this state.
Birdbath:	I am always neutral, as you know, in state affairs and I want to assure you again, as I have always assured you, that I am a lover and a friend of all Africans.
Nana Dziratuo:	I am also an African, but you are not my friend. You reported me to the Governor. They say you are M.A. Honours in mathematics. I must tell you to go home in this second world war, and use your mathematics in assisting to calculate the correct number of atoms in the bombs that your uncle, Sir Winston Churchill, and your people will use in bombarding the Germans, who are now determined to capture your Island. This is better, my friend, than using your mathematical brain in misgoverning and ill administering this Kokoroko State here!

Birdbath:	It is left to your own people to determine who is the better administrator, you or I.
Nana Dziratuo:	Yes, you know now why they are here! I must tell you, Mr. Birdbath, you have connived with these my people, and you have not only thrown this small Kokoroko State into disorder, but also disturbed my peace of mind and sleep in my bed. I thank you sincerely for all these. Good afternoon.
Birdbath:	Fine afternoon, Nana.

Car moves away

Kuma:	Okyeame Kakraba, let it be conveyed to Nana that—
Nana Dziratuo:	Yes, this small Linguist Kakraba too. Old Linguist, 50 years old, still moving under the name of Kakraba—a small man, small with his small little philosophical head! Kakraba indeed! I must tell you, Kakraba, and you all those in league against me, that I have handed you to the great gods of this land, gods that control the Black Volta whose waters we drink, that at any time you drink or bathe that water, you should vomit blood and dangle your legs to hasty death!
Corporal Bonsu:	Open Confession! Conspiracy damnable!
Amoah:	Hang him!

Hustle and bustle

Adjei:	Silence! *Muntie*! Silence!
Kuma:	Linguist Kakraba, I say, let it be known to the chief—
Nana Dziratuo:	I don't want to hear the voice of this plotting, philosophical small man! Don't want to hear him here!
Yaa Mansa:	What has my uncle done you? What has he done!
Christie Asantewa:	He insulted me twice in a crowded *Akwasidae* festival by pushing me with his linguist staff. I, Nana's wife. But I, Christie, a member of Christ Apostolic Church, I've forgiven him and ask God's Hallelujah, and mercy for him. Hallelujah! Nana, beg pardon, listen to them.

THE COUNTRYSIDE

	I say, give time and ear to what they have to say. Okyeame Kuma, speak on.
Kuma:	Now Secretary, give Nana a copy of our charges and our resolution which we have now submitted to the Governor.
Nana Dziratuo:	You can submit it to the King, Queen or Emperor, whoever rules us! Christie, Okyeame Manu, let's away.
Kakraba:	Nana, good-bye.
Nana Dziratuo:	I say, go away.

Beating of drums and singing of state songs

Christie Asantewa:	Is it not surprising that your State Secretary, this dirty natured Kwasi Quansah, forging documents, whom you saved recently from ignoble imprisonment when this same George Birdbath threatened to imprison him—it's surprising, that he should also be in league with these people!
Nana Dziratuo:	No matter. I am not a child. I am old enough to know that this is one of the perplexing paradoxes of this wicked world. Okyeame Manu, get Akua to call me my first wife Abena. Christie, we must think of how to avert the evil plans, the wicked machinations of these hooligans. What advice can your wisdom, your sound head give in these difficult times? Ah! Abena, you are come, be seated. Christie, you are a member of the Apostolic Church. People commend your pastors as wonderful people in prayer?
Christie Asantewa:	Yes Nana, I have the mind to tell you that I spoke to Pastor Godson Kwapong, our able Apostolic Pastor in town, on this affair. I asked him to pray fervently on your behalf. If it is not against Nana's plans, I wish we visit their service this evening. This Saturday is one of their biggest days, and the spirit of Christ is invoked to come down to heal and dispel all the difficulties of those who sincerely believe.

Nana Dziratuo: Well, I can also believe. Why, I am also baptised in Christ's great name! We'll go there this evening. Hum, how is it with me? My great courage begins to fail me. It's the mention of that Governor's name that shakes my strong nerves so. This Governor vehemently disagreed with me in one of my state boundary disputes with one of these N.T. boundary chiefs. Hum, our present Governor has been so strict on matters relating to Chieftaincy in this war time. They say he is an arch diplomat, hiding his wickedness in his diplomacy. He last deposed my next friend along the N.T. border, Nana Krante Oduro II, and threw him down mercilessly from his stool. Ah! what shall I do?

Christie Asantewa: Courage, Nana, God is great, His wonders to perform.

Nana Dziratuo: We'll visit the Apostolic prayer meeting this evening. Now Abena, what do you say about this?

Abena Konko: I am for consulting the great sorcerer Kronsu and his great oracle. He is a wonderful man. I discussed this with Okyeame Manu here yesterday and he holds the same view.

Nana Dziratuo: You can also consult him and enlist his assistance. These affairs need a united action. Driver!

Driver: Nana!

Nana Dziratuo: Get that old car ready. We are for the Apostolic Church this evening.

Driver: No petrol inside, Sir, Nana. The spring too be bad, Sir.

Nana Dziratuo: Look here, get help from my wife Asantewa for petrol. Can't that spring help us slowly thither and back? It's only about two miles.

Driver: I go try Sir, Nana.

Nana Dziratuo: Hum, broke, broke in all things—no pecunia—money, cash I say. Broke! Wanted to sell that stool farm this morning and get some cash, but this tricky chief Linguist Kuma came and

THE COUNTRYSIDE

	foiled my plan. This mathematician D.C. Mr. Birdbath, also in league with my elders, withheld my salary. What do they want me to eat? Well, Mr. Birdbath can keep the salary and be calculating it as long as he can.
Christie Asantewa:	It's almost time to start going. The service starts at 6 p.m. Driver, are you ready?
Driver:	Ready, Madam.
	They get into the car and it starts off
Congregation:	(*Singing*) Nyame san'o, san'o, one live. Nyame san'o, san'o, san'o. Come down, Jesus, Come down. Nyame san'o, san'o, Awuradi san'o, san'o. Praise God, Hallelujah!
Pastor Kwapong:	Dear brothers in Christ, Hallelujah!
All:	Hallelujah!
Pastor Kwapong:	Dear brothers in Christ, this evening we shall consider this short passage in St. Luke's gospel. The Gospel according to St. Luke, chapter 18, second half of verse 14. "For every one that exalteth himself shall be humbled, but he that humbleth himself shall be exalted." My friends in Christ, Hallelujah!
All:	Hallelujah!
Pastor Kwapong:	These words are spoken by Jesus Christ to all of us, both rich, poor, great and small. It is a great lesson for me and you to learn. When King Nebuchadnezzer boasted and vaunted himself, he was humbled by God to eat grass. In this world, whatever a man sows is what he reaps. But God is merciful and assists and never pays us in the same coin. If you sow seeds in humility, never boasting—
Nana Dziratuo:	Christie Asantewa! Let's leave these preachers casting indirect insinuations against men above their status. Can't tolerate this nonsense!
Christie Asantewa:	Why, Nana, he speaks not against you.
Nana Dziratuo:	You are all of the Apostolic Church. You can defend him. Look here, Pastor Kwapong, if I am proud it's my own concern.

Christie Asantewa: Oh! Nana, he speaks not against you. It's for all of us.

Nana Dziratuo: I can't stomach this! It's because he learned that I would be coming, hence he selected this text against me.

Christie Asantewa: I never informed him that we were coming! Oh! Nana, what's wrong?

Nana Dziratuo: They say some of these Apostolic pastors are prophets. Look here, Pastor Kwapong, let not your prophecy reveal to you things about me, the paramount royal blooded chief of this state. My subjects call me a boastful and proud chief. You have also heard it and have now told me in my face in the midst of this large congregation of about a hundred people. If I am to eat grass like King Nebuchadnezzer, why it's a herb all right. Many people eat herbs, it's a healthy food. Driver!

Driver: Nana.

Nana Dziratuo: Let's away.

Car moves off as Nana Dziratuo speaks

Some of these pastors talk politics in the pulpit. Pastor Godson Kwapong is one of them. I'll drive him and his religious politics congregation out of this town. If I am to walk on my hands and body, I am not the only example in a world full of millions of suffering, struggling people. I am ready to reap what I sow. Christie Asantewa, since I took you, a sufferer, from that coward, vagabond Corporal Bonsu, two years ago, I never once disagreed with you, but today I must tell you, I never liked your taking me to the Apostolic prayer meeting, to be soundly abused by this Pastor Kwapong. Tomorrow early at dawn, you must go and tell him not to pray for me again. The tricky Governor can depose me or even hang me at Ussher Fort. I am not better than those deposed. I'll get other people, who will not abuse me before praying for me, to offer prayers

	on my behalf. I am baptised a Basel Presbyterian. My Presbyterian Ministers can also pray for me and I will go to heaven all right!
	They reach the palace and get in
Christie Asantewa:	Oh! Nana, what's wrong?
Nana Dziratuo:	Nothing. Now Okyeame Manu and my wife Abena, what says the sorcerer Kronsu and his oracle?
Manu:	He says all will be well. He prescribes these medicines which we now bring to you. But he advises that you abide by the following injunctions and prohibitions. You should stop smoking your pipe for six months, and leave off taking *fufu* for the same period, as you use the medicines. You should live mostly on slices of yam, or *ampisie* and herbs. If you abide strictly by these, all troubles will soon be off your head, and you will live and reign happily many years in this state.
Nana Dziratuo:	This is worse than deposition! What! Not to smoke my jolly pipe and leave off enjoying my sweet *fufu* for six months. Why! Has he not prohibited my drinking and inhaling God's free water and air also? I'd better go to the Apostolic pastor Kwapong to be abused, and later prayed for. Yes, none of these silly heathen restrictions and prohibitions in Christ's merciful religion. None!
Abena:	Nana, the oracle promised to aid you himself to pass through successfully all these difficult ordeals for the six months.
Nana Dziratuo:	No more of that nonsense. But—Perhaps I might give it a second thought.
	Knocking
Christie Asantewa:	Come in.
Christie Asantewa:	What's sad. Speak, man!
Messenger:	I heard the D.C. just called Okyeame Kuma and the Odikro in his office, and informed them that the Governor has sanctioned their petition,

	and approved also the old Commission of Inquiry's report into this matter, that Nana be destooled. This is the letter given me by one of the D.C.'s clerks for Nana.
Nana Dziratuo:	And this is the success and long prosperous reign predicted by this dirty oracle! No matter. Messenger, put the letter down there. Look here Asantewa my dear, give me that bedroom key. I am now tired of this hopeless life.
Christie Asantewa:	What is Nana saying?
Nana Dziratuo:	I say, call me my other wives in the next house. Okyeame Manu, kindly go with the driver, and call me my elder brother immediately, there.

They depart, chief opens the door

It's always my strong belief that if a man is tired of this dirty plotting, wicked world which some are enjoying, but some find difficult to enjoy, that man must find a way, fair or foul, to end that life. Let the tricky, diplomatic Governor, the mathematical George Birdbath and my plotting subjects depose or hang my ghost. Oh! merciful God, I, Samuel, I, a sinner, render my wearied soul to thee.

He shoots himself

Christie Asantewa: What's that! What! in Nana's room? I am done. (*Bangs on the door.*) Ah! Ah! Nana has shot himself.

Weeping

The Town

There! up-side, and standing on their heads!
Tumble-down woods in a tumble-down world.
The sun was still a-bed; the wind asleep;
And slumberous sprawled the lake
So calm and yet so treacherous.
There, like a belly-full python with room for more,
Scans the lake with meek sardonic smile the world of men—
Herself the mirror of the world that lives by her.   In it
The tumble-down world of trees and hills and the sky,
Double-living in regions twain. The blades of grass so still.
Palm and bamboo leaves so staid. No waft of wind disturbs
The mighty flood. Not a ripple, not a shimmer. All, all calm.
The tumble-down woods so still!
From the stillness and the hush,—from the depths of the lake come
  voices none
May hear, but all, all understand.

G. Adali-Mortty

Tough Guy In Town
By M. Cameron Duodu

He walked up and down the pavement smoking cigarette after cigarette, his talking shoes making a tap-tap click on the hard ground. He scanned the streaming cars with his eyes. It was seven o'clock in the evening, and he had a little difficulty in reading the numbers of the passing cars. The sight of a black Kapitan made him start, especially when it bore the " Taxi " lamp. He was engaged in reading the number of such a car when he bumped into a man walking hurriedly by. All his pent-up anger came forth now, and he grabbed the man's shirt and asked in a booming voice. "What do you think you are doing, kicking me around like that? Are you going to beg me or not?" The man, short and shabbily-dressed, looked like a dwarf beneath Tough Guy's huge frame. He was stout in spirit, however, for his answer betrayed no fear.

"What have I done to be shaken like that?" he said, "You rather, who bumped into me do not give an excuse, instead you hold my shirt and shame me. Is that your good manners, impudent boy?"

" Good Gracious! " shouted the surprised Tough Guy. " Is that what you say? And you have the impudence to dare say I am a boy. Okay, I will show you whether it is you who feed me ". He was in the act of carrying out his threat when the loud blast of a horn made him leave the man and jump for dear life. In his fury, he'd forgotten that he was standing in front of a Taxi Station. A driver who had spotted a man and a lady coming from the opposite direction was speeding up to them to see whether they would come in for service. The zeal with which he was accelerating was such that had Tough Guy wasted another moment he would have been hit. He jumped clear, however, and landed in the sand at the station, to the complete satisfaction of his would-be victim. The latter strolled away wondering what was wrong with this generation. " The whole fact is that they ain't got no ethics, that's the whole trouble ", he mused as he walked away.

Tough Guy got up and began to shake off the sand from his clothes and from within his shoes. His encounter had made his feelings worse, and puffing furiously clouds of smoke from his cigarette, he began to reflect on his situation. " Ah ", he thought, "the old men were really wise who said "Travel and See ". Who could have thought that, I, Tough Guy, whose real name of Kwasi Asamoah is brushed aside for this heroic one, would have fallen into such a plight ? The guy at sight of whom the Kroos in Takoradi run like mad, the King of Pilot Boys, the audacious ' Toughie ' who has eluded the Police for years! Oh! it's incredible. But still as this is Accra and not Takoradi, I must wait like a baby and see whether anyone will turn up to meet me".

The thought of his situation made him more furious, but he had to content himself only with smoking harder and harder. In fact he'd just landed from the Kumasi Train at five and had made his way from the station, hauling his suit-case true 'hobo' style. Yes, there was no doubt about it—Macrato had said: it was the Atukpai Taxi station at Adabraka. So he'd come there and enquired. The Taxi Drivers admitted that Macrato parked his car there all right, but as to his whereabouts, they were silent. Tough couldn't explain their behaviour. Yet he knew nobody in Accra with whom he could put up, save Mac. He was tired— dead tired,—and sleepy. He'd come to Kumasi from Takoradi in the sleeper, but there had been so much romance—that is, conversation and exchange of drinks—with the girl sitting close by him, who said her name was Pat—that he hadn't been able to snatch any more sleep than an occasional doze off on the way. It was now 7.20—exactly two hours twenty minutes since he landed in Accra—and still no sign of Macrato. " These Taxi Drivers really know how to invite friends ", he thought sarcastically.

At that moment, the sound of a car coming at top speed was heard and the rhythmic blowing of an Opel horn. The Taxi Drivers came out of their cars and shouted " Do it! Do it! if it spoils, the garage will repair it and bill your master ". When they saw the car's number, they all shouted " Macrato–o–o !" Tough Guy's heart leapt, he put his fingers to his lips and let out a shrill whistle the real " tireman " way—" whae-whee !" The whistle re-echoed faintly from the speeding car, its brakes screeched on the tarred road, and before it had become quite still, it was backing up full speed to where Tough stood, causing a bearded Busman to brake suddenly and jump down, leaving the bus in the middle of the road. The cars behind the bus began to hoot, one tried to pass it, and braked sharply to avoid a collision with an on- coming Mammy Lorry. There was a real pandemonium!

Meanwhile the Bus-Driver had come to the station and was threatening the Taxi Drivers. They jeered at him, and when he turned to go back to the bus, he was greeted with hooting of horns from the now long line of traffic that had gathered behind him. The scene was not without its humour. The Busman twitched his beard and moved off, amid more hooting of horns and men.

All this while Macrato and Tough Guy were unconcernedly engaged in shaking each other's hands and grinning amid semi-audible murmurs of greetings, apologies and explanations all combined. " Oh Mac ", said the over-whelmed Tough, "I've waited pretty long here. I've had an awfully bad time. Where've you been ? " " Yeah, Paddy ? I've been to a dropping service at Bekwai—I was sorry because I knew you'd drop along, but you see a dropping service to Bekwai for £13 was too good to miss in these hard up days. I'm just going to do my accounts, as if I'd been working in Accra all day. My master doesn't know I've been to trek. So £3 will do for him. The rest minus petrol costs will be my tchobo."

" Say, " said Tough, " what is meant by tchobo ?" " Oh, chicken-feed !, it's the Taxi Drivers' word for Bonus. As I was saying, if I deduct £3 for petrol it leaves £10. £3 for accounts leaves me with £7, and by the way I got four passengers from Kumasi who paid £2. That makes it, nine solid pounds. A cool job ain't it ?"

Tough replied " Oh, it sure is. Now I'm hungry, let's get going." And so they went home, dined on " Rice-gun " bought by Mac's girl-friend, talked politics and reached the point of being estranged, but the situation was saved by Tough's remembrance that he wanted to dance at the Night Clubs.

Eight-thirty showed them at Lido, fully dressed. Mac's only shortcoming was that his face was too small for his large green-glass goggles: he looked like an imp ! Tough was a complete " Teddy Boy " in his large tailed over-coat and tight coffee gaberdine trousers. He meant to show off very well in Accra. The Bar at the club as usual, was crowded, but, as Mac put it, they wanted a cool place where they could drink their sorrows away. So, to " Super-Service Inn " they came. A Radiogram was blasting " Rock City Boogie ", and Tough Guy, unable to contain himself any longer, caught hold of a slim copper-coloured gal by the waist, and began to " swing " with her. Apparently, the gal was an adept in the swing business, for she responded admirably to Tough Guy's tossings. Tough Guy, encouraged by the cries of admiration emanating from the people in the Bar, who had now formed a circle around them, demonstrated very well his skill, which he had picked up at the Takoradi pubs. He jived and shook his waist, went back body bent as if about to fall down, leapt up suddenly, and held on to his partner's hands and it began all over again. It was hot, and it seemed as if Tennessee Ernie had specially composed ' Rock City Boogie ' for Tough Guy. The song ended : and a warm applause burst out from the spectators of this free exhibition.

Tough was offered drinks all round, congratulated here and there, and patted on the back by his happy pal Macrato. He was walking on air, for this was exactly how he had pictured "Tough Guy in Town".

"Howdy Mac! say me pal", he shouted across the table, "what about our going to blow our fuse down there at the Week-end in Havana? I've sure heard a lot about it down there in Takoradi. They say there are plenty damn cargoes there".

To the Week-end therefore they came, the Rhythm Aces welcoming them with a beautiful Mambo. Tough Guy was really in town tonight. He soon had the floor under his command with his sweeping, stylish steps, dancers left off dancing everywhere to admire him. Soon ladies were swarming to him to beg a turn with him. His ego was indeed expanded.

Later on, tired, he walked abruptly from his partner and went to the bar to buy a fag. "Barman, let me have a coupla packets of Luckies" he shouted to the sleepy Bar-keeper. "What are Luckies?" "You Limey, you don't know Luckies d'ye? Well I'll show you. 'Lucky Strike' an American cigarette." The Barman said: "We have none". Tough replied: "Okay, give me 'Havana'." Bar: "Out of stock". Tough: "Caballero". Barman: "Finished", and began to doze. Tough Guy's brutish instinct was aroused. He aimed a left hook to the dropping head of the Bar-keeper. It sent him crashing to the shelves, bringing a dozen bottles crashing down. He was no less wicked. He grabbed the pail in which glasses are washed, aimed it at Tough Guy and let go. But Tough came from Takoradi. He knew every trick of the game of single-combat. Quick as a panther, he'd ducked aside and the water and glasses had crashed into the faces of the inrushing floor-members. They were checked long enough, to let Tough Guy jump the counter, and knock the Barman out cold, with two terrific smashes on the jaw. Then he turned round and faced—the police who gave him several weeks in prison in which to remember his first day in the big city.

In The Streets Of Accra
By Andrew Amankwa Opoku

This is the road!
This is the main highway!
Shouters, we are in the street!
Shooters, restrain your guns!
This is Accra.

This is the town,
The street of the municipality.
Strangers, we are in the streets.
Townsmen, stretch out your sleeping mats
This is Accra.

This is the beach,
This is the pilgrim's haven—
A vast town, but where is the sleeping place?
A great crowd but where is an acquaintance?
This is Accra.

Why this tumult in the street?
Where are the pursuers
That harry every one so?
Let me join the throng.
This is Accra.

Why this head turning
Or is something approaching
That makes you turn jerkily
To look round about you?
This is Accra.

What is this buzzing noise?
What means this paa! paa!
Is this where you walk daily?
And you have lived so long!
This is Accra.

Stay let me have a look.
If such a collection of merchandise
Crowd even the streets so,
What of the market?
This is Accra.

What does this ringing of the bell signify?
This shouting and tinkling noise
This running in the blazing sun
This sweat that is skimmed off with the hands?
This is Accra.

Could women monopolise a street so?
In vain you try to elbow your way through
If you stop they will roll over you
If you turn away a vehicle is knocking you down.
This is Accra.

THE TOWN

Step out, son of the valiant,
When you look about you too much
Okete's children will mark you for a rustic
No one shuns the simple fellow for a bargain.
This is Accra.

Bestir yourself always
When someone pushes, hit him back
When someone bullies, scare him in return
Stranger and citizen are both alike.
This is Accra.

Vast expanse of water but where is the sleeping place?
This great great great town
Where could an eating place be
That Stomachtown has become so devastated?
This is Accra.

Oh, benevolent one, ferry me over,
If you would lead me round the corner,
Madam will drop in a ball for me.
When you are shy, you grow lean, but
This is Accra.

I have fed, but the food does not stay,
The wind is blowing, yet I feel hot.
Once we are on the beach
We sit in the sand.
This is Accra.

I see interesting things, yet I am unhappy
My heart is throbbing
Yet I have not committed any crime.
I'd better go and get myself drunk.
This is Accra.

Finery to the right and left,
Kwakye's beautiful thing—
It is money that did it.
Borrow to eat, borrow to pay!
This is Accra.

Society and friendship
That made the crab to go without a head!
Show me your friend
And I will show you your character.
This is Accra.

This vogue and fashion!
It is a taboo to stay when your colleagues are going out,
Yet the vulture's soul differs from that of the crow.
The cockroach does risky things, yet it never gets hurt.
This is Accra.

Step out, son of the valiant one,
If you look about you too much
Ɔkete's children take you for a rustic,
Who would not prefer to do business with the ignorant?
This is Accra.

If it is like this on the edge, how will it be in the depth?
So grand as it is at the backyard
How will it be inside at the dance?
How the electric lights scintillate!
This is Accra.

The dance has become grand indeed!
If you would permit my going in
I should join in too.
No one denies himself his favourite unto death.
This is Accra.

Madam, make room for me to sit!
I only came to have a look
The stranger does not carry the head side of the corpse,
Neither does one go to a strange place to proclaim oneself a saviour.
This is Accra.

Is it for the little I have
That you keep pointing at me, and
Spearing me with your fingers?
Is the dripping of fat from the curing eel a sign of wealth?
This is Accra.

Snuff And The Ashes
By Frank Parkes

Kofi Dzeseefo, in a pale blue nylon shirt, whose transparency afforded an excellent opportunity for the exhibition " red notes " in each breast pocket, walked majestically into the large drinking bar of the " Tsui Shito Tavern " with the self-confidence of one who was definitely not new to night club activity.

By his side strutted his chum Ebow, a good looking enough young man of about 23, broad of shoulder, sharp of wit, though not so quick of tongue. He was of an amiable disposition, this Ebow, but tonight, he was all sighs.

" Good evening ", the one in nylon said to the tall chocolate-skinned man behind the counter.

" Good evening, Kofi ". The bar-tender lifted up his eyes, and his face just sufficiently to reveal an accustomed smile.

" A large Guinness, three bottles Club Beer and a packet of cigarettes " Kofi ordered.

Outside in the open air pavilion, the band was playing a really hot High Life, *Odo ye wu*, while on the dance floor, young gentlemen and ladies were wriggling their bodies, like worms.

Once settled, Ebow sighed, " Bo, its all gone haywire between Arafuah and myself."

" You don't mean it," said Kofi incredulously.

" Read this then," Ebow retorted, thrusting a crumpled envelope at his friend.

Kofi ran his eyes across the blue cream woven page addressed to Ebow Nyametsiase, Enville.

" Well ?" Ebow queried.

Kofi smiled, folded the letter carefully, and put it in his wallet with a look on his face which in officialese would read " For necessary action ".

" Don't let this set you on edge Ebow, I'll see her some time for you ", Kofi promised, giving his friend a pat on the shoulder.

On Monday morning, as soon as he got to his desk at the Ministry, Kofi dialled 0006. An alluring female voice at the end of the line said " Hello " caressingly, so caressingly indeed, that thinking it rather inviting, Kofi was almost tempted to seek her name. But instead he asked :

" Can I speak to Miss Arafuah Mensah ? "

" Hold the line ", the female voice promptly advised.

While he " held the line ", Kofi thought about female telephonists in general. He felt they would make ideal brides with their lovely faces and entrancing voices, only, and there he felt was the rub, only if their stock of English words were not confined to the construction of sentences like, " Hold the line ", " No reply ", " Line engaged ", and so on and so forth without anything to relieve the monotony of their style. Anyway there he was at last.

Later that evening, a young man and a well-groomed girl were seen walking under the moonlit skies of Chorkor beach. The man was expostulating, chiding, pleading.

" Well ?" questioned the girl.

" You want me to change my opinion about you ?"

The girl cast a worried glance at Kofi. Down in her rich brown eyes there lurked a deep sorrow. She brushed aside the shadow of a tear from her brow. Her heart was full, too full for words. Finally she said through closed lips,

" Wherefore all this cross-examination ? Why all these comments on my fate, which fills my eyes with tears ?"

She could say no more.

" Don't be a big baby, Afie."

There was a long silence which gradually began to be oppressive. Kofi fidgetted with his silk American tie; pulled out an elegant cigarette case and offered her a cigarette. She refused. He smoked. She talked in her high-flown way.

" Pray tell me Kofi, had I been your sister, *onye musu mli bi*, would you have advised me to set our quarrel to rights ?"

Kofi smiled and pointed out, " You're simply making a mountain out of a mere mole hill."

She tried hard to suppress a sob. " Indeed ", Arafuah exclaimed. " You think it a mole hill, Kofi, that I should hear from the mouth of another girl, a secret that we, Ebow and I, both treasured like an Ashanti man his Great Oath ?" She braced herself and continued.

" I am by no means jealous. I always loved Ebow. But this, this revolting conduct has shattered my affection " Forever ".

" Beyond repair ?"

" Ever."

" You won't forget it ?"

" Me ? *Mihie kpan no gbikogbiko* ! "

From the finality of her tone, it was evident that whatever existed between Ebow and Arafuah lay deeply buried under those four words.

Kofi surveyed the scene before him, the golden sands, the silvery sea, the pale azure sky above his head, the moon which pierced through the cloudlessly clear canopy of heaven and blended with the lapping of the waves on the still shore.

Suddenly he hissed in her ear, " Arafuah, what would be your judgement if, as Queen of Olympus, you saw two mortals, an Adam and an Eve, standing before such an ethereal prospect, as we now, charged with a wanton waste of moonlight, stars and what is more, such sublime music of the sphere ?"

She could hardly believe her ears. The pompous clerk mistook her silence for acquiescence in his views. He used words that he thought she would like to hear.

" Afie, I could scarcely comprehend your motives when I saw you moving about with a man like Ebow. He is a ne'er-do-well. The proverbial rolling stone. He can promise you many things but he can't fulfil those promises."

She was so engrossed with her own thoughts that she found no time to be even slightly shocked. He drew in a long breath from his fag and then proceeded to splash a few more vivid colours on to the irresponsive canvas of her mind.

" I am, as you should know, a product of the University College, a local " beento " to be precise. I am " carful ", and it is commonplace knowledge that I qualify for the term " fridgful." In pity for the awful treatment this semi-educated boy Ebow, (who by the way is not fit to be my steward boy if you don't mind) has meted out to you, I am giving you an opportunity. I hope you appreciate how much the better it would be for you if you agreed to be my friend."

" Good night, Mr. Dzeseefo." She turned to go, but he shot out a restraining hand. She stood as still as a rock.

" Affuah, you can't just leave me like that. By no stretch of imagination could I have arrived at the incontrovertible logical conclusion that you are so dumb. I am sorry I have to say this to a lady, but it has always been my inviolate principle to face facts square. You talk of love. Can you eat love ? Can you chew love ? Can you fry love in sauce pan ? Of course not ! You do deserve every particle of ill treatment you have received at the hands of that abominable boy Ebow."

He was almost out of breath, like a man who has just run a three-minute mile. However, after a little respite, made the more unbearable by her absolute stillness, Kofi continued, more to ease the oppressive silence than anything else:

" You can get into the car for a lift home although you will agree with me that after your display of unbridled incivility, you deserve no such favour. It was a poet who said—what was it ?

" Shall a man understand,
He shall know bitterness . . . "

This time she was off, like a shot from a gun. She was frightened at her own speed. On, on, she ran, along the golden sands. She looked at her watch. It was ten. Tarred street at last. Better than sand she thought.

"Service", she shouted unconsciously. Brakes screeched. An open door. Awful. Comfortable cushion. Delightful.

"Osu. Last Bus stop."

"I will charge you twelve shillings", the driver shouted. "If you know that you cannot able pay, then go down."

"Never mind. It doesn't matter how much I pay to get back home."

Kwesi Oyeadieyie, Chief Reporter of the *African Ambition*, was Ebow's trusted and tried friend. They came from the same place, Kromantsi, a fishing village one hundred and five miles away from the capital. The two had at one time shared the room Ebow now occupied.

Kwesi walked into his old 'home'. The sight that greeted his eyes gave him pain.

Ebow was sitting on the edge of a sofa, with dejected head and gloomy gait, like an oak felled, a reed shattered, a deer that has been hunted down its dark recess in the plainy outskirts of ancient Winneba by men who needed it both to win the day and to awake the sleeping shrines of their primitive gods.

"You are sure of your love for Afie?" Kwesi questioned after listening to his friend's story.

Ebow did not reply. His bearing and eyes were eloquent answers.

"You certainly want her back?"

"Even if it means Federation and a unified Ghana becoming happy bed-fellows," Ebow revealed, "I shall get back my Arafuah."

"Come along then", Kwesi said and lit a cigarette.

Ebow took up his eight-yard *Kramo mentsi Hausa*, and passed it under his right armpit, across his chest and over his left shoulder, shaking free his imprisoned left hand by a backward movement. He was ready.

"How easy and quick it is to go the native way!", Kwesi remarked in a little mental hum.

Kwesi piloted his friend through a labyrinth which even Theseus might have found difficult to negotiate without a piece of string. In the worst slums in the whole of the capital, James Town, they stopped before an uninviting portal.

Kwesi walked in, his friend following close. The darkness was menacing and the fact that the two friends had only a minute before walked in the uninterrupted glare of a blazing African sun worsened matters. Ebow, a total stranger to the area, was temporarily blinded so that he could see neither the wrinkled old man who sat in Yoga fashion on an elegant sheepskin in the far corner of the dark room, nor the regalia of talismans, telling beads, and idols of wood and stone, his stock in trade.

When the old man therefore greeted the two friends, Ebow was startled.

The old man gave them no time to state their case but asked forthwith:

" Which of you born Tuesday ?"

Ebow was now really shocked. He was born on a Tuesday. And he could not hide this trivial fact from a man who seemed to know so much.

" Ha ", the old man ejaculated, " you are being given snuff, Snuff eh ?"

Without giving him time to think of a fitting reply the shrivelled jujuman added:

" All right, two and six."

After some eerie chants and incantations the medicine man gave Ebow a small parcel.

" Your matter be small boy play for me—this be a charm for love," he explained, " this powder ver powerful—I make am with vulture feather and some leaf dey for bush for twelve midnight for cemetery—put inside for any lavender you like—talk your plaber for top—take rub your face all—then if you go talk for dan woman face to face he no agree I no go chop kenky and fish again."

The echo of the old man's laugh resounded in the dark room, giving it a sinister ring.

Ebow, though incredulous, poured a shower of thanks on the old man and the two left, with a determination in the heart of the afflicted one to put to the test this pocket size Cosmic Bomb from the old man's quaint repertoire.

" Arafuah, set me as a seal upon thine heart, as a seal upon thine arm," Ebow whispered over the potion in the secret of his room, " for love is as strong as death and jealousy as cruel as the grave. Many waters cannot quench love neither can the floods drown it." In the secret of his room Ebow finished with his invocation, put on his suit and set out for Afie's home. When he reached her door, he almost decided to retrace his steps. The door opened. Their eyes met. Neither spoke. But the gaze, it was fixed. Some strange electric force had created the optimum atmosphere—fit for love, not hate.

Radio Dance Hour
By Chapman Wardy

Not an hour of continuous music
For all tastes,
But an hour of continuous music
For all lovers.
With only a partner for a gate-fee
Lovers go.
They dance
To drown all their cares and hopes,
They dance
Away their disappointments and fears,
They dance
While trumpets blare and saxes drawl,
The drums beat and bongoes bark
Heads turn dizzy and tearful eyes gleam;
Lovers wheel round at every turn,
Till Leo wearily shouts farewell,
And the band lustily plays its last;
"Yea man!" in wild chorus they yell,
"Enjoy radio dance hour to the last."

This Is Experience Speaking
By Peter Kwame Buahin
1. The Inmates Of My Room

  Should I blow or should I not blow my own trumpet? That is the question. It is very unfortunate, but it still remains a fact that the person who blows my trumpet has very unceremoniously left me. Not because he was not sufficiently paid but rather because he could not develop sufficiently strong and projecting cheers to make my trumpet heard amidst the din and bustle of Accra City life. And now, in his absence, I must willy-nilly sound this trumpet however faintly.

  By way of introducing the first note, I am a man who always faces facts squarely and is frank even to the extent of being imprudent. I am very short when it pays to be short and I am very tall when it is useful to be tall. "All weather" is my nickname. I am an intricately complex mixture of all that it pays to be. I am a Bachelor of Arts (B.A.), first class honours in ancient and modern Palmwinology; a master of all drinkables except coal-tar, cascara sagrada and turpentine; a fellow of the Royal Institute of Alcohol;

and Head of the Faculty of Immunity against Intoxication in the International University of Sparkling Bubbles. I am a man with green blood in my veins and with a more fertile brain than Erasmus'. In a word therefore, I am a very important person who is now soliloquising, with a mind in a cloudy puzzlement, to find out why the Government did not make it possible for me to drive in any of the luxuriously modelled and fashioned cars provided for the VIPs during the celebration of our Independence.

I stay at Accra New Town, in a house where lizards and bats and mice enjoy such first class but highly unharnessed democratic freedom that they freely and easily and impudently spit at and excrete on me, and even go to the sad extent of at times sharing my bed with me. I go out and come to meet them, carelessly relaxing in my bed, in a bossing attitude. Poor me, how dare I question them. It is just inviting them to multiply their trespasses. What is worse, our desires never harmonise, they are always at loggerheads, always conflicting and always quarrelling.

When I feel like taking my siesta, they feel like having sports. If they would be kind enough to allow me to lie on my back quietly, as an I-cannot-help-it spectator, whilst they do the high jumping and the running and the pole vaulting on the field beneath which I sleep, I wouldn't mind because that would mean training me to be more tolerant. But the pity of it all is, they don't. Sometimes the high jumpers miss and the pole falls on me. At other times too, they themselves lose their equilibrium and fall heavily on me —thus bruising me with their weight and polluting me with their pungent smell. And of course, when such unhappy cases occur, I, the poor victim, have to run to the doctor to cure my bruises and see the ever-ready-to-squeeze-out-money storekeepers for some Milton to wash off their acrid smell. All this is a big agent of erosion on my economic resources.

At times too, when there are no sports, Miss Sun, the residential bread-baker, bakes her bread and the oven being perpendicularly above my head, I am often more baked than the bread in the hot oven. It is impossible to convince this nagging woman to bake her bread at any other time except twelve o'clock.

Of course, with Miss Sun, I can say " there is comfort in every situation however wretched ". She never fails to give me ice cream in the evening, so that is a big consolation. But the lizards and the mice . . .

Talk I must, and I did question and advise them to have some respect for my age, experience and learning, by stopping all that rank nonsense.

"You man, don't encroach upon our rights—don't dictate to us what we must do and what we must not do—know that dictators are out of place in a democratic world such as ours. You have rented the four corners of the room and we have rented the two sides of the roof—if you don't want the sight of us, and our unavoidable falls on you, then try to separate your four walls from our two sides of the roof by the thickest ceiling your academic degrees can devise—if you fail to do this, our best advice is, don't be silly."

Thus rebutted I humbly approached the landlord with the characteristic humility of a tenant and poured forth in a profuse strain the litany of the gross offences committed against me by the mice and the bats and the lizards.

The landlord, who has an epidemic terror for any thing that sounds like "Expenditure," was not prepared to embark upon the project of ceiling my room.

And yet, suggestions and remarks, however much they may be rebutted in the beginning, sometimes bring home some rich curative effects in the end. My appeal to the landlord to get my room ceiled, which seemed as tasteless as a cube of sugar in the mighty ocean, in the long run effected something good. To escape belling the cat, the landlord suggested that I should rather employ a qualified steward, who could solve the heart-rending situation within a twinkle of an eye. This meant, of course, taxing my economic resources and not his. I had to choose between staying at the old premises and employing a steward whose salary would perpetualise my economic instability; and leaving the house to face that awful problem of finding a room in Accra which often compels honest people to shun recognising old faces (when they are suddenly confronted) or to dodge all familiar faces (when they are the first to see such faces) for fear these faces might know that they are roomless Johnnie Walkers.

A beggar has no choice but here I was an exception. I had a choice and therefore chose the former, and employed a highly recommended and best capacitated steward, Mr. Cat.

In fact, Mr. Cat proved to be efficiency personified. Within just two days, the co-tenants at the naked roof had become as dumb and as noiseless as a blank wall and as still as still could be. The slightest self assertion they displayed meant the loss of their individualities, and the felicious augmentation of the honourable steward's morsels and capacities. His sharp whiskers were ever on tip toe, his bright keen eyes were ever yearning and itching for action. His claws were ever sharp and ready to claw, and to tear to sumptuous morsels any mouse or lizard or bat who even posed as a pole vaulter or high jumper.

The few that managed to keep their heads by remaining actively passive were very bony. Their skin assumed a supernatural transparency, and their ribs could be counted. They were living skeletons, speeding precipitately towards annihilation.

Conditions began to take a happy turn—they grew from worst to worse, and then to bad—and so to good, and from good to better—but very unfortunately, they never became perfectly vee-shaped. Before I could score the superlative conditions of affairs, something very sad happened.

One fine Saturday morning, a very faithful precursor of a jolly good Easter day, when the sun filled the earth, with its charming and fascinating festive smiles, I decided to take that Easter Sunday smile with broad smile of a banquet. I bought a guinea fowl, for a guinea, and sent it to Miss Kind to make it appear at my Easter table.

I chose Miss Kind because I trusted her cooking capacities. Miss Kind, the Headmistress of Domestic Science in the Amalgamated School, displayed all her tactful dexterity and skill in translating my wishes into a concrete reality. Thus the long expected Sunday, arrived, accompanied by the well toned guinea fowl, gracefully clad in a rich brown swimming jersey and swimming in a delicious pool of sauce, wonderfully seasoned, palatably and sweetly embellished with first class spices and ingredients. Every nose that smelt the discharge of the highly scented and sweet odour of the dish was bound to grow wild with uncontrollable anxiety. My teeth began to water, my tongue instinctively began to jump about and even my eyes could feel, how exactly I don't know, the most categorically assured palatability of the dish.

I therefore determined to compose a befitting atmosphere for gourmandising, and to break that day the record established at my table. I left the dish happily resting on the table, and made for the nearest canteen ("Eat All Canteen," it was), to buy "You are lucky today wine", to accelerate the already quick flow of my saliva, and to heighten my agile appetite. Meanwhile, Mr. Cat the steward was standing faithfully by—watching. Before I left, I asked him to chase away any intruder who might visit my dining room in my absence. I traversed a distance of seventy-seven yards and still I could smell the sweet scent of my dish. If men were to serve their country with the straightforwardness and the conscientiousness and the anxiety with which I set off to get the "You are lucky today," we should enjoy such first class rapidity in our progress that our world could be most accurately described as a social, cultural and political paradise. I got the bottle and I was on my home trip—I was fifty yards nearer and I did not smell anything. I blew my nose, thinking my nostrils were not clear. And still I did not smell anything. I drew nearer still and I heard nothing. This time I breathed in heavily, and still no scent of the sweet dish.

I ran home as fast as my legs could serve me, and there I was—dish and everything gone. If you had been in my shoes, what would you have done?

With eyes sparkling with anger and disappointment, with a voice vibrating with painful disappointment and with a tongue suffering from the pangs of deprivation of such a *bonum delectabile*, I volleyed questions at my steward. " I found it to be a disturbing intruder, so I chased it out, as you directed me to do," was all the answer I got.

" Did I ever say so. And if yes, how can a dish be an intruder ?" said I.

" It filled the place with its unharnessed odour, and fearing it might pollute the air, and therefore mar the happy-go-lucky mood of Easter, I just got rid of it." "How?" " Good Heavens above; by simply removing it from the table and by keeping it where its odour would not be felt." I plucked up hope and quietly asked for the place where the dish had been kept.

" Goodness me, why brood over spilt milk, I have kept it in in my stomach ", said Mr. Cat.

"This is gross misconduct—I thought you could construct a line of demarcation between the intrusion of the mice and the innocent objects of my delight—I thought you were efficiency personified, not knowing that you are a helpless monument of harmful inefficiency. Truly, a fool will be a fool, whether he goes to school or not."

I made a very clever move to catch hold of that mighty and saucy steward, and thrash him as mercilessly as I could give vent to my anger. But he quickly took to his heels, and I was left without a steward and back to my A.B.C.

So I decided to leave the house and find a better place to stay.

2. The Search For A New Room

I spent my Easter Monday moving from house to house, eagerly trying to get somewhere to settle.

Quite unexpectedly, I found myself behind a palatial building which was a living advertisement of the splendour and the beauty of modern scientific and architectural achievements.

I entered with a great air, and asked to see the landlord. I met him quite happily having a drinking bout. He wore a mighty moustache which had been purposely grown to play the role of a sieve when he was drinking thick palmwine. His eyes moved as actively as the hungry eyes of an eagle, and the palmwine had made him more eloquent than Dingle Foot, and more actively lively than an American. I noticed there were two types of people in that drinking bout—the quick and the dead. Either quick or dead they had to be. From the way the landlord responded to my good afternoon, I got to know that he did not understand a word of English. And I do not know why he took me to be a Ga speaker; he very seriously spoke Ga to me and his Ga was Greek to me. *Oblayo* was the only alpha and omega I understood.

He looked at me and I looked at him. The silent trade is actually out of application when one is after a room to rent, otherwise I must have applied my knowledge of it. In the long run, I got a gentleman to communicate my intentions to him and I became very sorry, for his *Oblayo*, meant, I looked too young— was unmarried and therefore girls (the *Oblayos*) would be haunting me if I came to stay there. I regretted I had told him beforehand that I was a bachelor, otherwise I might have told him that though I look young, I have a wife and two children.

Any way there was much sense in what he said. He wanted a married man to stay there, so that the wife might take charge of the house, sweeping and lighting fire there. These two things are very dear to an old Ghanaian.

I saw my mistake. I shouldn't have said I was a bachelor. But before then, I was made to believe that stressing the fact that I was a bachelor would quickly find me a room to rent. But here this information did not work efficiently. There I was in a very big dilemma. Should I change my tongue or should I not change it? I asked my interpreter to tell the landlord that I wanted to modify what I had just said; that is, if I said I am not married, it does not necessarily mean that I am not engaged to a woman. I am, and I am going to get married. This week would see me a married man and so if he could—he might settle matters with me, and I would come with my wife the following week and that would fully qualify me to be his tenant. My wife would sweep the house, light fires there to make the *Asamanfo* happy, whenever they paid their visit.

Getting married that week, became a *conditio sine qua non* for my occupying the two chambers and a hall of the first floor at the monthly rentage of £12. I knew I had not engaged any woman, so I planned with the constructive advice of bosom friends, to visit a night club—where I could as quickly get a wife as I wanted to get married.

At last I came to the club. I increased my store of experience by many rich deposits of face-facts-in-the-face incidents. I stoutly called for a bottle of stout, and two bottles of beer. I lighted my Town Hall, and began to play the big man. I had thrown in the bait and I was expecting a good catch. My expectations were answered.

As I enthusiastically sat stouting and beering my spirits, two attractive ladies made their advance towards me. My heart was filled with brightly smiling prospects. That was already the beginning of a good enterprise. They greeted me nicely and my heart leaped with joy.

One of them started to address me with a big *Ofane* and I beg your pardon, *Minu Ga* was my quick reply. They smiled and I returned a broader smile as I realised there was a world of meaning in their smiles.

While still standing, one of them opened a stream of heart-to-heart conversation with me. " Please, it seems I know you " was the next sentence. " Of course, sweet ladies, I have travelled the length and breadth of Ghana, I am a big viator. I am sure it is quite true you know me and I am glad you have made this remark. I nearly made the same remark." They looked at me and smiled very confidentially.

They came up to my fancy. They were exactly the types of ladies who could call forth a young man's sensibilities. From the sparkling beauty of their faces—from their blooming rosy cheeks made more rosy by pancake—from their sweet lovely lips made lovelier by lipsticks—and from the superfine sweet fragrance which graced the air about them, I quite logically deduced the following:—

That they were specialists in the fascinating modern plastering arts of "Pancaking and Lipsticking and Love-inviting." Doctors of Lavender—Sprinklology they were.

There they stood before me—their sweet eyes swimming in a jolly pool of love, and not a bit in a hurry to leave me. I essayed to invite them to sit down, but again I was seared by their appearances. They looked so very dignified that my much boasted dignity did not seem commensurate with theirs. They bloomed and blossomed with dignity and grace and splendour. Very reasonably tiny-waisted, slim, flexible, smooth-skinned and in fine they were a wonderful tapestry skilfully woven with the interlacing threads of all that is existable in the thrillingly sweet province of Lady Beauty.

"Will you give me the honour, sweet ladies, of sitting down by me?" And scarcely had I ended the wording of my invitation, than I saw these ambassadors of beauty sitting one on my left and the other on my right. Every repeated glance I cast unveiled a new world of beauty.

They were as bright as the sun, lovely as the moon and as terrible as they were flirtatious. With sweet fingers and with finger nails glistering with masterly manicure, they rang glasses. I had the exclusive monopoly of paying for the drinks, and I executed that self-courted troublesome task with interlocking consistency. They had the privilege of constantly placing orders for this brand and that brand. It was indeed very expensive to bid them company.

Besides being great cosmeticians, they were highly qualified Fellows of the Royal Institute of Alcohol.

They drink with masterly poise all brands of drinkables—except cola, which was too strong for their weaker sex. The atmosphere was quite serene and aesthetic. Many more ladies, some of similar and others of dissimilar description, began to pour in.

A dance soon started. My two ladies who were so advantageously slim, so conveniently tiny-waisted and so tactfully flexible, quickstepped and mamboed and calypsoed with characteristic flexibility and elasticity of rubber. So light-lipped that those delicate lips could wear nothing heavier than charming smiles.

Yes, I should not lose light of the patent fact that Lido is not a garden of beautiful flowers only. According to the Akan proverb *Kurow biara Mensa wo mu* which being literally interpreted means—In every town there is a third born. I encountered some ladies whose descriptions were in conflict with those already described.

The *Mensas* (Third Born) of the night club looked so thick-lipped that their lips could easily suspend a fat bottle of beer in the air, and still render the force of gravity absolutely incapable of doing anything about it—a passive on-looker it must willy-nilly be. So bulky and so heavy and so superlatively the opposite of flexibility and elasticity that they moved about and danced with the flexibility of a big timber log. What a wonderful ocean of difference I witnessed in their typologies. But, however greatly they differed in appearances, they had, as correctly as facial expressions could dictate to me, a unity of purpose—and that was to be very "Sikaditious" and never to be in a hurry to get married to any young man who was sufficiently in a hurry to get married with the big "UT of purpose," namely to get a house to rent. They were all after a lily of the valley *affaire de coeur*—a love affair which is strictly a nine-day wonder. No amount of wording or bossing could convince any of them about the usefulness and the necessity for doing what Adam and Eve did. No lady in the catalogue was prepared to have a husband, even for a period of one week.

That is always the case—men are more often than not interested in women, and women in men. I was by no means an exception that day. I did not mind those of my sex and moreover I knew from experience that they could not help me; or even if they posed as helpers, they would only be developing the axe they might have to grind in so doing. At best, they would be arranging things for themselves.

I left the place completely broke—without any balm for the pangs of my wounded ambition. I abandoned the old idea of getting accommodation in that house whose walls welcomed only the married.

The apple was sour—after all, this was not the only building that observed good architectural norms—and therefore it was not the only beautiful building in town. After all, it was too remote. That was how I cheered up my sinking spirits.

Try, try, try again became my slogan, and I tried and tried and tried again. This time, I was ever on the alert to study circumstances before voicing out anything. At long last, news struck my enquiring ears about a house to let.

After what I called a serious study of the circumstances of the place—I drew the conclusion that a married person would have more chances of success than a bachelor. So I put on my big D.B. coat, lighted my big cigar, all to make me appear rather special, and I set out on my adventure. With a friend's child resting in my arms, I arrived at the house—this time I was welcomed by a landlady who looked superbly wicked and nagging. I told her what I had come there for, avoiding all premature information about myself.

And she asked me, "Is this your child?" and I said yes. And she said," Is it a product of your unharnessed lust or is it a legitimate child?" And I said, "Be sure I wouldn't do anything that is illegitimate—that is to say, the child is a legitimate son." And she said, "May I therefore understand that you are married?" And I said, "There is no harm in trying." And she said, "You are married, and you want my room—anybody who is married is no friend of mine and therefore cannot be a tenant here." I was trying to scratch my head in protest when she proudly left me, to entertain the furniture if I cared.

Married or not married—that is the question—and the answer lies in your star and not in yourself, for whether married or not married, you can be given or be refused a room to rent.

Palm Leaves Of Childhood
By Gyormbeeyi Adali-Mortty

When I was very small indeed,
   and Joe and Fred were six-year giants,
My father, they and I with soil
   did mix farm yard manure.
In this we planted coconuts,
   naming them by brothers' names.
The palms grew faster far than I;
   and soon, ere I could grow a Man,
They, flowering, reached their goal!
Like the ear-rings that my sisters wore
   came the tender golden flowers.
I watched them grow from gold to green,
   then nuts as large as Tata's head.
I craved for the milk I knew they bore.
I listened to the whispering leaves:
To the chattering, rattling, whispering leaves,
When night winds did wake.

They haunt me still in work and play:
Those whispering leaves behind the slit
On the cabin wall of childhood's dreaming and becoming.

Hot Day
By Kwesi Brew

The sheep are laid in mid-day slumbers
    And drizzling heat cumbers
      The flying of the clouds:
No cloud flies, no wind shouts
    In the mumbling noon.

The molten heat shivers on the space,
    The white egrets make pace,
      The purple starlings sing:
Their shoulders roll, their cries ring
    In the mumbling noon.

The Literary Society
By Henry Ofori

Narrator: The story takes place in a little town in the interior of the country. In such places well known in Ghana, people from other parts, because of their various occupations, are compelled to live in this town, Akutuase, and pursue their daily duties under the most austere conditions. The literate folk in the town find it necessary, in order to make life more pleasant, to run a social and literary club. The club in fact is the academy of learning in this little community. To show how earnest the members are in the deliberations, we present to you one, just one, incident in the club-room.

It is evening in Akutuase and as that day happens to be a club meeting day, we find a group of the members in front of the cocoa shed (which is used as the club house), waiting for the President in order that the day's business may begin.

Nkansa: I wonder what is keeping the President at home. I am sure he is still drying his cocoa beans ... ha ... ha ...ha.

Asante: You cannot say anything about anybody without making fun of him. I wonder what is wrong with you.

Nkansa: You mean what is right with me. There is nothing wrong with me but there is everything wrong with you, my dear Asante.

Asante: Don't call me " My dear Asante ", you are not even half my age, yet you think you are my equal.

Nkansa: God forbid ... imagine me being of such a mental disposition as you are.

Asante: What do you mean by that, eh ... what?

Nkansa: If you don't understand the language, I am afraid I am not going to teach you now. (*Laughter.*)

Asante: So you are laughing, are you? You always encourage this boy to be proud. I must warn you that if he abuses me again and I decide to beat him, no one should interfere.

Sokportie: I cannot understand why you two people are always at the point of fighting. I shall recommend to the President that we buy some boxing gloves for those who want to try out their strength ...ha ...ha ...ha ...!

Effects: (*Conversation lapses and a Mammy Truck passes by.*)

Asante: Honestly these drivers are at times reckless. Look at how that fellow drove past, and he is passing through a town too. That is how they come to knock down our goats.

THE TOWN

Sokportie: Last week four sheep and one goat were killed by passing mammy trucks. I wish the police would make a law to make killing sheep a crime.

Nkansa: The police have better things to do than make such unnecessary laws. Sometimes it is the fault of the sheep and goats.

Asante: Which reminds me that some human beings behave like sheep.

Nkansa: By which you mean . . . ?

Asante: Have I mentioned your name? Are you the only human being here? Why are you always so proud?

Nkansa: I think I am a human being and I think that you are not mad to talk to the wind, and that you were addressing yourself to us.

Asante: And if I was addressing myself to you all, are you the spokesman of the group? (*He moves threateningly towards Nkansa, and Mr. Sokportie comes between them.*) You must be careful, you hear. You must be very, very careful.

Sokportie: Oh Mr. Asante, don't do that. What are you two doing, are you small boys? (*The President, Mr. Osafo, arrives and moves up to them.*)

Osafo: What is happening here, are they fighting?

Nkansa: No, President, Mr. Asante and I disagreed to agree and we were actually trying to show each other who was the wiser. (*Laughter.*)

Osafo: Is everybody here? We should go in and do business you know, time is far spent.

Nkansa: (*Aside.*) As if we have been delaying the meeting and not himself. (*They all troop into the club-room and seat themselves.*)

Effects: (*A bolt is drawn and gates clang open—Furniture is dragged—Then Silence*)

Osafo: (*Clearing his throat.*) I declare the meeting open. The Secretary may read the minutes of the last meeting.

Addo: On point of order, Mr. President, you forgot to say prayers.

Osafo: O, I'm sorry, gentlemen—shall we pray, gentlemen?

Effects: (*Chairs Creak.*)

Osafo: O Lord who has brought us into this little bush town in order that we may gain our daily bread in order to get strength to do thy good work, we pray you to bless our little club and keep us all along the path of righteousness so that we may learn something from our meetings.

	Bless this meeting tonight so that everything ends well ..... Amen.
Chorus:	A A A A-men!!!
Osafo:	I would like to advise members that though this is not a church we must learn to respond to prayers in the proper manner. What was the use of saying A A A A-men?
	I now call upon the Secretary to read the minutes of our last meeting.
Secretary:	Minutes of the meeting of the Akutuase Literary and Social Club held in the club room on Sept. 10th, 1957 under the Chairmanship of the Vice President Mr. Akosa. The minutes of the previous meeting was read and after necessary corrections had been made it was approved and adopted. The main matter of the evening was a lecture by Mr. Osato, President of the Club and manager of the Providence Cocoa Syndicate Limited. His topic was China.

As Mr. Osafo said at the beginning of the lecture, "No one could talk about China without talking about Japan, for the two", he maintained "are like Siamese twins". In fact, he continued, the last time he saw a Chinese and a Japanese (during the first world war in East Africa) he could hardly tell one from the other.

Mr. Osafo said that as the two countries had the same people, it was much easier to describe life in Japan as the Japanese were the same as Chinese. He said that both countries write their literature in the same manner ... that is from right to left and upside down. This made it difficult for other people like us to understand them. He said Japan had an Emperor but the Chinese had none but that did not make much difference since the Chinese had their first emperor called Jino Teno about 6000 B.C., long before the Japanese had any.

Mr. Osafo said that because Japan is an island, most of the inhabitants are sailors but China was one large land mass and as a result most of the people are farmers. Touching upon the question of education, he said that the Japanese were more clever than the Chinese for they could make aeroplanes out of bamboo sticks. He said he himself bought in the year 1933 a Japanese bicycle made out of bamboo for fifteen shillings at Accra and that the machine served him for about ten years.

THE TOWN

The Chinese on the other hand, he said, being farmers were only concerned with the production of farm products and were not interested in the manufacture of articles. He said that it was the Chinese who first discovered how to make pork. He said that there were two brothers in China called Bobo and Oti who kept pigs as domestic animals. He said one day, the pig-sty caught fire and before they could save the poor animals the animals had been killed by the fire. He said that Bobo and Oti were sad that their pets had died and so they went into the pig-sty after the fire to have a look at them. There they saw that their flesh had been roasted to a very appetising brown hue. Oti then tore off a piece of the flesh of one of the roasted pigs and ate it. He found it very tasteful and therefore asked Bobo to try it too. Bobo tried it and liked it and soon the whole village grew to like the taste of pork. In concluding his talk on China the President said that what always reminded him of China was the discovery of the palatability of roast pork.

In thanking the President for his brilliant exposition of life in China the Vice-President said that it was true that knowledge is powerful but experience is more powerful, for as he maintained, the President Mr. Osafo had never been to a Secondary School, but yet was capable of meeting any secondary school scholar in any field of study.

The meeting was brought to a close at 7.45 p.m.

Osafo: Well, gentlemen, you have heard the minutes read, if anyone has any correction or amendments to make, let him say so.

Nkansa: Mr. President, I have two corrections to make.

Asante: He always has corrections to make, as for this boy ...

Nkansa: Will you please shut up? If you have anything to say, address the chair.

Asante: Are you talking to me?

Nkansa: Of course, yes. Who are you?

Asante: And who are you, too?

Osafo: Please gentlemen, I resent any such exchange of bad words. You must remember we are all big men in our houses. I don't understand why you, Mr. Asante, should interrupt when someone is on his feet speaking.

Nkansa: That is what he always does when I get up to speak.

	I don't understand it at all.
Asante:	When did I interrupt your speech, eh when?
Osafo:	All right, all right, go on, Mr. Nkansa.
Nkansa:	Thank you, sir. As I was saying, I have two corrections to make in the minutes. I was not here myself during the lecture for I was on holidays, but I know that the Japanese never make aeroplanes out of bamboo. In the second place neither the Japanese nor the Chinese write upside-down. Its rather the Russians who write upside-down.
Secretary:	I remember very well the President saying that the Japanese make aeroplanes and bicycles out of bamboo and that both the Japanese and Chinese write upside-down. I therefore see no reason why I should change the statements. If . . .
Addo:	I very well remember the President making such remarks.
Osafo:	I do not remember ever making these statements which you now put in my mouth. I remember saying that the Chinese were the first to discover that pork was good to eat, especially with rice.
Sokpo:	Yes, I also remember the President saying that thing about the pork.
Secretary:	So you people mean to say that I imagined what I wrote down in the minutes book. If that is the case, then I am not suitable to be the Secretary and you can ask someone else to take the office.
Asante:	As for me, I shan't say anything. Whenever I say something, they say I am interrupting.
Nkansa:	You don't happen to talk at the right time. This is the time for you to say something, for you were here on that day.
Asante:	Was I addressing you eh? . . . be very careful, you Nkansa. What you want to see you will soon see.
Nkansa:	Prpprppprpprpp. What can you do?
Osafo:	Not again, Mr. Nkansa. If you and Mr. Asante continue like this I shall have to use my powers as President to ask you to leave this room. Why are you two always quarrelling like women? (*Pause*) And now about this China thing, I never said those things so they may be deleted.
Secretary:	But Mr. President I distinctly heard you say that when you saw a Chinese and a Japanese during the world war in Burma you could hardly tell the difference.

Osafo:	Of course I said that, but what had that got to do with bamboo aeroplanes ? I was just referring to the physical features of the two peoples. Any more corrections ?
Asante:	If people are going to say one thing today and change their minds tomorrow because a small boy just out of College thinks it is wrong, then this club is not going to have any future.
Osafo:	Mr. Asante, I strongly resent your statement. It is in fact a deliberate attempt to discredit my integrity and character. It is good that I am the President, otherwise I would have considered it so personal that we would have to settle the case outside this house. I gave the lecture and know what I said. Why try to baffle me by putting things that are not true in my mouth, eh .... why ?
Secretary:	Is it the general wish of the house that I delete those two statements made by the President ?
Nkansa:	You should not say " Those two statements made by the President ", because he denies ever having made them.
Secretary:	I suppose you would be a better secretary than myself ? All along I have noticed how you have intentionally tried to discredit me, so that you may be offered the post. I am not being paid to do this and if you want to take over, you can take over right now.
Nkansa:	Of course, I would be a better secretary. For one thing I shall not put fictitious statements to the credit of people who haven't made them.
Secretary:	All right then, come and take over the post right now. (*Secretary gets up as if to leave the room.*)
Addo:	Mr. Secretary, don't do that. You know we have in our constitution how secretaries may be appointed, removed or may resign. What you are trying to do now is not in the constitution. If therefore you feel you have been offended so much that you want to resign, you have to go through the proper formalities. You don't just get up and say, I have resigned.
Secretary:	So I am not being constitutional ? All right. I shall hand in my resignation to the President after the meeting.
Osafo:	If there are no more corrections or amendments, will somebody please move for the minutes to be accepted as the correct proceedings of the last meeting. (*Silence.*)

Nkansa:	I move that the minutes as corrected be accepted by the house.
Addo:	I second the motion.
Osafo:	Those in favour say Aye.
Voices:	Aye Aye Aye (*about five voices*).
Osafo:	Those against...? Since no one seems to be against the motion, I shall sign the minutes book. Well, to today's business. The Treasurer has to give us a report on the state of our finance.
Secretary:	On point of order. I think it is the duty of the financial secretary.
Kublenu:	No, it is not the financial secretary who should give such a report. It is the duty of the treasurer. After all he keeps the money. How can I give a report on our finance if I don't know how much we have in our coffers?
Nkansa:	I think he is right, gentlemen.
Asante:	I think he is wrong.
Nkansa:	Of course you always think wrongly. (*Laughter.*)
Sokportie:	I don't mind if you ask me to give the financial report. I know how much we have in the coffees.
Osafo:	In the what fees?
Sokportie:	In the coffees, Mr. President.
Osafo:	Oh coffers.
Sokportie:	Yes coffecs. We have three pounds sixteen shillings and ninepence halfpenny. We at first had four pounds.
Nkansa:	What do you mean by, at first?
Sokportie:	I mean this morning we had four pounds. But this morning the secretary came for three shillings and threepence. The three shillings was for writing pad and a minutes book. The threepence was for the bottle of ink you see on the Secretary's table.
Asante:	If that is the situation, then how came the halfpenny in the account?
Sokportie:	Well, this morning when I opened the tin box in which I keep the money for the club, I saw a halfpenny in it. I asked my wife whether she put it in, but she said no. I was not able to find out where it came from.
Asante:	In other words, your wife knows where we keep our money?
Nkansa:	And why not? They both live in the same house and if he does not tell her about it, she may go and take some money out of it.

Sokportie: In fact, she gave me the tin box which used to contain chocolates.

Asante: Then I suppose one of your five children went and put in the halfpenny.

Osafo: Mr. Asante, I don't understand why you are making all this fuss about such a small matter. The treasurer is not short of money. In fact we have made a profit of a halfpenny. I personally don't see anything wrong with that.

Asante: I see a lot wrong that. Today he is halfpenny surplus, tomorrow he will be two pounds short. What sort of accounting system is he using? If I find a halfpenny in my pocket, I certainly would know how it got there.

Nkansa: Everybody here knows that. (*Laughter.*)

Asante: It is important that our treasurer should know how to keep our money so that it does not mix with other people's.

Osafo: All right, Mr. Asante, we shall tell the treasurer not to mix our money with other people's. Mr. Sokportie, you may continue with the report.

Sokportie: Unfortunately, not all members have paid their dues up to now.

Addo: How many have not paid?

Sokportie: Two have not paid. One member has been on trek since a month ago but he wrote to me that he will pay as soon as he gets back here.

Addo: And is the other man who has not paid here in town?

Sokportie: Yes, in fact he is in this room.

Nkansa: This is a shame. Even I have paid.

Asante: What do you mean by, even you? Are you not working like everyone else?

Nkansa: And what about you? Are you not working? Have you paid your dues?

Asante: I have not paid but that is not my fault. I told Mr. Sokportie that at the end of the month he should come and collect it.

Osafo: But Mr. Asante, as a responsible adult and a gentleman, you do not have to wait for the treasurer to come to you for your dues. You should have brought the money with you to this meeting. I would advise members not to give too much trouble to our treasurer.

	He is not being paid for this job. Members should always help him by sending their dues to him. He is a very busy man indeed, as you may all know.
Asante:	We are all very busy men.
Addo:	Don't say that, Asante. I am a busy man too, but I always send my dues to Mr. Sokportie in his house.
Osafo:	I think the matter is settled and Mr. Asante should bring his dues to the next meeting. (*Laughter*.) We shall get on to the next item on the agenda. Membership—I regret to say that the membership over the last two years has been dropping gradually. At the beginning of 1955 we were fifty strong. Now we are only nineteen. I know several people have been transferred from this town to other parts of the country but others have come here to take their places. I cannot understand why we have not been able to attract these people into our club.
Asante:	I know why. We do not plan interesting activities, on the other hand when we come here, the meetings develop into a discussion of personal matters. No one would like to come into a club of equals only to be laughed at or abused by small boys.
Addo:	Your reasons, Asante, are not sensible.
Asante:	You see what I was saying . . . abuses . . . that is all we hear at these meetings.
Addo:	Perhaps I used the wrong word, but what I was trying to say was that your reasons for the refusal of other gentlemen in this town to join us are not realistic at all. I think the reason is that these people are more interested in getting drunk every night than in coming here for intelligent discussion. Here is the storekeeper of the U.A.C. shop, ask him how many times these people call on him to buy drinks. When a man is interested in getting drunk, nobody but a missionary can make him put a stop to the practice. I personally do not see why we should worry because these people refuse to become members. In such matters, I think it is the quality of the members and not the quantity that matters.
Nkansa:	Hear, hear!
Addo:	We may have seventy members, but if they are of the wrong type, you will soon see that this will become not a Social and Literary Club but a boozemen club.

All:	Hear, hear, hear!
Sokportie:	I agree in toto with what the last speaker said. Even with our small number of members, you all know the amount of trouble I find for myself when it comes to collecting dues.
Asante:	This has nothing to do with dues. We want more members and you get up to talk about dues. I bet if someone else becomes the Treasurer, you will give the same amount of trouble if he comes to collect the dues from you. (*Laughter*.)
Osafo:	Do I take it that it is the wish of members to restrict the number to what it is at present?
Voice:	Yes!
Osafo:	On the other hand I had in my mind a bright idea for making our membership balanced. What I mean is this: you see all the members are males. Every time we hold a dance we always have to ask a lady (my wife) to act as the M.C. with one of our members. I think it will be a good idea if we had some female members. What do you think?
Addo:	I think it is a good idea, but from where are we going to get the ladies?
Osafo:	I was coming to that. Fortunately this year we have had the fortune of being blessed with three female teachers in the primary school. Apart from these, a midwife has come to set up her practice in this town. The Government has kindly sent a telephone operator here too.
Nkansah:	But I understand the post master wants to marry her.
Asante:	Marry who?
Nkansa:	The telephone operator.
Asante:	What has that to do with us? We want female members and the telephone operator is a female, that is all that should concern us.
Osafo:	I don't think in this particular respect the problem is as simple as all that. You all know how antagonistic the post master is towards this club. When we want to bank our money in the Post Office Savings Bank, he is always insulting because he says he knows we would constantly be coming to him to withdraw part of the amount. What is more, ever since we refused to allow him to come to our last dance without a ticket, he has stopped talking to me. In that case I shall not be

	surprised at all if he refuses to allow the woman to become a member.
Asante:	But the woman is not married to the post master yet.
Nkansa:	But they are friends. He is always in her house.
Asante:	He is always in her house and so what? You are always in the house of one of the female teachers but does that mean you are her friend?
Nkansa:	You see how he is trying to twist everything to suit his evil mind! We are talking about the telephone operator and you come in with this accusation. If we are to make accusations and allegations about some of us here in relationship with these female teachers, some people here will be having trouble with their wives in the house. *(Laughter . . . Uproar.)*
Osafo:	Gentlemen, the matter is an important one that concerns all of us and I will not allow personal remarks to be made. You two, Nkansa and Asante, seem to be great rivals at something. I hope it is not about one of the female teachers. *(Laughter.)* Gentlemen, I think the best thing to be done in the case of the telephone operator, whom I am sure we all find very charming, is for one of the younger men to cultivate her friendship and draw her into the club.
Nkansa:	And what about the post master?
Asante:	What has the post master got to do with it? We want the girl, not the man. *(Prolonged laughter.)*
Osafo:	Seriously, gentlemen, I think that is the best way to get the young woman into the club. I have been in this sort of thing in several towns, and every time, I found that we had female members only when the women were interested in some of the men.
Addo:	May I suggest, Sir, that Mr. Nkansa who is the youngest and most handsome among us be asked to make it his task to woo the young woman.
Asante:	You couldn't have suggested a better man. *(Laughter.)*
Nkansa:	President, I resent the statement made by the last speaker and I am asking him to withdraw it.
Osafo:	Oh Mr. Nkansa, but that was a compliment. We are all aware of the immensity of your attraction and amorous propensities. *(Laughs.)* In fact I am sure you will not be surprised to know that I think you have been experimenting with your talents on my eldest daughter. *(Uproar in the house.)* It is bound to

	happen in the life of every young man, expecially when he is as intelligent as he is handsome. We all did that when we were young.
Asante:	Tell him more, oh father, tell him more.
Nkansa:	Tell who more ? You are happy that I am being labelled as a lady follower. What about you ?
Asante:	What about me ?
Osafo:	All right, all right, let us stop there. What about the lady teachers ? I am sure being teachers, we shall not find it difficult to get them in as members. I hesitate to suggest who should contact them on the point, but as Mr. Nkansa is also a teacher in the same school, I am sure he will find the task easy.
Nkansa:	On the other hand, Mr. President, there are some people in this room here who are more intimately connected with the ladies in question. There is one man here, who though he is married, can be found always hanging around the houses of these lady teachers. (*The Club room becomes uneasily quiet, only broken by the distant titter of one or two members.*)
Asante:	There is a Twi proverb which says " words fear the beard ". Mr. Nkansa, if he is really a man, he should come out with the facts of the case instead of casting insinuations.
Nkansa:	If the cap fits you, wear it, so says another popular proverb.
Asante:	You are a coward, why don't you mention the name of this married man ?
Nkansa:	I have said what I have said. In fact I will say more. This married gentleman in question was on one night thrown out of the room of one of the female teachers (*laughs*) and not only that but the gentleman in question knocked his forehead against the door and had a deep cut. So let us see who in this room has bandaged his head. (*Laughter... as Asante rushes to where Nkansa stands and slaps him.*) So you have slapped me !
Asante:	And I am going to slap you again.
Osafo:	Mr. Asante, stop that childish behaviour. (*Nkansa slaps him back and the two get into a huddle.*) Mr. Asante, stop that.
Asante:	But didn't you see him slap me ?
Addo:	But you slapped him first.

Osafo:	Separate them, somebody! This is very disgraceful, two grown ups... hey, mind what you are doing, you are overturning my table. (*The two men struggle while the other members try in vain to separate them. Mr. Nkansa lifts Asante up and throws him on the President's table, thus overturning the bottle of ink on the President's clothes. Pause.*) Look what you have done. You have ruined my white trousers with this ink.
Secretary:	We just bought this bottle of ink and look what you have done to it. Overturned it all into the President's trousers.
Osafo:	This is no laughing matter. You know how much these trousers cost me? I ordered the suit from England, now look what you have done. What am I going to tell my wife? This is very disgraceful. Two grown ups, fighting like market women. The club should suspend you two gentlemen now.
Addo:	Yes, I think they should be suspended.
Sokportie:	And be made to pay for the bottle of ink. But, Mr. President, I think they should be made to shake hands so as to forget what has happened.
Nkansa:	I am not going to shake hands with that ass.
Asante:	Who is an ass? Hey, look sharp, you see. (*Rushes towards Nkansa again.*)
Kuble:	You are being foolish, Asante. The mere fact that you give me eggs from your station farm does not mean that I should back you when even I think you are in the wrong. After all, don't I pay for the eggs and vegetables you send to my wife?
Asante:	So I am foolish, all right, I'll say nothing, I leave everything in the hands of the father above... what I have done to you people to merit this hostility from you all!
Osafo:	That is a very stupid statement, Asante, and I am saying this not only as the President of this club but as your uncle as well. You have behaved very disgracefully today and I wish you would do what everybody expects of you, that is apologise. After all, you were the first to slap Nkansa, against whom you had already made allegations similar to what he made against you. You must be ashamed of yourself.

Secretary:	Mr. President, I suggest that we appoint a committee to go into the matter and suggest the measures we as the members of the club should take.
Addo:	I think that is a good idea.
Osafo:	Now that order has been restored, may I suggest that we deal with the last item on the agenda . . . The salary of the watchman and caretaker. The caretaker came to see me this morning to lay a complaint. He said he had not received his monthly salary of one pound ten shillings for the last three months. I know we have not enough money in the coffers but we must all the same pay him, for an agreement is an agreement. What do members suggest?
Nkansa:	I suggest we all pay a special levy of five shillings per head for the purpose.
Voices:	That is a good idea.
Osafo:	All right then, I shall empower the treasurer to collect the amount from you, starting from today. In the meanwhile I am going to pay the caretaker myself and shall collect the money we contribute into my pocket. Has anyone anything to be discussed before we adjourn the meeting?
Addo:	Yes. May I suggest that we buy two pairs of boxing gloves so that the next time any members want to fight, we let them do it in the proper manner? (*Loud laughter and fade.*)

It's Ritual Murder
By Lionel K. Idan

In bed I lay one chilly night,
My eyes weighed down with heavy sleep,
A host of bells with all their might
Were running riot in the deep.

It screamed with joy, each noisy bell,
So did all men in sinful bane,
For, this good news the noise did tell:
Our Lord today is born again.

But, as I listened in my sleep,
To this uproar of bells and men,
Some strange noise forced my mind to peep
Into an old deserted pen.

And there I saw, much to my shock,
Two sheep, two turkeys and two hens,
All grouped together like one flock,
Speaking as though in a conference.

" Why must we die," began one hen,
" Each time the Lord is born again ?
They spill our blood—these sinful men—
The Lord's arrival to proclaim."

" E'en since the day that Adam fell,
And might began to chase the weak,
We home-kept birds have lived in hell,
There's none, not one, who'll for us speak."

The next hen spoke in a mournful tone:
" When shall salvation reach us too ?
When shall we call our souls our own ?
When shall we know just what to do ? "

" Soon man—proud man of dev'lish plots—
Shall pounce on us our blood to spill,
Our flesh he'll boil in big black pots,
An ancient custom to fulfil."

With head bowed low and eyes in tears,
One turkey spoke, I heard her say:
" Our case is worse than yours, my dears,
Few turk's e'er see the New Year's Day."

" On Christmas Eve when all is Christ,
Men put poor turks in great distress;
They kill and eat our flesh with rice,
It's ritual murder, nothing less ! "

With tear choked voice the next turk' spoke:
" Strange things occur on this strange earth;
The frog perspires in his cold cloak
When lizard chews pepper in mirth."

'Thus we poor birds who are for peace,
Are made to pay for Adam's sin,
While Eve's real serpent lives in peace,
Himself and all his next of kin. "

A sheep then spoke in great dismay:
"A cruel world we're in, my friend!
Last Christmas Eve man took away
My parents and they ne'er returned."

" Yet Christ Himself so loved his sheep
That He became the Good Shepherd.
Our lambs His bosom there did sleep
When home from pastures green He led."

At last I heard the last sheep scream:
" Enough, my dear! Enough I say!
My salty tears unfettered stream,
When sorrow on my heart does prey."

Then saw they cruel man appear,
And all gave out one deafening cry;
It was a cry that told of fear,
The fear of death that was so nigh.

Big drops of tears rolled down my face,
As these poor things were marched away.
I tried in vain to plead their case;
But this last prayer my heart did say:

" Dear Lord, reveal to them who feast
On meat, what sin and harm is wrought
When'er they kill and bury beast
Inside their stomachs, there to rot."

The Wrong Packing Case
By F. K. Nyaku

Some years ago, Mr. Atta-Yao was a Senior Civil Servant in a certain department in Accra, and was put in charge of over 100 labourers and a few junior clerks. As he always asked a bribe of his subordinates by using the general formula, "do something", he was nick-named, "do something". This great bully dismissed labourers for the least mistake, but reinstated those who could give him a bribe. Whenever he had to recruit labourers or some junior clerks, he chose not those who showed promise but those who gave him bribes. Some applicants who were too poor to give anything were employed on condition that they should give half of their first month's wages. And that was not all. When the applicants got the employment, on pay days, Mr. Atta-Yao summoned the labourers one by one to his office where he paid and asked each one to "do something" with, say 10/-. Those who refused, he dismissed immediately.

One afternoon, all the labourers met and sent the following petition:

> Dear Mr. Atta-Yao,
>
> *We, the humble labourers working under you, beg to put this our humble petition before you. We beg you to call all of us together on pay days and to give us all that the Governor has given you to give us. Do not force anyone to "do something" again. We hear that your pay is about £60 a month, car allowance extra—if you sleep outside your house, the Governor pays you 10/- every night for sleeping. Kindly therefore leave our poor wages alone.*
>
> *We beg you not get angry and so sack all of us, but to consider this our humble petition.*
>
> > On behalf of all the labourers,
> > We remain
> > > Yakari Busanga,
> > > Johnson Kpakpo,
> > > Kwabena Akuamoa,
> > > Ayigbe Kofi.

Unfortunately, this petition failed to achieve its aim. It rather greatly offended Mr. Atta-Yao. The four labourers who signed the letter were dismissed instanter.

The day after this incident, a very poor but good-looking secondary scholar, by name Amoako, applied for a job in the Clerical branch. Mr. Atta-Yao was willing to employ Amoako if only Amoako would "do something". So he summoned Amoako to an interview and said:

"Well, Amoako, you want to be a clerk here eh? Are you prepared to do something?"

"Yes Sir," replied Amoako, "I am prepared to do anything you may ask me to do."

"You do not understand my point," said Mr. Atta-Yao. "I mean do something. Don't you know the meaning of "do something"? You want employment, "do something". Are you prepared to do something?"

" Yes, Sir," replied Amoako. " I am prepared to sweep your office everyday and to clean your car apart from my clerical duties."

" Nonsense "! shouted Mr. Atta-Yao. " Don't you understand Accra English?"

" I do, Sir, Master. That is the same English we use in Trans-Volta," replied Amoako.

" What do you mean? Go away!" bellowed Mr. Atta-Yao.

" Yes, Sir, Master, thank you Sir," said Amoako turning away.

At the door he asked another question:

" Please, Sir, may I come here to start work here early tomorrow morning?"

" Look here!" shouted Mr. Atta-Yao, " Don't be silly. You must do something before!"

" Please, Sir, what then am I to do?" asked Amoako.

" Go and ask your friends to tell you," said Mr. Atta-Yao.

" Please Sir," replied Amoako, " I came here only yesterday; I have no friends yet."

Mr. Atta-Yao now got annoyed and said, " Do not trouble me. You must do something. Go and ask my messenger. He will tell you. If you are not prepared to "do something ", never come here again. Troublesome fool!"

The messenger who was well trained in advising such applicants about doing " something " came and led Amoako to a quiet corner and explained everything to him. The messenger advised Amoako that since he, Amoako, wanted to be a " real clerk " and not a "common labourer" he had to give say £5 or to give a note promising to pay £6 at the end of the first month.

Amoako left the yard and went to his brother, the Zoo-keeper at Achimota. That afternoon the Zoo-keeper had caught a live snake which he meant to sell to the Professor of Zoology at Achimota. He put the snake into a packing case and nailed the lid onto it securely, after having made some holes at the sides to let in air. He placed this packing case on the floor in a corner of his food-store.

Amoako and the Zoo-keeper discussed at length what they would give Mr. Atta-Yao. Money was out of the question for they were very poor. At last, the Zoo-keeper decided to send one bottle gin and two live rabbits. The rabbits were bought and put into a packing case which was closed and ventilated. This second packing case containing the rabbits was placed on top of the one containing the snake. The Zoo-keeper warned Amoako several times that he should send the upper packing case to Mr. Atta-Yao.

Early the next morning, the Zoo-keeper left the house to feed his animals without carrying the snake away. He warned his brother Amoako for the last time to take the upper packing case.

When Amoako was ready to leave, he put the bottle of gin into his straw hand-bag and, remembering his brother's constant warning, took the upper packing case, and left for the office. As soon as Mr. Atta-Yao saw Amoako, he said, " Hey, you this troublesome boy, you are here again ! Are you now prepared to do something " ? " Yes sir," replied Amoako, " I am prepared now to do something, though I have not brought anything of much value; just two rabbits and one bottle gin, ' Old Tom Gin '. Kindly accept these from me."

Mr. Atta-Yao accepted the presents and employed Amoako. He opened the gin at once and took now a gulp, then a sip, alternately. After about 20 minutes, he finished about one-third of the bottle. While feeling tipsy, he got out of the office, shouted at two or three labourers, insulted four or five and threatened six or seven. He returned to his office and continued drinking. When he had drunk about half of the bottle, he suddenly remembered the rabbits. He got hold of a crow-bar, opened a part of the lid, put his left hand in to get hold of the ears of one of the rabbits, when he felt a very sharp and crisp bite. Being amazed at the kind of rabbit which could bite so severely, and now being completely intoxicated, he peeped into the box through the opening. The rabbits spat into his left eye, then in the right eye, almost simultaneously. He raised a very sharp alarm and several clerks ran to his aid.

Mr. Atta-Yao told them that he had been given a present of one bottle gin and two wonderful rabbits which bit his fingers and spat into his eyes. A labourer also rushed there and managed to open the packing case with great trembling. A big snake was seen inside it. Mr. Atta-Yao was rushed towards the Korle Bu hospital, but on the Korle Lagoon Bridge, he died.

The case was reported to the police and Amoako was arrested in his office. Just as Amoako was about to enter the Police Car, the " Go Inside ", the Zoo-keeper and his servant arrived with the Professor of Zoology, bringing along a similar packing case containing two rabbits. All these people were taken to the Charge Office at the main Police Barracks. Amoako's statement was taken but neither the Police nor Amoako nor the Zoo-keeper knew how it came about that the wrong packing case was taken. The Zoo-keeper blamed Amoako for not taking the upper packing case.

Amoako assured him that he had taken the upper packing case and accused the Zoo-keeper of placing the wrong packing case at the top. At the height of this argument, the Zoo-keeper's servant said in a trembling voice; "I beg you; it is all my mistake. I did not know that the packing cases contained different things and were placed in a definite order. When my master went to feed his animals and Brother Amoako went to take his bath, I went to sweep the food store. I removed the upper packing case and placed it on the floor where I had already swept. I removed the second one which was originally placed on the floor and placed it on top of the other. After sweeping the corner I simply pushed both of them together, in the new order, back to their place in the corner. I never knew I had made a great mistake."

Amoako was granted bail and requested to appear before the High Court. That fortnight was a time of stress and strain for Amoako. Rumours circulated that as he was the cause of Mr. Atta-Yao's death, he would surely be hanged. He became as lean as a shadow and his brother as thin as a pencil.

At last the day of judgement came. The court was packed full. A certain lawyer pleaded for the deceased for about 30 minutes, and made almost everyone sure that Amoako would certainly be hanged. Amoako was not a stammerer, but when he was asked to speak he stammered, just like a perfect stammerer. He trembled, perspired profusely, and admitted that he was guilty of giving a bribe but explained how he took away the wrong packing case and thereby gave the snake to Mr. Atta-Yao instead of two rabbits. He pleaded fervently for mercy. There were a few moments of complete silence, during which time everyone, except Mr. Atta-Yao's relatives, suffered severe mental agony on behalf of Amoako. At last, the judgement was pronounced. Mr. Atta-Yao was found guilty of accepting as bribe, one bottle gin and a live snake. His gratuity for his many years service was therefore forfeited. Amoako was also found guilty for giving as bribe, one bottle " Old Tom Gin " and a live snake mistaken for two rabbits. He was therefore asked to pay a fine of five pounds there and then, or to go to prison for two months with hard labour. Amoako looked appealingly to his brother the Zoo-keeper but the brother signalled to him that he had no money. It was the Professor who lent him money and thus saved him from imprisonment.

Amoako is still working in the office. He is climbing slowly but steadily.

Lines On Korle Bu
By Kenneth Macneill Stewart

'Tis 4 o'clock—at the Hospital's Gate
A crowd of visitors, in long queues, wait
Admittance to the many Wards that be,
On missions full of tender charity.

The gate is opened !—and they surge in, fast.
The last becomes the first—the first the last:
Each to a ward, in anxious haste, depart,
To tell a tale of home—and of the heart !—
A tale to charm the sick man on his bed,
And ease the fever in an aching head !
A smile would often ripple down a face,
That seemed so altered by the sick man's case,
Where deepened lines of pain in furrows show,
What he endured and suffered, here, below !

Beneath yon sheets and coverlet of green,
Stretches a weakened body spectre-lean,
With truant hope yet beaming in sad eyes
That lose their lustre as the fevers rise;
Or grow still dimmer as the pulse-beats fail,
As though man's help may prove of no avail !
The Nurses, ever quick to mark a change,
As quick the necessary things arrange.
The startled visitors are asked to go,
And diverse orders in succession flow.
Hot-water bottles and hot-pads appear;
And artificial oxygen is there,
While glittering in a square enamel tray,
Surgical instruments are in array.
Screens are pulled round the bed for privacy,
Such the procedure in emergency.
The Doctor, summoned, hastens to the scene,
And tense the lagging moments pass between
The drama o'er the bed where burns a light,
And men with death in mortal combat fight.
Under the breath, the Doctor's orders go;
And, silently, the Nurses, to and fro.
The perspiration covers his fine face.
As steadily he battles with the case.

Sometimes, there is a silence that appals,
That's only broken when a forceps falls
Into the tray with a metallic sound,
Or when some foot-step shuffles on the ground.
At least, the Doctor smiles—a sign of hope,
And tests the patient with his Stethoscope . . .
He bathes his hands, looks at the patient's face,
And satisfied, walks slowly from the place !
Such scenes like these, in Korle Bu, each day
Are treated as routine in their own way.
Well-trained and disciplined and well-behaved,
A fine staff works—and many lives are saved.
Here, gowned in green, the busy "S.R.N.",
Competes in knowledge with the seasoned men—
The "C.R.N.s"—who, also, play their part,
To make nursing, in Ghana, a fine art,
By raising to great heights—second to none—
A service that is brilliant—and well-done.
The pupil-nurse—the little girl in blue—
She, also, plays a part as splendid, too.
The zealous youth, that is in training, yet,
Let us not *his* services forget—
The youth with a fine, kindly, manly touch,
Forever willing—and he does so much
To help a patient ever in distress,
With comfort, nurtured in a charmed address !

At 5 o'clock, all visitors retire,
Leaving such gifts as patients may desire—
Like fruit, a tin of milk, sugar or bread,
While some leave monetary gifts instead.

At last the ward is cleared ! The evening food,
On a wheeled-trolley comes, and all things good
Are served to every patient in his bed,
Each to his choice, whether beef-broth and bread,
Kenkey, yam, rice and stew—what'er there be,
And a fine service goes on splendidly.
The dinner o'er, to beds lined in a row
Well-fed and cheerful, smiling patients go.
Then, the Night Staff bustle to relieve
The Day Staff that prepare to take their leave.

First, round the ward the Senior Nurse-in-Charge
Takes her reliever, there, explaining large—
As they stop at each bed—each patient's case,
Consistent with the practice of the place.
And as the long, expiring day is done,
At 6 o'clock the main lights are turned on.
A high fan helps to cool the sultry air,
And give more comfort to the patients, there!
The Nursing Sister, capped and gowned in white,
Inspects the ward to see that things are right.
The Night Nurse, now in charge, takes her around
Explaining every case with reasons sound,
Couched in respectful terms, with clarity,
Good judgment and responsibility.
The Sister, calm and pleased, nods her assent,
Greets every patient with a compliment.
From bed to bed, shedding a kindly light,
Goes this fine ebon angel of the night.
Th' inspection ended, with serene accord
She signs the Log—and, smiling, leaves the Ward!
The Nurse, now, seated at her table, reads
The notes containing every patient's needs.
She checks the medicines with careful ease;
Measures the doses—and more things than these—
Prepares the Hypodermic Syringe, too.
And so, the night's routine goes smoothly through.
In bed, the patients lie quiet and still,
While draughts of sleep their weary eyelids fill,
As on some blissful, health-exhaling shore,
In sleep, e'en those in pain, these realms explore.
Freed temporarily from its griefs, the brain
Grows numb to the sharp, piercing stabs of pain!
In sleep, a smile adorns the suff'rer's face,
Forgetful, even, of the time and place,
And the grave dangers which he, lately, ran
When, first, his frightful sufferings began.

As the still night wears on, a sigh—a groan!—
A cry of pain! a deep, but feeble moan
May break the silence with a pang of dread,
And bring the Night Nurse racing to a bed!
The sufferer put at ease, the Nurse moves on
To give attention to another one.

Sometimes, a patient in a horrid dream
May startle the whole Ward with a loud scream !
And springing bolt-upright, trembling in bed,
Stare into space and hold his aching head !
Such are tricks some frightful fevers play,
A worry to the mind by night and day !
The unforeseen is, always, ever near;
And the inevitable, too, is here.
In Hospital, the staff moves on its toes,
On the alert for dangers cramped with woes !
Blest are those ebon Florence Nightingales,
Whose patient service never, never fails !
Blest are those gentle hands, grown gentler, now,
That bind the wounds and soothe the aching brow;
That mother, just the same, the rich and poor,
And for each one a mother's kindness bore !
Blest is such everlasting charity,
Twice blest is all that lovely sympathy.

From somewhere, floats the clarion of a cock,
And, solemnly, there strikes a distant clock,
They, both, tell that the night is dying fast,
And in the grips of dawn it breathes its last !

Dawn, and the bustle of the Ward begins,
With sounds of buckets—and the sound of tins:
The shuffle of those well enough to walk:
The chatter of those strong enough to talk.
To the bath-room, in lines, patients repair
To have a bath and comb and dress their hair.
Around the Sterilizer, to and fro,
With buckets for hot-water, there, they go !
This movement goes on till the sun, and day
End the procession in a gentle way.

The Day Staff takes up duty, here, once more ;
And life goes on as it has done before.
The beds are tidied and the Ward is swept;
An atmosphere immaculate is kept.
The Nurse-in-Charge, to a chart, has arranged,
And order of the beds are quickly changed.
This is done for convenience—and they say,
'Tis done because it is the " Theatre Day ".

The " Theatre Day " . . . momentous day of all,
With its anxieties both great and small;
The complications with which these things are rife;
Its climax in a battle for a life !
These passing risks, doctors and nurses know;
But confident, about the task they go.

Now the wheeled-stretcher is brought to the bed—
The patient, half afraid, yet, smiles instead—
Nude, save for a white wrap, he's gently laid
In the cold stretcher and, at once, conveyed.
Into a spotless room the stretcher goes,
And robed in white and masked, standing in rows,
The Theatre staff attendants linger by.
Without a smile or murmur or a sigh !
The room, th' adjusting table, globes that shine,
Look like a studio in every line,
But a glass cupboard, showing instruments,
Tells the true story of the room's contents.
The scent of chloroform floats on the air.
What a tense silence hovers everywhere !
Ah, on a chilly table, they have laid
The patient, ready, for the Surgeon's blade !
Aproned and masked, silent and thoughtful—stern,
The Surgeon enters ! . . . It's not, yet, his turn.
The Anaesthetist finds the patient's vein,
And in ! the needle goes without much pain.
The patient, next, is asked to breathe in deep !
And something snaps ! . . . Then, darkness, silence—sleep !
Man-made eternity, like man-made death;
But with the soul, still, giving warmth and breath !

What happens next, no one has ever known,
Except the Surgeon and the Nurse, alone !
Ah, this great way, how many men have passed !
For many, too, this way has been the last.
But surgery is such an art, today,
There are less risks along this narrow way.
Long hours after, with a scorching head,
A parched tongue, pillowless—and deep in bed,
The patient, under strain and mental strife,
Slowly, with growing strength, returns to life !
Revived, the mind goes back into its prime,

Bewildered! lost to place—and even time!
And the wheeled-stretchers, rushing to and fro,
Bring and take patients with them as they go.
The patient leaves the Ward in life's full flush,
And comes back a still form cloaked in a hush!
Grand, tireless fellow! master of his art,
With all humanity in his large heart,
Theatre cases oft, all day, go on,
Before the Surgeon's heavy task is done.
He puts such trivial things as self behind,
And does his duty, nobly, for mankind.
He never stops to worry or complain,
And his best moments are, relieving pain!

Haven of mercy! sanctuary, too!
Realm of loyalties—such is Korle Bu.
Since the great Guggisberg gave birth and place
To this asylum, symbol of the race,
Its fame, from Ghana, through the world is known,
With fine distinctions, unique, of its own.
The age shall make that reputation grow,
Enshrined with a new glory, here, below!

Pay Day
By G. R. Hagan

Mr. Kofi Jackson, a book-keeper working in the firm of Industrial Agents Ltd., was receiving £35 a month. He saw an advertisement for a similar post offering a salary of £45 a month, so he applied. He was interviewed and three weeks afterwards received an appointment letter asking him to assume duty on the 1st February. The letter was dated 23rd January.

"Good show!" he exclaimed as he scanned the lines, thrilling with success.

"I'll surely be punctual! Let me write an acceptance of the post now!" After the first few moments of sensation his face darkened into sadness as it dawned upon him that he could resign from his present appointment only after giving a month's notice or refunding a month's salary in lieu of notice.

"Gracious!" he sighed giving the letter a more serious reading.

" What the deuce is this! Hm!" He folded the letter, put it back into the envelope, and sighed again. He looked into space and thought hard.

"No, a loan won't do; only last month I went in for thirty pounds for forty pounds—ten pounds interest!" His wife's baby was due early next month.

He got up, paced up and down.

"Stop the noise over there, infidels", he shouted to the children through the window.

"Kofi, you look exceedingly tired today," said Mr. Jackson's wife who had entered the room unnoticed. There was a pause as Mrs. Jackson thought about their problems.

"I saw the midwife this morning. She said these should be bought."

"All right! Put it somewhere," said Kofi, still looking through the window.

"There it is."

Having racked his brains without finding any way out, he turned round and threw himself into an arm-chair and temporarily ceased to think about his problems.

At dinner as Mrs. Jackson observed the unusually slow manner in which he ate his meal, she realised that her husband was disturbed.

"Kofi, what is worrying you?"

"It's nothing; I've left some work undone."

Mr. Jackson had a rather sleepless night.

The following morning he decided to see the Manager's wife. The manager himself was serious and bureaucratic, but his wife had shown kindness and a desire to talk to the staff whenever she visited the office. So Mr. Jackson was encouraged to go and see her. He marched to the bungalow.

"Is missus in?"

"Yes; you wait here," said the steward boy.

"Who is that?" the Manager's wife called.

"Myself, ma'am"

"Oh I do recognise your face—"

"I am Jackson, the book-keeper."

"Oh yes, Oh yes; what can I do for you?"

"Please, missus, I beg you, speak to your man about my pay. A man like myself with a family of six, I get only £35 a month. Please do try to get for me, say forty-five pounds—"

"What! An increase of ten pounds a month! It is unthinkable! If at all there will be any help, it will be one or two pounds."

"Ma'am, but try for me."

"Well, but you should understand—"

"But ma'am, have compassion on me—"

"Well, as I say I'll try but don't hope for anything so large."

"All right, I'll go."

" Good-bye. "

The Manager was shocked to hear that Mr. Jackson had asked his wife to intercede for him to obtain an increase in pay—a huge increase. He was particularly annoyed at Jackson's audacity in doing so.

The next morning the Manager sent for Mr. Jackson. Sternly he warned Jackson never to approach the Manager's wife in any circumstance. But Mr. Jackson was not shaken either by his sternness or his words.

" Manager, I suspect you don't pay us as much as the Company has authorised," declared Mr. Jackson standing akimbo instead of his usual curtsy of hands behind him.

" What ! " exclaimed the Manager with eyes wide-open, hair standing on, sweating immediately. " What do you mean ? Whoever told you—"

" Nobody has told me anything—"

" Are you suggesting that I am defrauding the Company by—"

" I am not suggesting anything like that. What I mean is that you forced these meagre salary scales on the Company."

" Nonsense ! Leave my office ! "

Mr. Jackson left instantly looking very much annoyed but rejoicing in the disturbance he had created for the Manager. He went to his own office and simply sat down without any intention of working.

" Messenger, buy me some cigarettes," he ordered.

He got the cigarettes, and began to puff smoke all over.

" Jackson, I understand you are proving refractory these days," said Mr. Coke, the Assistant Manager, surprised to see the smoke, which was forbidden. "The Manager reports you were insolent to him this morning ?"

" I was not insolent; I just asked for an increment."

" Well, the line you took was not appropriate. I'm disappointed in you."

Mr. Jackson was desperate; he did not feel like working. He got up and walked to the office exchange to talk to Lucy, the telephonist. That continued and the cordial reception which the telephonist always gave him encouraged Mr. Jackson. At lunch time he invited her to meals at the office canteen.

Lucy was herself sociable and did not object to any entertainments Mr. Jackson offered; at any rate she had not taken a serious view of Mr. Jackson's sudden approaches. But whether as a mere showing off or whether as a serious friendship he did not make plain, Mr. Jackson always tried to let Mr. Coke see that he had some intimate connection with Lucy.

On one occasion Mr. Jackson was conversing with Lucy during office hours. When he saw the Assistant Manager coming, he put his hand gently on Lucy's shoulders.

" What about an hour at the Ambassador Hotel tonight, Lucy ?", asked Mr. Jackson with an air of pomposity as Mr. Coke passed by.

" Oh yes, I'm free. "

Mr. Coke overheard them, and he blushed. Though he was generally known to be kind and affable, he was also jealous and sentimental. When Lucy was first employed he paid great attentions to her and sometimes invited her to the night clubs. Coming back from the other end of the verandah he saw Mr. Jackson still conversing.

" Jackson, will you see me in my office ?"

" All right."

Mr. Jackson followed him directly.

" Well, Jackson, I'm sorry to have to break—"

" Oh, don't worry !"

" Jackson, I—I don't know how to begin," Mr. Coke hesitated, took off his spectacles, and started to polish the lenses. " Eh – – – – what was I saying," he said, as he got up from his chair and walked to the window as if he really meant to see something outside. Then he turned round, looked at the floor, and up again looking directly at Mr. Jackson. " Yes, eh – – – Jackson, you are one of the oldest members of staff this Company boasts of. Last year when the General Manager arrived from England, you may remember, how well I spoke about you to him – – –"

" But Mr. Coke, what have I done ?" queried Mr. Jackson taking careful note of Mr. Coke's attitude.

" You must be patient for a minute. What I want to tell you is that within the last few days your conduct has been growing from bad to worse – – –"

" Because I was talking to Lucy or what ?"

" Well, that may be an instance of irresponsibility."

" How ?"

" There is no harm in talking to that girl but you, as a senior man, ought to set a good example. You mustn't hang about. Is it the way you think a Manager will be encouraged to grant an increase in salary ?"

" Mr. Coke, I see that you are jealous because you saw me talking to Lucy – – –"

" Jealous ? Why ?"

"It's all right, I'll have no more of this." And so saying he went out.

Three days before pay day, Mr. Jackson was busy in town seeing many friends. Some came to the office and stood on the verandah with him and had some discussions; the other members of staff wondered what it was all about.

The following day those very people started tripping in to see the Assistant Manager. The first among them came early in the morning.

"I want the Manager," he said.

"You can't see him like that; you have to see the Assistant Manager first," said the messenger as he took him along.

"Please, sir, this man – – –"

"Come in. What can I do for you?"

"Please, that your clerk, eh – – –Mr. Jackson is owing me five pounds for about six months now."

"Is that all you are after?"

"Yes, sir."

"All right, come in two days' time," replied Mr. Coke thoughtfully.

On pay day people crowded at the office waiting to collect debts from Mr. Jackson. As soon as he got his pay he went directly to the Manager's office. Without announcing himself, he entered.

"Please, sir, so you didn't grant me any increment; you are after all not human; you are selfish, you are wicked—"

"What the deuce is all this! Coke!" the Manager shouted.

"Yes."

"I think you have to agree with me that we must dismiss Mr. Jackson. Ask the cashier to pay him one month's salary in lieu of notice. I don't want his services again."

"But, Manager, I must speak my mind. The pay is too small, and I must ask for more?"

"Get away from my office. I have terminated your appointment."

And so on the 1st of February Mr. Jackson assumed duty as book-keeper in his new office no less rich than before.

The Walk Of Life (Agbezoli)
By Israel Kafu Hoh

It storms and rains relentlessly
From morn till night in life.
The earth is as slippery as slime,
Winds do blow and the sun doth shine,

The rainbow stretches across the heavens.
So while you move with the egg of life,
It is wise to step off cautiously.
When you move about with the lamp of life,
Do cover it very carefully.
May you always remember that
" In the midst of life is death ".

Peace
By Lebrecht Hesse

Peace, Peace, a thing so dear to all mankind.
Whose meaning and looks are true and kind,
Whose reign on earth are known to two,
Adam and Eve, who flouted her law,
To live and reign like gods on earth.
Come, come, for voices are drowned in fear,
When we remember the day of thy wrath.

Peace, Peace, where livest thou now ?
Or hast thou fled the earth ?
Where once thy glory and honour stood,
Before that Dupe severed man from you.
Listen now to our shameful call
In this tormenting age of rage,
When every atom splits in space
And leaves mankind for ever daunted.

Peace, Peace, we pray thee once again.
Forget for ever those sins of old,
Which veiled that sacred face from all mankind.
Send again that soothing breath of health,
To heal mankind from mortal fear,
And reign again with thy calm glory
On this deserted world of woe,
Sailing on the seas of our common foe.

Peace, Peace, thou hope of mankind,
King of heaven and Lord of earth.
Forgive thy erring sons and daughters,
And deliver them from their own created fears.
Lord of earth show us again thy kindness,
And lead us to thy former kingdom of old
Where mankind can find glory in thy presence.

Heaven Is A Fine Place
By Adolph Agbadja

Hear the voice of the wayside preacher: "Heaven is a fine place; Heaven is a glorious place; Heaven is a comfortable place. Anybody who reaches Heaven will enjoy the most incomparable, superb, attractive and sweet smelling scent of life there, beyond utter description. Things there are incomparable with the practical, material, and visible things we see here, in life.

The bedecked houses, the towering mansions, which we see here, on this plane of life; the elaborate palaces of Kings and Queens; the mighty and magnificent cathedrals, the Domes, the Theatres and many other attractive establishments, on this earth, are merely the counterfeit imitation of Heavenly Habitations.

The hurrahs, the toasts, the ovations, and the various commemorations in which we jubilate, on this earth, are just the partial and divisional displays of the superabundance of Heavenly Design.

The luxurious cars (amongst which we can mention the Studebaker, the Opel, Zephyr, and the Jaguar), the spacious shining buses, the electrical or coal-engine trains, the buzzing and noisy aeroplanes, the Helicopters, all in magnitude and diminutive, are just inventions and artificial creations subtracted from the spiritual world.

As soon as a man enters Heaven, or has reached the threshold of entering there, he at once looks down upon these material and corporeal inventions, as futile as the sand.

The artful painted Damas, the wormlike looking velvets, the decorated *kentes*, which we preciously value; the soft smooth blankets, the dazzling woollens and palmbeaches, which we constantly procure and wrap our bodies in, are only the fallen leaves, from the top of the tree of Life, in Heaven, upon this earth. The man-made gods and goddesses: the gold, the diamonds, manganese, bauxite; uranium which man values so much, are mere drops, deposits, and evacuations of angelic superfluities.

The joys and merriment that we occasionally experience, and indulge ourselves in, are but the remnants of Heavenly festivals, which operate there at all times.

He who spends one day in Heaven, and has enjoyed himself there with its perpetual concomitant fragrance, aroma, and melodious music, sharply condemns and despises a thousand years of earthly reveries and orgies. Everybody, small or big, rich or poor, learned or unlearned, tall or short, must unceasingly fight from now onwards to secure the ticket, the passport, or the licence to enable him to reach Heaven.

May God bless us all, Amen."

This sermon seemed to me an extraordinary description. It thrilled me from my head to my toe, whilst I listened with treble attention to the preacher. The definitions and ascriptions he touched on in the preaching set me thinking madly, how I should reach Heaven in the shortest available time, so that I could attest and enjoy myself, with the blissful attributions and functions, which the preacher said were going on there continually.

I made this affair, " of reaching Heaven " at an earliest hour a primary desire. Returning to my residence, which was on Labadi Road, I started to put questions to my parents: " Papa, Papa, I wish to ask you some matter ". " Yes, Kofi, I am at your disposal, go on with your petty question." " Well, please (being afraid) can you show me where to buy a ticket which will enable me to reach Heaven, in the next forty-five minutes; can you exactly show me the location, and the centre, where to go and get the ticket ?" " What! absurd, nonsense! Kofi, what's the matter with you, are you hungry ? and thus losing your memory ? Ama, Papa bring some *kenkey* and *kinam* to Kofi, he is very hungry ".

" Oh dear father, I am not hungry, nor am I going insane, never; I am normal. Only I am after a unique desire, and I am just requesting your guidance, you being my father." " Yes, surely, I am your father, and I am responsible for all your requirements. But, just now, you are not talking sense. Who can go to Heaven by buying a ticket ? " Well " I interrupted, " the preacher said so ". " Which preacher ?" " If any preacher said so, it was a spiritual talk, leave it out of your mind, banish at once that frenzied idea." I kept quiet and left my father alone. I never discussed the question with him again. I could not indulge myself in any other assignment, in the house, than finding all avenues by which I could fly to Heaven; and to see with my naked eyes, exactly things there in the accordant vivid preaching I heard from the preacher the past Sunday.

" I must see how Heaven is like, by all means ", I encouraged myself. This divine yearning filled me so much, that I turned a "crank " to my parents and brethren, in the house. All the inmates of our house, including my own parents, soon started to form a queer opinion about me and were finding fault with me. " Kofi, is by himself, his mind is deranged, who can see Heaven with the naked eyes?" said one of my younger brothers, as he looked at me, and reported my behaviour and mood, to my mother and father one day. My parents called me, and strongly advised me to refrain myself from this mysterious desire. They told me that there was no Heaven, anywhere; therefore, I must relinquish the bogus and absurd feeling immediately.

Periodically I isolated myself from the house to a distant area, so as to avoid further disturbances, and discouragement from others. Occasionally, I refreshed my memory with this saying " Heaven is a fine place, that's why many must try to go there. I will be there very soon."

At one time, my father overheard me, and said " Absurd, nobody can see Heaven, unless in death." Still I never withdrew from my reflection. I concentrated and pondered over the question relentlessly.

The phantasmal thought had fully fledged in me. And one morning, I departed from home, set on an extensive search, for fulfilling my desire. I moved from office to office, visiting, and interviewing personnel and officials, in the Authoritative Departments in Accra.

At first, I went direct to the Passport Office, and demanded from an official there, that I had come there to secure a passport to go to Heaven. The officer in charge frowned, and looked at me, with an air of uncertainty and vagueness, and said to me " Look here, we are not playing here; we are servicing important people, who are after tangible requests, unlike your crazy desire ".

I stared at his face, and cowardly walked out with discomfort. I hurried to the Licensing Office of the Gold Coast Police, at the Airport. As I alighted from the Bus, I sharply and smartly entered into the charge office, where a police man was in charge, at the counter.

" Good morning, police friend." The response came " Good morning, fine young man, how are you?" " I am not all right." I replied. " May I just be sure if this is the Licensing Office?" I put to him. " Oh yes, it is, " came the reply. " What can I do for you?" " Well, I just want to obtain a licence ". " What sort of licence, are you after, we issue varieties of licences here— Car licence, Vehicles, and Trucks; and so on. Do you want a car licence?" " No sir, I haven't even a bicycle. I am on a different mission altogether. I want a licence to go to Heaven with; I am directed to come here for it. " " I doubt if we can satisfy your request, anyway, let me report it to the Inspector; here we do everything by order ". On reporting the matter, the Inspector in charge came out from his office. Peeping at me, he asked with a military voice: " Who are you?" " I am Kofi Abudu, from Labadi, I want a licence to go to Heaven with, I am told to be here for it ". He grinned at me and he shouted for two escort policemen, to restrain me, whilst he phoned for the Police Ambulance to come and take me to Asylum, to be examined.

The escort men laid their hands on me—dragging me into the cell. " Leave me alone, what have I done ?" " You are crez, master sey mek we holu you, you go go for Asulum." I started to shout " *Adzeei, Adzeei, Adzeei* !" This high noise, disturbed the white officer there. As he came out from his office, he ordered that I should be released, and be driven away instantly. As soon as I had been set free, I took to my heels. "*Hee na seke yelo, Na seke yelo, eyitso efite.*" This shouting meant that I was a mad man, my mind was deranged.

Returning to the Municipality of Accra, the last place where I went in frustration for obtaining a pass to Heaven was the Opera Cinema. The time was noon, when I reached the offices of the Cinema. As I arrived at where tickets were sold, the seller asked, " Yes master, what class of ticket do you want to buy ?" " Oh ! any kind that can usher me to the best seat in Heaven," I answered. The youngman selling the ticket never minded me at all any more. I remained there, looking into the air, calculating in my head, how many chairs could there be in Heaven, estimating the size of God's Throne. Looking behind me, I saw a long queue. " Hey, you ! clear away from the window and allow better people to buy the tickets, so that I can earn a huge commission, with which to attend the Evening Dance, at Tip Toe "—saying this, the youngman came out, got hold of me, and thrust me out from the yard.

My eagerness to go to Heaven still developed beyond measure. Indeed I had a prompt decision, of travelling to Koforidua in pursuance of my desire. Eventually, I arrived at Koforidua, that very day, at five o'clock. I started walking in the streets, taking minute care in reading the notice boards, in the town. All of a sudden, I beheld a sign board, rubricated with red letters, which read thus: " SPIRITUELLE LODGE " and it continued in small letters " All who are desirous of reaching Heaven, come to the Diocesan, without hesitancy ".

After I halted and scanned the notice board, my heart was replete with abundance of happiness. " Oh, thanks to Providence, I now get to the end of my long Desire." I impatiently strayed into the House, and I was directed to the Assistant Diocesan, to whom, I related my heart's desire. He in turn, sent me to the main lodge—a dome-like compartment, where I saw the Senior Diocesan sitting in a cushioned chair, calm and reposed.

Reaching him, I was quickly ordered to squat before him, and greet him, in the following words, which I repeated nervously. "Praise to your Honour, seated in Cushing Chair," and the response came out: " And blessing to you, son of Okankwei."

I was asked to fall on my face and state my needs to him. This I did. The voice came to me. " Yes, what are you after, you lost lamb ?" I related my story. " For long weeks, I have been imposed on by a burning desire. That is, I want to reach Heaven as soon as possible." I ended. " That's an easy task, you have touched the correct terminus. You will see Heaven only this night. Bring ten shillings, without delay." I carried a pound note with me. This I gave to him, and he returned the balance of ten shillings to me. He told me to wait till 8 o'clock, when I would be shown the way to Heaven. I was glad, hearing the exhilarating tidings from the noble man. I perched on a chair, awaiting anxiously, for the appointed time as a bridegroom, getting ready to be knotted to his bride.

The long awaited hour came. I had been taken by an attendant into a small room, by the main lodge. I was told, I had to sleep alone there for the night. My heart beat within me with fear. A camp-bed was fixed there for me to lie in. The room was dark, and we looked inside with a flash light which the attendant carried. He told me that, no light should remain in the room, in the night, and he would take the flash light away.

Before he left, he issued the following passwords to me. " In your sleep, keep on saying these words—HEAVEN OH HEAVEN ! HEAVEN OH HEAVEN ! At a certain period, in the night, as you continue repeating these words, you will be caught to Heaven by the Angels, without any consciousness of yourself, and you will remain there, a new man altogether, forever and ever." He left.

I slept in the dark room, expecting what could befall me in the gloomy night. It was more than being in the grave. I lay myself on the camp-bed, but I could not sleep profoundly. I kept on, repeating those watchwords " HEAVEN ". Unknowingly, a deep slumber shadowed over me; a complete oblivion and total eclipse it was.

Suddenly, unexpectedly, and in surprise, I perceived a flood of light in the room. It shone through a small window closed, streaming on me, in suffusion. In this glowing influx, there projected a ghostly figure, in a white apparel.

This prominent and luminous light, tore away the previous tomb-like state, in which I had been imprisoned. The small camp-bed shuddered under me. My whole body was shaking with fear. I raised up my head, but I was forced to put it down because of the powerful radiating light, penetrating into my eyes. This flood of light circulated in the room; I rolled with great amazement, in the bed. Up to a short time, the ghostly figure approached me. I felt a horrible terror, as this happened. As I stood on my legs to run away from the room, the ghost suppressed me from escaping.

Then the voice came. " I am the one you have long been searching for, and wish to see my dwelling place, you will reach there today." I became breathless and stunned, by hearing those words. My feet were feeble under me. I could not behold the two sparkling eyes, of the strange figure. Presently, the voice continued, " Fellow me ", the ghost moving away. It seemed as if both of us, had embarked upon a journey walking on a smooth path, in the bright light. Finally, we arrived at a delightful habitation, where I began to hear melodious music, which was in function there.

I beheld a huge and massive gathering, surrounding a mighty decorated round table, all were in white and resplendent gowns. As I looked round, I noticed with an untold joy, the excellency of the place. Everything there looked colourful, in a lovely manner of array. The roses, the chairs, the tables, and the different apparatuses and appurtenances looked glamorous, and were in an attractive set of order. The vivacity of the occupants there changed me completely from the dirty earthly state into a heavenly state. Everything on me was promptly altered. I was given an equal gown, like that worn by the Angelic host there.

The presentation, indeed, showed itself unique, splendid, and majestic. The order of life never faded and became irregular. "As it was in the beginning, is now, and ever shall be, without end." Said to me, by one of the Angels there.

Nobody entirely vacates his original position, except occasionally when he is sent out to go and perform a special duty, and he must return without much delay.

There exists perpetual bright light there, soaring over all the inhabitants. They no more need electrical lights, nor any sort of lights used here—on this earth. They never experience darkness there. The joy there is endless and superb. Marvellous life ! There is no fire, nor cooking utensils, yet sweet and sumptuous meals and tea are catered for each and every one, occasionally, and regularly.

No hunger to be felt; no labour; no quarrel to be seen there. Calmness; Tranquillity; Order; this is the great testimony to be borne, by any visitor, who has been there.

In fact, a blissful Domicile! The man sitting at the Head of the Council, occasionally came to me, to where I sat, and spoke into my ears. "Are you happy?" "Oh Yes, beyond description," I replied. And I was told that I would be taken to 'The King of Glory' in His majestic and monastic Sanctum, on the following day.

Then, at last, all of a sudden, I was aroused by a great noise. As I opened my eyes, I found that I was in my own small room, at LABADI, outside Heaven.

Ata
By Israel Kafu Hoh

Down the lane go the siblings of my friends,
Over the lee, the friends of my companions;
But never one of mine anywhere.
What of mine? What ails them?
Why must I be so lonely and blue?
Ata, dear brother, Ata,
I shall venture over every hill and dale,
To see your face before the night be dark,
That you might with me keep company.

Complaint
By E. K. Martey

Had she loved me
As she told me
When she scolded me
For being naughty
She wouldn't have died.

How now lonely
Do I only
Take a cold tea
This cold frost morn.
Why should she die,
Why should she die?

No more naughtiness
Mum, no more stealing.
No more delinquencies
Mum, no more pinching.
Come back to me.
Why should you die,
Why should you die?

Jack's got a mango sweet
Joe's balloon O, how neat.
None for me, not a bit.
Come back to me, mum.
Where have you gone, mum,
What does it mean to die ?

To My Mother
By E. A. Nee-Adjabeng Ankrah

Ah me ! My heart is choking up,
For comfort I cannot sit up;
The ground under my feet is burning, Ma.
Mother, break the coffin and come out, Ma.

And here come the rains in mid June,
Good when they start but bad their cold—
Alternate heat and cold is Afric's lot,
Survival of the fittest is the rule.

But today's cold is killing, Ma;
Hear the rains patter on the roof!
Biting cold brings reminding sorrow.
Mother, break the coffin and come out, Ma.

Now I know not how to call thee,
Both father and mother thou wert;
Still pray in the dark for thy loving touch.
Mother, break the coffin and come out, Ma.

My mouth's salty with tears of thee,
I no more thy sweet form behold;
I go round like fish in strange waters seen.
Mother, break the coffin and come out, Ma.

Dead leaves make the squalor and filth,
A rotten stenchy mud all over.
Most wonderful thou, detesting taint
Lie stately unmoved in such swampy sod.

I see thee only in mind's eye,
Better still I see thee in God.
God alone will sponge off these salty tears,
And make my lips sweet again to kiss thee.

In mind I conjure thee, darling.
What gruesome spectacle thy change;
Thy black loving eyes most mild and so sweet,
Have now sunk deeper than thy lonesome grave.

I shiver when such thoughts do come,
Fain unborn this doomed corruption tastes;
But truth it is, that flesh must pass such way,
A way so restful, but awe inspiring.

Orphan thou madest me by thy death,
Inured to thee ere this divide—
With thee and with father I loved so dear !
Oh ! this life, that thins with advancing years !

The rains over, the sun shines bright,
With beams that soon will wet us all,
Rejuvenating the old with vigour.
Mother, come out and take the cold off, Ma.

But soon, the basking times over,
The earth becomes hot as baker's oven.
My feet are coal black with each step I take.
Would thou had'st windows on thy coffin too.

Oh Mother, mother dear, come out !
Why bear these extremes of weather ?
Would I could thy coffin to pieces break—
But look at such frail limbs of body mine.

Steel me with that endurance thine,
And join thyself in my prayers !
Make thy coffin ever my wings, with
Jesus, thee and me ascending heav'nwards.

Oh! My Brother
By I. K. Ametsime

Oh ! my brother, my brother dear
    Your face before me cannot clear;
Though not even an image of you I have
    Yet my mind is always on you,
For you left me with your favourite hymn:
    Dzidzɔ wònye nam esi wodzim.

Your years were just eight, little brother,
    Just beginning to know of life
For your boyish brain was just starting
    To read your first tongue, and the A B C,
With the songs of praise I'll sing till I die:
    Dzidzo hawo madzi vaseɖe esi maku.

Brother, dear brother, my brother dear
    A mother's love we did not know,
For she left when you were just young.
    Had we had our mother even today I say
My ears would have a delight to hear you sing
    Avi sɔ aɡbɔ le afisia kple fukpekpe fũu.

Hundreds of miles between us lay
    And my letter to Pa . . . How's my brother?
Was written on the day you were gone.
    Oh! death! why deprive me of my brother
And his most loved song of praise:
    Ŋɔdzi ɡeɖe le aɡbeme vaseɖe esi miaku

Natural did all seem after those six months
    When I turned my face home bound,
But Oh! brother, my eyes were in tears
    For I reached the station where we last met
And found you not, but somebody
    Who could not give me your songs of praise.

Then at home—where is brother Kwashie?
    Nobody talked but I heard an answer,
Which sent me nothing but heart-break,
    And to your home was I directed—
Your father's home no more your own—
    But your songs of praise I heard you sing:
Avidzi ko mianɔ ne Xɔla meli o.

Where is my brother? for his place is so quiet.
    Oh brother! brother! are you alone there?
Oh no, with grand-ma and mother.
    But grand-ma and mother are dead.
Ah! I remember, I remember, brother too is dead
    Only his songs of praise can't die with him:
Mloeake la ava dzaa ale wofe asi.

My last gift to you, a forget-me-not tree
    Which at your head did stand
And your remains in its shade do rest
    And away again, away from you.
Good-bye, good-bye, dear brother, good-bye.
    But with your priceless gift with me I go:
Dzi la dzɔm teġbee 'labɛ nye nutila fa.

The Homeless Boy
By E. A. Winful

My father was an Englishman,
" Whose blood was hot from fathers of warproof";
My mother, a dark African
Whose blood was sluggish and deplasmatised:
But I, no African or Englishman,
I wander craving for Man's love:
Am spurned by African and Englishman,
And reap the hate I did not sow.

My father felt great Shakespeare's pulse;
My mother danced perpetually to tomtom
Or the xylophone!—But I, displaced,
And neither gong, nor golden verse
Inspire my breast and feet of molten lead.
And these once pirouetting toes.
Decline the ballet and barbaric dance.

I cannot blame my mother's love,
Nor cast a stone against the boy
Whose parents were both Englishmen.
I seek a home neither Africa
Nor British Isles can give, a home
Away from man and beast, who all disown
My kinship with their hearts of stone—
And yet one day another African
Shall seek divorce and separation from his kind
And seek the graces of an English girl:
And then, perhaps, " all passion spent",
And chastened by the voice of faith,
My brother shall be brother to the Englishman,
And I regain my home in Africa,
And yet desire the British Isles, which still
Remains my spiritual home:

No bastard now, no child of Ham,
My blood shall fuse the poles apart
And reconcile my parents' heart.
This is the vision of the boy
Whose mother was an African,
And heir of all the gold of India,
Egypt and the Western World,
This is the song of the lost mulatto,
And this the prayer of the despised quadroon!

The Lone Horse
By S. A. A. Djoleto

Now, right now in this great new country
Of sand, mud, grass and gold lives the lone horse.
He writes in a language not his own,
He talks about simple things that all know,
He likes the soil, the trees, the winds, men.
He sees them all with joy and knows them all,
He feels the way lies in singing about these.
He cries hard: " talk less and ring your talents more "
But those around him thrive, complaining louder:
" Oh the national culture is not unearthed;
Oh the world laughs at our glorious imitations;
Oh our folk tales linger cold and untold;
The rhythm of our music is unique,
It works wonders deep in us but spurned.
Our nation's history has too few chroniclers."
Yes, a band of doleful owls who sadly wail
While they hide edgeful knives that cut neat,
That slit to bits the papers of morons
Who've not had twenty years of deep schooling,
And if Western nations are fast ahead
And only experts know how to catch up
With them, what now have these experts done for us?
Such as these, except the few, do nothing;
They've big heads for books, small minds to create.
Loud-voiced pontiffs who talk and never scratch.
The lone horse living among these giants has
Success in his head, failure in his heart—
His way to achieve is to neigh crooked!

The Perfect Understander
By Albert Kayper Mensah
Lean and feeble, yet as keen
As an old god at its first sheep,
Mistaking pus for fat,
The young Freudian calls to keep
Another date for meal and chat,
Intent to use as evidence
What e'er she thinks she finds of me,
To make her sexual magnet swing.

The Woods Decay
By Kwesi Brew
O there are flowers in Tamale
That smell like fire.
The Harmattan winds twiddle and toss them
But they never blink a colour.
I see the cross on the hill
And your hair scattered on the grass;
The heavens covered us
And we were happy in our love.
That glow of laughter has left me:
I have lost the light.
I hear the hush of trees
In this palpable darkness,
I stand still:
Did I hear you say:
The stars may show the way
But you have lost your love?
Yes I have lost my love,
And my eyes are no longer
Oases of ecstasy.
I have lost you
I have lost myself.
But a vision of your lyrical bosom
Floats like a ship on the storm
Of my delirious mind.
I have waited,
My mouth dry for your warm kisses.
I have waited:
The snake slittered through the grass
Slowly, unheeded, silent like Time.
   have waited:

The winds bring no tidings;
They blow through the trees,
Through crevices and laugh.
But I no longer understand
The love-taught tongue
Of trees and winds,
The language I learned
In the childhood of our love.
I now speak the tittle-tattle of men,
Bewildered men meditatively kicking
White pebbles along unfrequented paths;
I speak their tittle-tattle
And the earth presses firmly against my feet.
Oh, I am tired of the winds;
And the long unheeded calls of a heart
Shrouded with pain.

On Parting
By Joyce Addo

    There to the sweet wild grass
And by verdant palm trees
    Let's bend our steps for the last
Or by turbulent brown streams
    Let's discuss our future hopes and dreams.
For the birds sing and the bees drone
    And O, the fateful hour of Parting.

    Do you remember that Sunday
That warm afternoon
    In the enchanting month of May
When with a smile on your lips
    And your crystal eyes searching mine
You pledged you'd be forever mine?
    Now the birds sing and the bees drone
And O, the fateful hour of Parting.

    Weep not, Amina
For Fate does true friends sever
    And leaves them Hope
Their greatest friend forever
    But time brings Age, ruler of Earthly Glories.
Time makes us old and leaves us memories.
    Now the birds sing and the bees drone
And O, the fateful hour of Parting.

By yon grey clouds
Birds teach their young to fly
    Helplessly hovering under Heaven
Until they leave the sky
    But back to Earth like mortals they must part
Each on its own true bearing its little Life to start.
    Now the birds sing and the bees drone
And O, the fateful hour of Parting.

    You have determined
To set out for your people once more
    Can I stop angry waves
From beating ashore?
    Much as I need you now, they need you too.
Loyal must you be to them and true.
    For the birds sing and the bees drone
And O, the fateful hour of Parting.

    Caught in Love's tender trap
Did I mistakenly believe
    That our future is without mishap?
Now we're doomed and I cannot retrieve.
    I ask for nought but a relic from you
In the years to treasure, and our pledge to renew.
    Now the birds sing and the bees drone
And O, the fateful hour of Parting.

To The Night Insects
By Albert Kayper Mensah

Chirping little insects in the ditch,
Who sing unheeded daylight pains at night;
Disturb the night! Disturb the sleeping rich,
The men whose only bother is delight;
Disturb the torpid conscience with this itch!
With cries of ill-born babies badly nursed,
Torn away from love, or bred in dirt.
Tell of babes, baptised in church, yet cursed
By ancient ills, and circumstance of birth;
Who lift a thinning arm in longing pain
To bare a naked rib, and withered armpit!
If infant spirits worship God in song,
Before our God, these others can't but cry.

The Blind Man From The North
By Albert Kayper Mensah

Here, in the sun, by the hot and dusty way
Sits a man from the North gone blind.
In his hunger, he intones from an ancient lay
Of the ways of an Allah left behind.
But the crowd pass on, too dense to care or stay,
Too deaf to hear the news of the Allah left behind;
Yet he begs, and recites, and salutes the inner Allah
He believes is within each passer-by
For he sings of what he sees
Of a life of love and mercy.
We should live in Allah's sight.

A Second Birthday
By Albert Kayper Mensah

I strolled along the Garfield avenue,
Past Knight, and the black abandoned pit latrine,
To where, way back, a bathroom could be seen,
But now, a barn house garage stands, all new.
Behind me was the road to Damascus;
Before, the College blocks, and a water-tower:
And as I walked, I saw a Lazarus
Emerge from a tomb, his death-clothes o'er his shoulder.
His powerful body freed from bandages,
A rising flame of life, from the night of death.
Uncertain yet how long the ravages,
The germs, and the million killing ways of earth
Will spare his new-found Life, his radiant grace.
And as he walked past me, I saw my face.

In God's Tired Face
By Albert Kayper Mensah

Each seeking aims
Peculiar to his feeling mind,
Should keep a record of the find
He makes, however wild the claims.
Some day, by these, maybe
Our world will wake to see
The image of its frightened face
With grim broken outlines of a tired race,
In the face of God, left on a lady's shawl.

The Executioner's Dream
By Kwesi Brew

I dreamt I saw an eye, a pretty eye,
In your hands,
Glittering, wet and sickening;
Like a dull onyx set in a crown of thorns,
I did not know you were dead
When you dropped it in my lap.
What horrors of human sacrifice
Have you seen, executioner?
What agonies of tortured men
Who sat through nights and nights of pain;
Tongue-tied by the wicked *sappor*;
Gazing at you with hot imploring eyes?
These white lilies tossed their little heads then
In the moon-steeped ponds;
There was bouncing gaiety in the crisp chirping
Of the cricket in the undergrowth,
And as the surf-boats splintered the waves
I saw the rainbow in your eyes
And in the flash of your teeth;
As each crystal shone,
I saw sitting hand in hand with melancholy
A little sunny child
Playing at marbles with husks of fallen stars,
Horrors were your flowers then, the bright red bougainvillea.
They delighted you.
Why do you now weep
And offer me this little gift
Of a dull onyx set in a crown of thorns?

Had I Known
By G. M. K. Mensah

"... But thou, if thou shouldst never see my face again, Pray for my soul," were the words with which I paid my mother when she had finished preparing me for school that morning.

I became conscious of something wrong and I wondered what on earth made me pronounce those words. When I arrived at the school I found that I was five minutes late. Afraid to meet my teacher, I hid myself behind a hedge just near enough to the classroom in order to overhear all that would be said.

I remained there with a mixed feeling of fear and pleasure because I had escaped my teacher's brutish and numberless lashes. Nevertheless, I regretted that I was not doing what my parents had expected me to be doing that day. Suddenly and half-disbelieving my ears, I heard my teacher scold and forgive a boy who was also late. In the next second, I was at the threshold of the classroom thinking that if a boy in the same category as I was forgiven, then I must also have the same treatment. But the reverse was the case. I had six good lashes on my bare back and I was told to keep standing with my arms raised to my shoulder-level for a score of minutes. Cruel, isn't it? Anyway, this affair had no relation to my words: "But thou, if thou shouldst never see my face again, Pray for my soul".

A few minutes later, at about 8.30 a.m., some elder boys of my class were selected to go into the woods to cut some bamboo. This at once aroused a spirit of jealous competition in me. I therefore resolved to all in my power to go with them. A series of questions began to chase one another in my head: " Should I ask my teacher? Should I leave the class and let my teacher find out for himself? Or should I remain in the school and allow my friends to go?" The last of the series received a big "No", the second was taken up with enthusiasm.

Five minutes after my friends had left, I stole out of the class-room and chased them hard. In the next three minutes I was conversing heartily with them. They knew me too well to be surprised at my action.

Soon afterwards, my friends were deprived of my interest in them by the surrounding grasses and shrubs. What attracted me most were the gaily coloured butterflies which flew from flower to flower in a way which quite adequately displayed the astonishing skilfulness of nature. I determined to catch one of the innocent butterflies. I followed the one that appeared to me most beautifully coloured.

I tried to catch it as it settled on one of the flowers. The creature behaved as if it could read my thoughts. It flew from the first flower and settled a bit further. I followed, but it flew further and further as I approached and the further it went the more the superfluity of its beauty increased. So I determined not to give up, but to pursue and catch the butterfly wherever it went. It was too late when I discovered that my friends had left me and that I had lost my way.

The time, as I conjectured, was 4.30 p.m. Fear began to rule me and I began to feel tremendously hungry and thirsty. I gave up the chase and started to find my way home,—no more into the forest for bamboo, but back home. I could not find my way. I cried, shouted and perhaps wept (I was not conscious of what was happening), for help from anybody at all. There was nobody to help. To make matters worse, the rain started to pour in torrents with thundering storms and dazzling lightning. The rain, however, quenched my thirst as I began to swallow drops of water from my hair.

I ran in any direction, only changing my course when I hit myself against a tree. I had given up all hope of life again and I was only thinking of what I had told my mother. " But thou, if thou shouldst never see my face again, Pray for my soul." Suddenly, in a flash of lightning, I saw a small hut, and at once I made for it. I knocked heavily at the door when who should come, but an old man. I approached him with a mixed feeling of fear and relief, and told him my story, without waiting to be asked. While I was breathlessly narrating the story, the clause " Had I known " flew from my mouth.

" Had I known, I wouldn't have followed the butterfly! Had I known, I wouldn't have run away from the class! Oh had I known." " Be calm," the man interrupted quite confidently. " You will soon find your Father." Then quickly he vanished into the hut. I waited to see what would happen next, when the man reappeared with two jaw-breaking loaves of bread and, handing them to me with a cup of rather transparent tea, he told me to eat.

I was still standing and as it was quite inconvenient for me to stand and enjoy my tea, I asked permission to sit. This was granted readily, and without waiting to be shown a seat, I found myself sitting on a dome-shaped clay-work which was one of two at the entrance of the hut.

Suddenly, I observed a flash of light in the man's face. "I have done something wrong," I thought. "What is it? Am I eating too fast or too slowly? Am I sitting in the wrong place?" These and similar questions raced in my mind until I was forced to stand up. The man had again left me. The transparent tea had been finished with one loaf of bread and I began to see things more clearly. "Ah! my goodness, I was sitting on an idol," I said to myself. " This man will avenge the idol." I began to recall stories I had often heard of a " murdering group " of fetish people who lived in the forest, and hunted for human heads and blood for their gods. I found that I was standing in a circle of idols all clothed in cowrie shells and red palm-oil.

I then decided to examine the man carefully, but before he returned I had seated myself at my former place, lest he discovered my realisation. Then I overheard a whisper from which I inferred that there must be a second man inside. " What, sitting on a god-servant?" I overheard a voice say, "Ah! little demon. He will see." Then a severely controlled laugh followed. " S s s s . . ., he may hear," cautioned another voice. I was in a terrible state when the man came out again. His skin was smeared with red, blue, and white clay, and he wore red parrot feathers in his hair. " Today be today," I thought. " Either he kills me now or I take to my heels when he leaves for his accomplice." " How do you find it, lad ? I mean the bread," he asked, looking very interested and innocent. I was no stranger to the world. " Oh! any more ? It is most palatable," I replied.

He returned for more. " It is now or never, and I must be quick about it," I said to myself. Then, throwing the remaining bread, heaven-knows where, I started to run away. The idols seemed to chase me or assure me that they would report my escape. I ran straight into the forest. The rain had stopped and as I discovered that nobody was chasing me, I sat down to steady myself a bit. "Oh! goodness! why did I go there ? Had I known, I would have run straight ahead. Had I . . ." Just then I noticed that the tree was surrounded by small pots buried to their rims. I saw that beside each pot was a piece of chicken.

I sprang back and at the same instant a knife pitched into the ground when I had sat only a second before. Above me towered a woman in the robes and ornaments of a priestess, her face distorted with rage. Before I could get past the tree, I felt the grip of the priestess's hands on my neck. " Oh, mammy, I didn't mean any harm. My friends made me do it. Oh! had I known, I wouldn't have followed them," I was reciting. " That has nothing to do with me," she replied.

Quickly I broke away from the priestess, running as fast as my legs could carry me, still saying to myself: " Had I known . . .". Then I heard a faint, motherly voice calling: "Kodwo! Kodwo! . . . Why is Kodwo still sleeping ? Mercy, go and wake him up ". Suddenly, there came a heavy knock at my door and in astonishment I opened my eyes to find that I was " running " in bed. The time was 8.30 a.m. "Gosh! Mercy, what have we got for breakfast ?" I asked.

Re-incarnation
By S. D. Cudjoe

They came by sea,
Innumerable like the surfs they came,
Dressed in sea-green robes
And cloaks of frothy white lace.
They came and went, and yet more came,
By night they came
On their fateful journey nowhere,
Weaving eternal patterns on the golden sand.

By land they came, the living dead,
To tidal threshold of new life.
I heard mysterious voices
Beyond my mother's heaving breath,
Beyond the wind's gentle tread
On the depth of night.
Until at cockcrow, Nature sang,
And Dawn beckoned me enchantingly
With dew bejewelled hands.

Ancestral Faces
By Kwesi Brew

They sneaked into the limbo of time.
But could not muffle the gay jingling
Bells on the frothy necks
Of the sacrificial sheep that limped and nodded after them;
They could not hide the moss on the bald pate
Of their reverent heads;
And the gnarled barks of the *wawa* trees;
Nor the rust on the ancient state-swords;
Nor the skulls studded with grinning cowries;
They could not silence the drums,
The fibre of their souls and ours—
The drums that whisper to us behind black sinewy hands.
They gazed,
And sweeping like white locusts through the forests
Saw the same men, slightly wizened,
Shuffle their sandalled feet to the same rhythms,
They heard the same words of wisdom uttered
Between puffs of pale blue smoke:
They saw us,
And said: They have not changed!

'O Forest, Dear Forest'
By S. E. Archibald-Aikins

O Forest ! O Forest ! Dear Forest !
There is happiness in the forest,
There is rapture in the lonesome valley,
There is unity, which none interferes.
In the dead night, strange shrilling sounds roar;
I love not man the less, but
Nature the more.

O Forest ! O Forest ! Dear Forest !
These interviews from which
I build my permanent existence;
To mingle with the universe,
And feel
What I can ne'er expose,
Yet cannot all conceal.

O Forest ! O Forest ! Dear Forest !
There is yet a place of shelter,
Where the enemy cannot come,
Where the battle trumpet ne'er
Sounded or the drum.
Twenty thousand battalions
Sweep through in vain.

O Forest ! O Forest ! Dear Forest !
Man marks the earth with ruin,
His control stops at the outskirts;
There are gallant soldiers,
There are potential natural weapons
Of war,
There is tranquillity and felicity.

O Forest ! O Forest ! Dear Forest !
Hark, O Forest ! I am the forest,
My realm is full of rich resources
Enemies ever try in vain to capture;
My defence forces are genuine.
The lofty trees point vertically
Towards the lovely blue sky.

O Forest ! O Forest ! Dear Forest !
My babies fall to the ground as they are old;
New babies take their places;
My babies are full of rapture.
In my lonesome world,
Hark ! Sweet songs pierce the air,
Beasts and birds make my world lovely.

O Forest ! O Forest ! Dear Forest !
Hark ! I am the forest;
There are wooden-built cities,
The seasons determine my existence's nature.
I am an isolated kingdom,
Man toils in my kingdom for wealth;
There is a rapture for man.

O Forest ! O Forest ! Dear Forest !
O Forest ! I conceal my identity,
To mingle with the universe;
Man destroys me to build great cities,
My vast realm man cannot destroy.
The armaments which thunder-strike
My city walls, no effect have they on me.

O Forest ! O Forest ! Dear Forest !
Birds and beasts, merry in my realm,
My realm is always full of joy;
Dear Forest, the kingdom rare to find,
The storm cannot destroy my realm,
I have strong resistance against destruction,
O Forest ! The realm rare to find.

O Forest ! O Forest ! Dear Forest !
The mountain has its own realm,
The desert has its own realm,
The animal has its own realm,
Dear Forest ! Man has his own kingdom.
Kingdoms exist, O Forest !
My realm is as typical as the world ever saw.

My Sea Adventure

By S. E. Archibald-Aikins

O Mighty Sea! O Mighty Sea!
I awoke one broad day
I was tossing at the south-west,
The sun being at its highest;
I descended to the sea
In formidable cliffs.

O Mighty Sea! O Mighty Sea!
The peak of adventure hill was at
My elbow; bounded with cliffs
Fifty to seventy feet high,
And fringed with great
Masses of fallen rock—

Loud reverberations, heavy spray
Flying and falling, followed one
Another from minute to minute,
That attempted to discourage my adventure;
My undaunted courage ne'er yielded—
O Mighty Sea! O Mighty Sea!

I ventured my sea adventure,
I beheld huge slimy monsters,
Soft snails of incredible bigness;
Copious, massing across
The bed of the mighty sea;
My vessel still forged ahead.

O Mighty Sea! O Mighty Sea!
I realised such creatures, your babies,
O mighty sea, your babies are harmless,
Your babies are formidable—
Your babies are rare to find;
They make up a great sea-bed-city.

O Mighty Sea! O Mighty Sea!
Starving at sea, still I preferred confronting perils,
The wind blowing steady and gentle ashore,
The billows rising and falling unbroken;
I was undaunted, I should ever succeed
In my adventure; O mighty sea!

O Mighty Sea! The weather was temperate,
I ventured advance ;
The night drew nigh, O sea!
I forged ahead across your mighty surface,
There was a full moon;
O Mighty Sea, I advanced to success.

O Mighty Sea! O Mighty Sea!
There was a strange and huge
Creatures ahead of me; that
Was the whale, the king of the sea,
And massing around it, were the
Young babies of the mighty sea.

O Mighty Sea! O Mighty Sea!
Long laborious miles I
Had still to accomplish;
Your babies ever happy to welcome me,
Lo! The sea-bed-city of marvels,
All of beauty, all of use, a planet could produce.

O Mighty Sea! O Mighty Sea!
There was a great city under the sea;
Polar marvels, and a feast
Of wonder, and shapes and hues
Of nature's arts prevailed;
O Mighty Sea! The city of peace.

O Mighty Sea! O Mighty Sea!
I entered a strange world
That was the land people talked about
The land of glory, the land of grace;
Ten thousand tumbled on my sides
To pave way for my successful adventure.

O Mighty Sea! O Mighty Sea!
If I were to fail, I would have failed originally;
Lo! There was the hope of success,
The peak of the high cliffs
Ashore were evident, they confirmed
My success in the adventure.

O Mighty Sea! O Mighty Sea!
That was the lonesome land
Which within its bounds, I was;
Strange eventualities prevailed
My undaunted courage ever
Empowered me with new spirits.

O Mighty Sea! O Mighty Sea!
Then faced me the real task
To accomplish, a real task;
At a distance situated the stockade,
Many efforts were made, all fiasco;
At length my efforts were glorified with success,
O sea, help.

O Mighty Sea! O Mighty Sea!
I was at the stockade, great
Corpses lay about with javelins in hands.
O sea! Satan was at hand
The stockade gate was shut with
Strong iron bars; within was the treasure.
Those were the pioneers
Those were the first victims of
The first adventurers;
Death had ended their efforts,
There was treasure, there was treasure,
I was in the midst of treasure.

O Mighty Sea! O Mighty Sea!
Through a long course of daily toil I'd to go,
My knees trembled and heart beat;
I had no huge buildings, where
Incessant noise was made by springs
And spindles, yet I'll gain more wealth
Ever made.

O Mighty Sea! O Mighty Sea!
Gains which severest toil seldom reached
There was the long-heard hidden treasure,
And there I was to make—
I broke open the stockade gate
There was the hidden treasure,
Treasure for me.

O Mighty Sea! O Mighty Sea!
My adventure succeeded after days of toil;
Poverty I deserted, hence
Wealth was mine, wealth was mine;
Home I returned with glory, O Sea!

O Mighty Sea! O Mighty Sea!
My undaunted courage had brought home my
Desire. My indefatigable efforts had
Led me into the world of joy;
My trees were hence evergreen.
O Mighty Sea! Great adventure, great wealth.

The Passing Of The King
(INTRODUCING " THE GOLDEN AGE " BY DR. ARMATTOE)
By Albert Kayper Mensah

All day, the drums say
" Ten years ago today,
The king turned, never to return. "
And while the air is all alive with song,
His Royal Palms wave greenish-golden leaves
Fair with the tenderness of long drawn hair.

Here, in the palace court,
Tall sad ladies sway in grief
To drummed notes of mourning and of love.

We mourn him most, who knew him best,
And loved him as the one link
Between the past and us...
A rare soul aglow with ancient pride,
The pride of a golden age, unremembered.

With fitting grace, he bowed his way from life,
Bidding us to build upon the past,
With pride of worth that only makers know.

But we have failed the King, and lost the past,
And seem now, a race
Sick with loss of memory.

O gentle dancers, dance his spirits back
Who taught us in our childhood to believe
If only we could feel across the age,
A race that made a kingdom might awake.

Patriotism
By Joyce Addo

Will I ever feel shy
To point to my land with pride,
The dear land of my fathers
Land of many wonders,
The land that gave me birth,
Endowed with rare treasures of earth?

Should we forget those who paved
The way that now we're saved—
Men by whose life-blood and heroic story
This dear land gets its history—
Men from whose lips came liberty,
By whose toils we now are free?

Many are the nations of the world
And varied the flags unfurled
When they all in great jubilation
Hailed Ghana into the Commonwealth of Nations,
With the red, yellow and green
This black star now stands supreme.

Let's take off our hats, it's an honour
For us to belong to Ghana—
Black Nation young yet haughty—
Alert in mind, strong in body—
Sons of Ghana pray for unity
And peace will bring prosperity.

Unity to harmonise with all tribes,
Peace even though we stand for rights,
Fraternity to teach us we're brothers
And sisters in this land of our fathers—
Love and strength for us to maintain
What others struggled to attain.

What was before is now no more—
Let's sink our faults to another shore—
A new era for us has dawned
Blessing for the living, hope for the unborn,
Praise the land of our fathers
The land of many wonders.

African Heaven
By Frank Parkes

Give me black souls,
Let them be black
Or chocolate brown
Or make them the
Colour of dust—
Dustlike,
Browner than sand.
But if you can
Please keep them black,
Black.

Give me some drums;
Let them be three
Or may be four
And make them black—
Dirty and black:
Of wood,
And dried sheepskin,
But if you will
Just make them peal,
Peal.

Peal loud,
Mutter.
Loud,
Louder yet;
Then soft,
Softer still
Let the drums peal.

Let the calabash
Entwined with beads
With blue Aggrey beads.
Resound, wildly
Discordant,
Calmly
Melodious.
Let the calabash resound
In tune with the drums.

Mingle with these sounds
The clang
Of wood on tin:
Kententsekenken
Ken—tse ken ken ken:

Do give me voices
Ordinary
Ghost voices
Voices of women
And the bass
Of men.
(And screaming babes?)

Let there be dancers,
Broad-shouldered negroes
Stamping the ground
With naked feet
And half-covered
Women
Swaying, to and fro,
In perfect
Rhythm
To " *Tom shikishiki* "
And " *Ken* ",
And voices of ghosts
Singing,
Singing!

Let there be
A setting sun above,
Green palms
Around,
A slaughtered fowl
And plenty of
Yams.

And dear Lord,
If the place be
Not too full,
Please
Admit spectators.
They may be
White or
Black.

Admit spectators
That they may
See:
The bleeding fowl,
And yams,
And palms,
And dancing ghosts.

Odomankoma,
Do admit spectators
That they may
Hear:
Our native songs,
The clang of woods on tin
The tune of beads
And the pealing drums.

Twerampon please, please
Admit
Spectators!
That they may
Bask
In the balmy rays
Of the
Evening Sun,
In our lovely
African heaven!

The Ghosts
By Albert Kayper Mensah

Listen . . . it is evening in Kumasi,
And the lengthening sunlight fingers stroke the town
In a final caress, and move away westward,
Drawing a blind across the sky
Behind them as they move.
Can you hear the dark blind moving?
Listen!
Listen to the groaning noises,
Wild, nightmarish, fiendish wails . . .
Voices of dreaming town
Dreaming now at nine o'clock.
At Kejetsia . . . the city's centre,
Bright new lights are on:
But here, where I stand,
In this deserted corner,

The lights are fading in our hearts,
And lovers have to part at sundown
If they want to meet tomorrow;
So let me go to Kejetsia
To get a taxi home.
Cars will cross at Kejetsia
If they dare not come near here.

They won't, or dare not come near here,
Because, from where you are,
You can hear
The offensive-defensive singing of a gang
And the clang and yell of slogans,
To keep their spirits up,
Or frighten attackers off.

Listen!
Did you hear it too?
The wailing of the pregnant woman
Caught under a crumbling wall blown up?
The children, terrified, and running away to safety
And the heavy clatter of the boots
Of a pair of racing police men?

Did you count the explosions too?
Five, I think, in a rumbling sequence,
The last, the loudest of them all . . .
And five more homes will bleed!
I must run to Kejetsia,
To the mocking brightness at the centre
Of the pregnant town in labour,
To get a taxi home.

Kejetsia was bare and quiet
Except for a lone figure ... waiting ...
Looking for a taxi home.
He moved away as I approached,
And would not speak to me.
His outstretched hand was thin and black,
And fluttered in the wind.

A passing taxi picked him up,
And picked me up too.
Then a curious pleasure flushed his face
To see me by his side.
We sat in silence for a while,
Then the driver spoke:
"I'll drop you, massa, at your gate,
And then . . . " "Thank you," I said.
" How long have you been in the town ?"
My car companion asked.
"Six years " I said, " a long time."
And he, "Enough to know the joys
Of the town in days of peace and plenty."
This, the driver did agree with;
(And I mourned that the town was ruined.
Ruined perhaps for ever).

Suddenly,
I seemed before an aged councillor.
For the weak old man
In a firm, wise voice
Spoke with the courage and the passion of a youth
In love with life
And said:
"Do you think that all is lost
Because your wailings reach high heaven
And your tidy, new-built mansions
Blown to bits over night ?
This is not a time for tears,
For mental failure or despair
Though opinion now is backed
By force that often knows no meaning
And any day,
Or so it seems,
Darkening clouds may break in blood
To flood the groaning city.
But this you can PREVENT and MUST !
By learning NOW to LOVE each other !

This is not a time for jesting,
But for living as they did,
When our forbears had to save
The very ethos of the race.

These are days when men must speak.
Shout the meaning of their souls
To the stone, the stool, the tree,
To the earth, the wall, and sky,
And the sun, when it appears,
But above all . . . to *Twedeampong*
Pointing to the blood of Abel
On the naked cement pavement!
You must speak to the heart that poured it.
And the evil hand that drew it."

Suddenly there was a silence,
And I wondered where I was;
But it did not last for long,
For his voice rang out again.

"Listen . . . you whose youth is strong,
Human ways delay and sway,
Till they take a stable form
Like a lake on a bed of clay,
Supporting life, and giving beauty.
What you suffer in your day,
Is the price you have to pay
As you try to come to rest
From the swaying force of change.

You must learn what life can teach you:
And remember this, my son . . .
We have ruled ourselves before,
Though in a much more simple world.
And if your heart is sound and strong,
You may triumph where we faltered
And avoid the mocking pity
Of the man who, in his heart,
Curses and despises you.

You deserve self-government now,
But you must avoid its dangers."

At this stage, he pulled me to him,
And in a whisper, said to me:

" If you want to make it work,
Do not fall a prey to daily
Fear of death, and sudden death.

Try, amid the blood and passion,
To discern a fitting answer
To the cry:
  '' Self-governing what?
  Self-governing whom?
And when an answer has been found,
With an inspiring present,
Worthy of your past and future,
And the genius of your blood,
You must leave the shifting sands
Of self-seeking and deceit
And erect far mightier mansions
On the rock of healthy souls.
Then . . . and only then, my son,
Will you sleep in peace at night fall,
And the lovers will be gay,
For the lights at the heart of the city
Will illumine every heart
And destroy all enmity.''

We had reached the College gate
But the driver would not take
The fare I had to pay him.
Instead, I saw his face transfigured
As he smiled to my companion
Sitting in the taxi.
A chilly feeling made me shiver
Then as if I knew it all,
My companion said to me . . .
'' He was once my private driver
When we shared your world.
He and I, and countless others
Look to you to save the day . . .
Some of what we left must die
But love and keep alive the best
And let that common love
Make you Friends.''

While he spoke, the taxi left;
And as I stood and shook with fear,
I saw two black and ghostly hands
Fluttering in the wind.

The Herdsman From Wa
By Kwaku Poku

I was returning to Kumasi from Akomadan, on the Kumasi–Wenchi road, after inspecting my polling stations. This was the day before the Elections. The road which I was travelling was described by the Assistant Government Agent as " P.W.D. maintained road ". You have to travel on it to appreciate this dry brand of official humour, but stripped of its jargon, it simply means that it was a jolly bad road but it might have been worse. It was a dusty narrow road, full of deep pot-holes which on a rainy day could easily be death-traps for the unwary.

It was on this road that I overtook two dusty herdsmen driving unwilling and emaciated cattle. The herdsmen, who looked wizened, were using their whips vigorously and liberally. As they spat, not once or twice, each displayed a set of teeth yellow with kola and neglect. The faraway look in their eyes told a story of fatigue and hunger, but these herdsmen showed not the slightest sign of succumbing to the ordeal: an ordeal which was in no way mitigated by the fierce blaze of the sun that beat mercilessly on them.

As I sounded my horn one of them signalled me to slow down, waving his whip excitedly. Then swish! swish! went the whip of the other herdsman, in a futile attempt to bring order and discipline among the brutes. I thought this display of brutality was uncalled for, because I was quite willing to stop while the cattle cleared from the middle of the road. But of course he knew his own cattle better.

When I drew nearer I observed the cows a little more closely. Their legs were thin but strong, their skins taut and shiny, and their eyes, glassy with the heat. In short they were ugly beasts. For a moment my sense of beauty got the better of me, and I thought that they deserved their whipping. Their bodies were branded with broad marks, but whether they were tribal marks, like those of their masters, or whether they merely signified official pleasure and approval, I couldn't tell.

I greeted the herdsmen amiably and tried to exchange pleasantries with the more intelligent-looking of the two. But at this point, I suddenly heard the angry hooting of two taxis behind me. Knowing from painful experience that taxi drivers have a large stock of rich and appropriate vocabulary for communicating their feelings on occasions like this, I quickly drove forward past the cattle and parked on the left side of the road. One of the drivers who had not recovered from his fit of bad temper, raised his left thumb at me, as he drove past, and shouted something about my mother. These chaps don't leave you in any doubt about their feelings, especially if you happen to be what they call " I drive myself ".

"Warm work!" I greeted the herdsman. He mumbled something in return, and grinned, showing his yellow and dilapidated teeth to disadvantage.

"Massa has got fine car; massa has plenty money," he said, when at last he found his tongue. Massa, massa, always massa, I thought to myself. Just because a fellow rides in a car he hasn't finished paying for, he must be the object of such embarrassing respect. In the meantime the other herdsman looked on, amazed that his fellow tribesman could use the Queen's English with such precision. As the conversation grew warmer, his face assumed a permanent grin, with his mouth half open.

I conceded that my car was fine, but about the plenty money, well, I wasn't half so sure; for as a matter of ascertainable fact, the car was bought for me by the organization in which I served, and it would take me at least four years to pay for it. He thought I was being funny, and he would have none of it. He had placed me on a pedestal, and there he would have me remain. And there on this pedestal of vicarious opulence I remained throughout the conversation. Needless to say that I felt a little dizzy.

It turned out that he wanted a lift to the nearest village to have some food. He certainly needed it. I opened the door for him and he came and sat down rather timidly, afraid perhaps that he would soil the seat. I offered him some of my sandwiches which he politely but feebly refused. Did he smell a rat, I wondered. Well, my sandwiches were spread with sardines and eggs and I didn't see where the rat came in. But if he didn't want them, I couldn't very well push them into his mouth, could I ? Surprisingly enough I caught him once or twice eyeing the sandwiches longingly, as if he wanted to change his mind. I left the door open for him.

"Any time you change your mind, old man, you'll be welcome to it," I said, He cocked his ear.

"Did massa say something ?" he asked.

"You heard me, you old rogue. Go to it and don't spare yourself." No better signal for attack could have been given to an army. My friend the herdsman attacked the sandwiches with a gusto that made me half regret my generosity. He made eating a joy to watch. He took two sandwiches at a time, surveyed them carefully and then pushed them smartly into the right side of his mouth, where a few teeth survived. If the sandwiches proved a little unmanageable by moving to the wrong side of his mouth, he would thrust his right forefinger into his mouth and slowly guide it to the right side. And after that it was one steady munching all the time.

The grub put him in a genial frame of mind, and loosened the bonds of his tongue. His talk flowed on without interruption save for the prolonged and thunderous belching that erupted from his belly now and again. Thus, I am sure did the Olympian gods express their pleasure after one of their sumptuous feasts. Each time he belched, he slapped his belly to indicate the source of his geniality.

A Chev. de luxe driven by a chauffeur whizzed past us without warning. I recognized the car. It belonged to one of the influential men in the district who was returning from a rally organized by his Party to ginger things up for the Elections. As his car whizzed past us, I recognized his bald turbanned head shining from the glass behind his car. The cloud of dust trailing behind him slowly settled on the leaves, adding to the accumulation already there.

As we emerged from the blinding dust, we were greeted by a whiff of cool air, like a gracious benefaction in this roasting heat.

The herdsman after this rude interruption, resumed his talk. He had walked all the way from Wa with his cattle—a distance of about 400 miles. When darkness overtook them, they hurried to the nearest village to spend the night there. When it rained they managed as best they could; sometimes they got as much as 25 quid for a cow, but that was rare as his cows were puny little things. Some of their customers were decent chaps who paid you spot cash: others, well they just didn't bother; but one got to know that type instinctively. Above all, he said, the sale of cattle called for the exercise of the most skilful oratory, because some of the customers were very close with their money and you had to coax the extra quid out of them.

As the Elections were uppermost in my mind, I tried to manoeuvre the conversation into politics. He didn't seem to know much about the great events that were convulsing the country, and the political parties that were stumping the country for votes. He had of course heard of some of them, but on the whole he seemed to have a most comprehensive ignorance of the politicians. They were just a lot of fishermen fishing in waters that were best left alone. Whenever he passed, he said, he saw large crowds of people listening to men who looked too well fed to want anything themselves, talking and gesticulating. He disliked these crowds intensely because he thought they were loafers who would be more gainfully employed on their farms, if they had any; and what was worse, these crowds frightened his cattle with their noise and numbers. That always made the cattle very difficult to manage afterwards.

And what did those crowds want any way, he asked. I confessed that sometimes I myself wasn't quite sure that I knew what they wanted. But I tried to explain as simply as I could all the important issues at stake. He listened attentively, and even respectfully, but it was obvious from the expression on his face that he wasn't at all impressed by the weighty matters that engage the minds of public men. He wore a puzzled look, as if he couldn't connect all that I had said with his cows. It all seemed too remote for him. " Only connect . . . only connect " I whispered audibly to myself.

" What is massa saying ?" he asked.

" Nothing at all, nothing at all, just a silly idea occurred to me."

" Well, whatever it is they want, I hope that when they get it, they will leave me and my cows alone." After saying these words I understood instinctively that he had exhausted the subject of the public life, and he had no further interest in the matter.

We were so deeply absorbed in our little chat that we drove past his destination without realizing it and so we drove five miles back to the village. When we arrived, he took his kettle and stepped down, beaming with gratitude and a full belly. I told him to look me up any time his cattle strayed to the south. He agreed, and after shaking hands, he announced his name in deliberate tones: "Comfort Issaka is the name."

The clouds were scudding along, banking up ahead of me so I stepped on it, determined to beat the rain before it started.

Finally I arrived in Kumasi. The road from Soame to Bantama was littered with stones and broken bottles, and the police were having a busy time trying to disperse the remnants of a bloody bottle fight. That certainly was an unorthodox way of settling a political argument, I thought to myself. And then suddenly, the wisdom of Comfort Issaka's words dawned on me, and as I looked at the broken bottles, his words assumed a deeper and ironic meaning. I realized for the first time that I had been honoured with the company of a simple man, who ignorant of the doings of this vast and eager world, firmly holds on to the simple truths of experience.

" Whatever it is they want, I hope that when they get it, they will leave me and my cows alone . . ."

Well, I hope that they do.

Pa Grant *Due*
By P. E. A. Addo

The nimtree drops its dead,
And soon is old with age.
And man too drops his head,
When weak and old in age.

So Pa, our Pa, is gone,
The place we cannot tell.
But yet his work is done,
The work he did so well.

We laid him down to rest,
And mourned his silent death,
In earth we made a nest,
But left out all his wealth.

We can say *Mo* with pride,
And he deserves that praise.
To fire the youth he tried,
From bondage us to raise.

Oh *Damirifa*, Grant,
An image we shall make,
The highest place to plant,
To be our Freedom gate.

The 6th of March we know,
You never saw on earth,
But heard it said we know,
Before your painful death.

So while you rest in peace,
The chain of years may slip,
Never effort cease,
And not again to sleep.

The Mosquito And The Young Ghanaian
By Kwesi Assah Nyako

" Agya-e-e-e !   Agyaa-e-e-e-e !   poor mosquito !
Why dost thou bite me
In this unforgettable midnight ?
When the great church-bells are being tolled,
To mark this historic sight,
Vision of the national flag,
The three colour flag, the black star,
Hoisted high over the new Parliament of Ghana,
And the imperial flag lowered ?"

" Young Ghanaian !   Young Ghanaian !
Art thou up in arms against me ?
But I too celebrate this day,
No blood, no celebration for me ?
" Young Ghanaian !   Young Ghanaian !
Be cheerful, Be cheerful,
Else thou spoilest the beauty,
The beauty of this great day."

Young Ghanaians !   Young, young Ghanaians !
Let's praise my ancestors, the great mosquitoes,
Killed thousand invaders of West Africa,
Thereby released us
From settlers, land problem, colour bar."
" Praise be your ancestors, cheerful mosquito,
There is great hope for Africa."

Unity In Diversity
By F. K. Nyaku

All men are like choristers, singing just one song;
Some may sing Baritone, others may sing Alto,
Some may sing Tenor, others may sing Bass.
Whichever is your part, with others harmonise.
Unite in diversity, we are all but brothers.

All men are like instruments in the same orchestra;
Some may be strings, others may be wood-wind,
Some may be brass, others give percussion,
Whichever you are, with others always blend.
Unite in diversity, we are all but brothers.

All men are like footballers, playing on one side.
Some may be forwards, others may be halves,
Some may be backs, one may be the goal.
Whichever is your part, always help your team.
Unite in diversity, we are all but brothers.

All men are like students, studying various subjects,
In Training College, or in Technical School,
In Secondary School, or at the University.
Whichever is your College, be a diligent scholar.
Unite in diversity, we are all but brothers.

All men are like citizens of our dear Ghana,
Some are from Trans-Volta, others from the Colony.
Some are from Ashanti, others from the North.
Whichever is your region, be a good citizen.
Unite in diversity, we are all but brothers.

For all men are passengers, going to one end.
Some may sail in ships, others go by train,
Some may fly in aircraft, others go on foot,
Whichever is your lot, try to reach the end.
Unite in diversity, we are all but brothers.

All men are tourists, passing through this world,
They will all go six feet, where they all will rest.
And will sing forever, no more diversity.
Thenceforth, and then henceforth, though lots now differ,
Unite in diversity, we are all but brothers.

The Journey To Independence
By Isaac B. Dadson

Drums

Narrator I: The Second World War with all its horrors is over. The green caps have returned home to feast on their fame with their loved ones.

Narrator II: Brave men who went to battle with songs and fell with their faces to the foe. The Victory at Myohaung —their enviable prize. Their conduct and their deeds are a pride and a source of inspiration to the sons and daughters of Ghana.

Narrator I: Some of them fell, but their bleeding feet are yet beautiful upon the mountains of honour, and the scars on their bodies are diademed with glory. We shall remember them.

Narrator II: Takoradi Harbour was the scene of great jubilation —Troops disembark and they march through the streets to their camps.

Military March and Cheers

Narrator I: The Gold Coast troops are discharged. They meet their loved ones after six or seven years' absence. Resettlement Advice Centres are opened under Col. Whitcombe, popularly called by the veterans, " master and good friend ".

Narrator II: Work is found for hundreds of them in Government Service—Special concessions are made for ex-servicemen in Government contracts, 25 per cent of the labour force must be ex-servicemen.

Narrator I: Scholarships are awarded to Lieutenant T. K. Impraim and Sergeant Arkhurst. Major Seth Anthony, de Graft Hayford and others are given senior appointments—

Narrator II: But for many their military life cannot easily fit in with their new surroundings.

Storm Music

Narrator I: The veterans come together to form Ex-Servicemen's Union to cater for their needs. The Gold Coast Legion becomes unpopular. Their representative in the Legislative Council, Mr. Robert Ben Smith, is greatly disturbed by the growing discontent among the veterans.

Narrator II: The Ex-Servicemen are now seething with discontent and an outlet is needed to give vent to their feelings.

Narrator I: Meanwhile the Burns Constitution, popularly described as out-moded at birth, is on trial.

Narrator II: 1947—the Birth of a new Political Party.

Narrator I: The United Gold Coast Convention is formed at Saltpond with the aim of Achieving Self Government in the shortest possible time, with Mr. George Alfred Grant, popularly called Pa Grant, as National Chairman. Dr. J. B. Danquah, Messrs. Ako Adjei, Obetsebi Lamptey, William Ofori Atta, Akuffo Addo and R. S. Blay constitute the Steering Committee. Mr. Kwame Nkrumah is invited to become the General Secretary, and he addresses a record crowd at the Rodger Club.

Nkrumah: I bring with me greetings from friends in the United States of America, friends in the United Kingdom and Organisations working towards the final liberation of Colonial peoples from the yoke of Imperialism.

Cheers

And across the parapet I see the Mother of West African Unity and Independence, her body smeared with the blood of her sons and daughters in their struggle to set her free from the shackles of imperialism and I hear and see springing up cities of Ghana and becoming the metropolis of science, art, industry, scientific agriculture, philosophy and learning. And I hear mortals resound and echo with the rejoinder " Seek ye first the political kingdom and all things will be added unto it ".

Cheers

Narrator: I Nkrumah has kindled the fire of nationalism among the youth and the fire spreads like magic all over the country. The leaders of U.G.C.C. address ex-servicemen, and many provocative and emotional speeches are made, with particular reference to the reward given to the ex-servicemen after their sacrifices in Burma and India.

THE TOWN 233

Narrator II: On February 28, 1948, the veterans remember the fallen, their ordeals in the jungles. They resolve to present a petition to the new Governor, Sir Gerald Creasy, who has just arrived in Christiansborg.

Storm Music

Narrator I: The ex-servicemen meet at the Old Polo Ground and form themselves into orderly companies for the march to Christiansborg Castle.

Narrator II: The historic march begins

Burma Special—the Veterans' Song

Narrator I: The March continues—They remember their fallen comrades—brave men who fell with their faces to the foe. The unarmed but hungry ex-servicemen march on.

Drum Taps

Narrator II: Meanwhile Senior Government officials have been detailed to receive the petition at the Secretariat. The ex-servicemen deviate from the approved route and they march towards Christiansborg Castle.

Military Marching Song

Narrator I: The crowds of hooligans around the columns grow larger and larger. The small Police Post at Christiansborg Road is overrun.

Narrator II: 3 p.m. on 28th February, 1948. AT THE CROSS ROADS.

Narrator I: The 200 ex-servicemen, led by Sgt. Adjetey and Attipoe, arrive at the cross roads and are met by a detachment of the Gold Coast Police Force under Supt. Imray. Their advance is slowed down and Supt. Imray addresses them.

Imray: I have orders to prevent you from marching to the Governor's residence.

Shouts

Narrator II: The pressure continues and Supt. Imray issues a warning.

Imray: Unless you retire, I shall order my men to shoot—

Bugle

Narrator I: Hooligans begin throwing stones. A tear gas bomb is thrown. And then a clash and a crash—The final warning is given.

Bugle

Narrator II: And the order—Fire—
Shots

Narrator I: Sgt. Adjetey and Attipoe fall in the act of quieting their men, and trying to restrain the hooligans. Panic strikes all—The ex-servicemen retreat into the town to tell the story.

Narrator II: Women shriek and children run to their parents. Mischief is set afoot! Crowds pour into town. Commercial houses are set on fire, others are broken into, their wares looted.

Narrator I: Policemen and troops are rushed to various key points in Accra to protect life and property; and then the Governor speaks—

Governor: My first duty as Governor and Commander-in-Chief is to maintain law and order and I am going to do that with the forces at my command.

Narrator II: So a state of emergency is declared. All schools are closed down.

Narrator I: Riots break out in Kumasi and other places. The United Gold Coast Convention sends a cablegram to the Secretary of State for the Colonies.

Voice I: Civil Government broken down. Police unable carry out orders. U.G.C.C. prepared accept interim government meantime.

Narrator I: The Joint Provincial Council of Chiefs send another.

Voice II: Chiefs and people deplore action by irresponsible minority. Pledge our loyalty to the king and approve of Government action to maintain law and order.

Narrator II: Station ZOY comes out with the following announcements.

Announcer: By order of His Excellency the Governor the following people have been arrested in connection with the disorders. Dr. J. B. Danquah, Ako Adjei, William Ofori Atta, Obetsebi Lamptey, Akuffo Addo and Kwame Nkrumah.

Narrator: Local newspapers are censored, curfew imposed throughout the affected areas. A few weeks later, the Secretary of State acting on the recommendation of Governor Creasy appoints a Commission of Enquiry headed by Aiken Watson, K.C.

Narrator II:	The Watson Commission Report blames the leaders of the United Gold Coast Convention for the disorders and recommends changes in the constitution.
Narrator I:	A Constitutional Committee under James Henley Coussey is set up, with Messrs. Adu and Dickson as secretaries. It consists of Ministers of the Gospel, Chiefs, Contractors, Lawyers and Private Citizens up and down the country.
Narrator II:	1949—The split in the popular Camp.
Narrator I:	The steering committee of the U.G.C.C. remove Nkrumah from the post of Secretary. At Saltpond another cross-roads. The younger elements urge Nkrumah to resign. He does so, and makes a statement to the country.
Nkrumah:	We have made the cause of the people our very own. We have really and voluntarily taken on ourselves the sorrows and griefs of our people. We have snatched a torch from the Omnipotent and placed ourselves between Him and the people, we have taken on ourselves the part of the Emancipa-, tor, yea the Agitator, and God has accepted us through the people. There come in all political struggles rare moments, hard to distinguish, but fatal to let slip, when even caution is dangerous: then all must be set on a hazard, and out of the simple man is ordained strength.
Narrator I:	12TH JUNE, 1949—The birth of a new party and the fulfilment of Dr. Aggrey's prophecy—There is a youth movement coming on in Africa that some day may startle the world.
Narrator II:	Kwame Nkrumah forms a new political party called the Convention Peoples' Party with its motto:—Forward ever, backward never.
Narrator I:	Various branches of the U.G.C.C. switch to the C.P.P. A powerful newspaper, the *Accra Evening News* makes its debut with the motto:—" We prefer self-government with danger to servitude in tranquillity ".
Narrator II:	Nkrumah calls for a Constituent Assembly, as opposed to the Coussey Committee, whose members were nominated. Invitations are sent to all youth

	organisations and councils, and Nkrumah addresses a record crowd, after the Asanteman Council and Joint Provincial Council, have turned down his invitation.
Nkrumah:	The proper body to draw up a Constitution for the Chiefs and people of the Gold Coast is a constituent Assembly made up of representatives of the people. The Coussey Committee is not representative. What we want now is a constituent assembly to draw up proposals for Self-Government Now. We want to manage or mismanage our own affairs; otherwise I shall declare what I term Positive Action. The chiefs are no problem for they will run and leave their sandals behind.

Cheers

Narrator I:	The Trade Union Movement now threaten a general strike.
Narrator II:	The Colonial Secretary, Mr. Saloway, meets Nkrumah and assures him that his views will be given due consideration by the Coussey Committee.
Narrator I:	And so to the year 1950. His Excellency the Governor Sir Gerald Creasy, leaves the Gold Coast and a new Governor comes, described as strong man—Sir Charles Noble Arden-Clarke.
Narrator II:	He arrives at a time when the declaration of positive action is imminent. Every attempt is made to avert the clash. Some leaders taunt Nkrumah for accepting vain and shallow promises from the Colonial Secretary. Nkrumah decides to declare positive action, and Dr. Danquah comes forward with a fatherly appeal in the press headed " Kwame don't do it ".
Narrator I:	On January 19, 1950, Nkrumah declares positive action, based on non-violence and non-co-operation with the Government. The declaration is followed by a general strike. Hundreds and thousands of workers join in.

Storm Music

Narrator II:	A state of emergency is declared. Two policemen lose their lives in Accra. Newspaper Editors, Trade Union leaders and leaders of the C.P.P. including a paramount chief of Sekondi are arrested.

THE TOWN 237

Narrator I: Nkrumah is sent to James Fort Prison. Meanwhile the Coussey Committee has completed its task. It recommends changes in the Burns Constitution of 1946 and the appointment of African Ministers. The three portfolios of Finance, Defence and Justice should be held by expatriates. An Assembly of 84 members should be partly elected and partly nominated by territorial councils.

Narrator II: 12th June, 1950—General Election.

Narrator I: The C.P.P. organised by Komla Gbedemah with their slogan " S.G. now " secures a majority of seats. The greatest surprise of the Election—the defeat of Nana Sir Tsibu Darku, Omanhene of Assin Atandasu, member of the Executive Council, by Pobee Biney, a railway engine driver.

Narrator II: In Accra, Kwame Nkrumah, Life President of the C.P.P., is released with all those imprisoned in connection with the Positive Action.

E. K.'s Song on the release of Nkrumah

Narrator I: The Governor invites Mr. Nkrumah to form a government and the following Africans are appointed Ministers for the first time in the history of the Gold Coast—K. A. Gbedemah, Minister of Trade and Industry, J. A. Braimah, Minister of Communications and Works, Asafo-Adjaye, Minister of Local Government, Kojo Botsio, Minister of Education and Social Welfare, Caseley Hayford, Minister of Agriculture, T. Hutton-Mills, Minister of Health and Labour, and Kwame Nkrumah as Leader of Government Business. Dr. Danquah becomes the unofficial leader of the opposition.

Narrator II: 1951—The opening of the new Legislative Assembly by His Excellency the Governor, Sir Charles Noble Arden-Clarke.

Anthem

Narrator I: The new Legislative Assembly is opened with all pomp and pageantry. A Speaker in the person of Mr. E. C. Quist is elected, with Rev. F. K. Fiawoo as Deputy Speaker.

Narrator II: 1952–53. The new Government takes shape.

Narrator I:	The title of Leader of Government Business is changed to Prime Minister. Two Ministerial Secretaries to the Ministers of Communications and Finance are imprisoned for bribery and corruption. The Prime Minister makes a motion for self-Government.
Narrator II:	25th November, 1953—A new Crisis.
Narrator I:	Mr. J. A. Braimah, Minister of Communications and Works and the only Cabinet Minister from the Northern Territories tenders his resignation.
Narrator II:	On 7th December, 1953, a Committee of Enquiry is formed under Sir Arku Korsah. It is to enquire into the circumstances leading to the resignation of Mr. Braimah and of the allegations of bribery and corruption against members of the Government.
Narrator I:	The Korsah Committee Report clears members of Government from all the allegations, but recommends the release of Mr. Krobo Edusei from his duties as Ministerial Secretary to the Ministry of Justice.
Narrator II:	12th March, 1954—The life of the first Legislative Assembly is almost ended. The Prime Minister rises in the House.
Nkrumah:	I do not wish to weary the House on this last morning of the Budget meeting but Honourable members will expect some remarks from me because this is also the last sitting of the Legislative Assembly under 1950 Order in Council.
Narrator I:	The Prime Minister pays tribute to the Speaker, the traditional members, the Special members for Commerce and *Ex-Officio* members.
Nkrumah:	I should like to pay tribute to your influence in maintaining the high standards of friendliness and dignity which are part of the tradition of the Gold Coast Legislative bodies. You have preserved an impartial position among the strains and stresses of the political combat.
Narrator I:	And the Speaker adjourns the Assembly.
Speaker:	Honourable members, we have come to the end of the last meeting of the last session of the Legislative Assembly under the 1950 constitution. Now we

	have to part and I wish those members who by reason of the order in council may not find it necessary to seek election, good luck and success.
Narrator I:	15th June, 1954—The 2nd General Election in the history of the Gold Coast.
Narrator II:	The people go to the polls to elect 104 members into the new Legislative Assembly under the new Nkrumah Constitution. It is, men think, the last phase.
Voice I:	Accra Central, Dr. Kwame Nkrumah, C.P.P.
Voice II:	Kumasi Municipality, Mr. Asafo Adjaye.
Voice III:	Sekondi, Mr. John Arthur.

Cheers and Shouts of "Freedom"

Narrator I:	The C.P.P. clears 72 seats, the combined Opposition and Independents poll 32 seats. Nkrumah forms his new Government with little change.
Narrator I:	But a cloud, a little larger than a man's hand has risen in Ashanti. The people realise that this is in truth the last phase—the British are withdrawing. The National Liberation Movement is born.

N.L.M. Song

Narrator II:	For two years and more, the debate in the country sways to and fro. White Papers are drawn up, experts come and go, the parties publish their manifestoes, both here and in the United Kingdom.
Narrator I:	But the journey to Independence has been launched and there can be no looking back. The dream of ages has become a reality. The Ghana to be is now in the making. Let us all unite, in honour of all those who made it possible.

Ode To The Hon. Dr. Kwame Nkrumah
By Prince Haasnem Nehrbot

    Lone figure on the stage,
      With lonely vision wild,
Changing the annals of our age
All in thy simple mien so mild.

    And myriads in thy train,
      Whose hearts are all aglow,
Declare that never stress nor strain
Can steal their love's perpetual flow !

    Where'er thy pathway bends,
      Thick crowds like flowers strewn
Devoutly on thy sway attend,
Such as world emperors great were shewn !

    Encircled everywhere
      With wreaths of heartfelt cheers,
Fresher than those the Caesars wear
In all their triumphs fraught with fears !

    Pent in thy bosom now,
      And undelivered yet,
A New Convenant to endow
The human race with dreams unmet.

    Nursed in thy bosom-base
      And unabated too,
The anguish of thy suffering Race
That sharpened thee to give the clue !

    Stately and all alone,
      With lonely vision wild,
That opens breach in bordered zone
To preach—" No Race shall be reviled !"

    Thy suave and silent power,
      Fenceless of armoury,
Hath taken citadel and tower
More than old days of archery.

Futile before such power,
  Stands modern craft of War;
And man-made thunderclap must cower
Before the Art men's hearts adore!

No General lost so few
  In warfare great as thine,
Where arms and squadrons come to rue
Like helpless craft on ruthless brine!

Self-disciplined, austere,
  A Creed unto thy soul,
Hath preached a Kingdom far secure
That eddies in the bosom whole!

The Nation's need art thou,
  As dew to the rainless field;
Their brimful knowledge hacks them now,
They dread the curbless Force they wield!

Unfathomed Messenger!
  Thy Mission half-confessed
Augurs New Day (whose Harbinger
Thou art) when all has been addressed!

Like phantom visitant,
  From some aerial realm,
Released in clay though hesitant,
To take our glorious Ghana's helm!

Like lingering Meteor bright,
  Flaring our Nation's sky,
Presaging omens good in sight,
And prosperous days unnumbered nigh!

Mortal, and not like one,
  Thrust on our age as such
By some propitious Chance or Throne
To change affairs and values much!

Unpleasant thou must be,
  Upsetting bowels and brow
Of rash regimes that disagree—
Old systems new ones must allow!

Few Victors ever lived
  To see their conquests thrive;
Thee Destiny has deftly hived
To rear, and reap thy mighty drive!

How many Heroes stayed
  To hear their glories' toll?
Thee Fortune has herself delayed
To see thy trophies all on scroll!

Long may She so delay
  Thee from untimely snatch,
That nations may be saved decay;
On better Creed their quarrels patch!

Long in our brief span
  May'st thou on Earth be spared:
Preserve our Customs and our Clan.
Enrich their usages impaired!

And while thou art with us,
  To guide our state affairs,
Improve our social measures,
Refill our national coffers!

Lone Figure on the stage,
  With lonely vision wild,
Changing the annals of our age
All in thy simple mien so mild!

The Dawn Of The New Era
By J. Aggrey-Smith.

A Grove named Prapratem and later the Town Hall, Cape Coast.

Horn

Herald: Ah! now—the sacred grove of Mother Africa—serene, retired, and weird. It's here I've laboured these forty years as Herald of Mother Africa; no service is sweeter than service to Mother Africa, bountiful patroness of the Gold Coast. It's 1948 this, a year of great national re-awakening, and the Mother yesterday told me that a few years are to roll by and then will appear the Dawn of a New Era for the Gold Coast. And this must be true! Great Mother Africa knows the destiny of men and of nations. In a year, she says, she will appear in human form to consecrate her people in their path to Independence, and recall them to their responsibility to Africa and the negro race. The clarion now loudly calls for unity and co-operation. O glorious Dawn, come, I pray you come—come and usher in this New Era—the era of hard work, ambitious experiment, successful enterprise. But what have I now in my hand? A proclamation! It's Mother Africa who orders this proclamation and I read it with a heavy heart:

"Be it known to all citizens of the Gold Coast that I, Mother Africa, who know the destiny of men and of nations, have caused to be issued this day, the 28th February, 1948, a summons to all who are fated to depart this life before the year in the 1950's when the New Era is to dawn.

"It is a unique privilege accorded these people in recognition of the significance of the Dawn of the New Era. A knowledge of their time for leaving life which is expressly stated in their summons will enable them to make preparations enough."

A bell rings

Death: Sorrow in the land, sorrow in the land. I, Death, declare it.

A sound of wailing

Herald: Ah, that's Death ringing his bell of woe. Alas, the hour has come and Mother Africa's summons are being served. Dust to dust, and ashes to ashes. Death is hard on his task. There's weeping and gnashing of teeth in many a home, as chief and commoner, rich and poor, strong and feeble, alike receive their summons. How distressing, how exasperating, it is to know that contrary to all one's expectations the hour of death is so near.

Approaching Footsteps

I wonder who is approaching the sacred grove of Mother Africa at this hour?

Heavy Knocking

Ah! Death himself, Death the leveller. Surely it's not for my soul you've come my friend? Thanks to Mother Africa, I at least am beyond your icy grasp.

Death: No, Herald, I have not come for your soul. I know of that enviable boon granted you by Mother Africa as her trusted servant—to live the life of a mortal, and yet enjoy immortality. No, it's to talk about these mortals I have come.

Herald: Ah, yes, these poor mortals! Dust they are and to dust they should return. And with you, Death, there's no discrimination.

Death: Ha! ha! ha! I am no respecter of persons! What is discrimination to Death? By my yardstick, I measure Chief and beggar alike. Men should only aspire to just and noble deeds, so that when I serve them their Summons, they may leave with joy; for often the hour comes to take a man away and he begs for time to turn over a new leaf or clings to his treasures or loved ones, and would not wish to part with them. But then it's all over, my duty I must do. Ha! ha! ha!

Herald: Quite true, quite true, you are the exemplary slave of Duty, Death. But remember, Man is prone to forgetfulness.

Death: Prone to forgetfulness! As man forgets not that he is alive, so must he not forget that Death also

	reigns. And as man knows that the time he watches not the thief comes, so should he remember that I come as a thief in the night to take him away.
Herald:	These are true words, Death. O that men may learn by good deeds and service to their fellowmen to lay up for themselves treasures in heaven.
Death:	Now, Herald. Fare you well. Bless Mother Africa, who granted you immortality, that rare boon.
Herald:	Goodbye, Death, and may you fare well in this your unenviable task. Now I must make ready for Mother Africa. I must kindle her fire and trim her lantern. I think I hear again the noise of tramping feet.

Heavy Knocking

	Who are these that invade the sacred precincts of Mother Africa at this hour? Ah, so it is Kojo Brown, my old friend Kojo Brown. What ails you, man, and who are these with you?
Kojo Brown:	Kojo Brown (*in a broken voice*). This woman is Ekuah Atta, my wife. And this man is Kwame Sika, my bosom friend. Ekuah is the youngest of my three wives—I married her only yesterday. I've spent a lot on her. But today I'am completely undone.
Herald:	What is the cause of your tears, friend Kojo Brown?
Kojo Brown:	Oh! Herald! Oh! Herald! I've received a summons from Death, and by this summons I die this day. I have come to see you if you can do anything to help me. I have here two bags of gold, one for you and the other for Mother Africa, if I may find an extension of my time, to witness the glorious Dawn of the New Era.
Herald:	Ah! Kojo Brown, much as I sympathise with you in your sad lot, I must tell you it's an impossible request you make. Death is no respecter of persons. The services of Mother Africa and myself cannot be purchased with gold.
Kojo Brown:	What then shall I do to be saved?
Herald:	All that you can do to be saved is to resign to fate and trust in God. You must count yourself blessed to be among the first to bear the happy news of the approaching Dawn to our fathers beyond the grave.

Drunken Singing

Herald: What fine evidence is this of respect and good manners?

Kwame Sika: But who is this? Paul Tom, the unemployed—look, dead drunk as usual!

Herald: See how unceremoniously he burst into Mother Africa's sacred grove! He'll surely be punished for that. He and his family today stand condemned. Society will abhor them.

Paul Tom: (*Shouts*) I am Paul Tom, Ha! ha! ha! Bless my stars, bless the day I was born, I've escaped the doom, no summons has been served on me. I live to see the Dawn of the New Era. Ha! ha! ha! Good luck to Paul Tom. Plenty of work in the New Era for Paul Tom the unemployed.

Kojo Brown: (*Sobs*) Ah! Brown, my fate is cruel, my eyes grow heavy. This wretch of a fellow adds insult to injury. See how he makes merry whilst I bemoan my woeful lot. Such is the course of fate that a despicable wretch like this can live and I should die. But I take good Herald's advice. I resign myself to fate and trust in God.

Ekuah Atta: Kojo, Ah! Kojo, what shall I do if you must die this day?

Kojo Brown: Ah! Ekuah, all is lost.

Kwame Sika: Do cheer up, Ekuah, do be comforted, Kojo. I, Kwame Sika, will see to your property and look after your wife. Be happy, for you have played a glorious part in the drama of politics, in commerce and in religion. You are sprung from no mean family. Was your grand father not one of those who signed the Bond of 1844? And your father, was he not an instrument in the formation of the famous Fanti Confederation of 1868? Did you yourself not draw up the Constitution of the National Congress of West Africa which had a United West Africa as its idea? An idea that may be realised!

Kojo Brown: Kwame, you are really inspiring.

Kwame Sika: And in commerce haven't you been a great business-man with a remarkable sense of duty and a reputation worthy of emulation? Your name is on everybody's lips. In matters of religion you acted as your conscience directed you: a keen church-goer, you paid your dues regularly and offered high bids at harvest-sales. Why need you fear death? Posterity will surely remember you and sing your praises.

Kojo Brown: Ah! Ah! Ah! Kwame, you have greatly cheered me up. I thank you very sincerely for these fine sentiments. May your eloquence and wit be of use to our nation when Independent. But Ekuah, I am leaving you behind.

The death bell rings

Death: Sorrow in the land, sorrow in the land.

Kojo Brown: Alas! that fatal bell, my hour is come; see—see—that's Death approaching. I see him, I see him, hold him. Ah, Ekuah, my all, my all, at last the hour of departure has come.

Ekuah Atta: Ah! cruel Death, take me away also. Oh! Kojo I'll be with you wherever you go.

Nearer my God to thee, nearer to thee. (A. & M. 277.)

Kwame Sika: Paul Tom, Paul Tom, wake up!

Paul Tom: But who are you?

Kwame Sika: I am Kwame Sika. Wake up and go to your house.

Paul Tom: Oh! where am I in the world?

Herald: You are in Mother Africa's sacred grove. And I that now speak to you, I'm the Herald of Mother Africa. You burst into our Mother's grove a short while ago unceremoniously and dead drunk, thus violating its sanctity. The sword hangs on your head, and from this day you and your family stand condemned. Society will abhor you.

Paul Tom: Ah! Ah! wretched Paul Tom, I'm doomed. May Clement's Everlasting Palm Wine Bar never prosper. My family is doomed—the Herald has spoken. What shall I do? True it is—" Wine is a mocker, strong drink a brawler ".

Kwame Sika: Oh! Paul Tom, this is the result of your waywardness and disrespect. Like many other misguided people, you consider our expected Liberation the beginning of lawlessness, and disrespect for institutions. Come now, and let us go.

Music

Herald: Now I'm left alone to beguile the time—these nine years that are to roll by before the Dawn appears. But Oh! these mortals—how queer their ways are. One comes in, an old man, a few inches from the grave, wanting to bribe Mother Africa and myself to prolong his days in the world; who ever heard of this before? Oh! that men may learn to live by honest means, and come to the end of their days unmarked by wanton scars. And this old man comes with one he calls his bosom friend. A friend indeed, whose main interest is in the money, and the young lady the old man leaves behind! What times are these? Fitting enough are the poet's words:—

> Rapine, avarice, expense,
> This is idolatry; and these we adore:
> Plain living and high thinking are no more.

Another comes, Paul Tom, unemployed, heavily drunk, and reels into Mother Africa's sacred grove. Heavy is our responsibility, for this our little country has now become the beacon light to other colonies, this political experiment. What shall I say? Aha! how time flies. Look, it was 1948, a short while ago but now it is 1953—Five years have already passed away and I scarcely took notice. One year, two years, more four years more, in fact, and the Dawn of the New Era appears. True, many things have happened and many more are still happening in the nation's path to Independence, but they all come as birthpangs in the birth of a new nation. It's a credit to my nation that wise counsel has always prevailed. This is the secret of its growth in political stature. But the Dawn is fast approaching and what does this Dawn imply?—Of course it implies changes in the nation's affairs. The country is to have internal self-government. Members of the Assembly are to be elected directly by universal adult suffrage; there is going to be a cabinet composed entirely of African ministers with an African Prime Minister at the head. This indeed is the last stage to Independence. Let me have a look outside.

Music. Shouts

Herald: Hurrah! Hurrah! Hurrah! the long-awaited Dawn has broken. The sun has never risen more gloriously than today. The dawn is here. This is the unique occasion, the occasion on which Mother Africa will appear in human form to her people. It's my duty now to announce the joyous news to the whole country; my horn will come to my aid.

Shouting, singing and drumming

Herald: Now the hour is at hand and Mother Africa is to meet Statesman and some others of his people, at the Town Hall. I go to meet her at the appointed place and escort her thither.

Drumming

Herald: Hail! Hail! Here comes Mother Africa; those eyes are blessed that behold her! Hail! Hail!

Kwame Sika:
Ekua Atta: } Hail! Our great Mother Africa.

Statesman: Our bountiful mother, I that speak to you, am Statesman. On behalf of my people here, and the whole nation, I bid you welcome on this occasion that the Gold Coast takes her last step to Independence. Your presence is significant of this unique occasion. We are highly honoured, gracious mother.

Mother Africa: Thank you for your kind words of welcome. Statesman, I have all along been your unseen guide. I made you all rouse up your people to action and announce to them the approach of the Dawn of the New Era. Yours will be the great task of leading the men and women of this nation to freedom. The path to Independence is spread not with roses but with thorns. The eyes of the world are on you and if you fail, remember you have nailed the doom not only of your own people but also of the entire negro race. For a pattern of sound democratic government, go to Britain—learn of her ways, study from the pages of Churchill and Attlee, belonging to different camps but brothers. Independence is a means to an end and not an end in itself. Here, receive your staff of office and may God be with you.

Statesman: Thank you, Mother Africa. I promise to do my duty, so help me God.

Mother Africa: Now, I have a message. Three of your distinguished heroes and one heroine on the other side of the grave have sent you a message—Casely-Hayford, Aggrey of Africa, Tete Quarshie and Yaa Asantewa have sent you messages. I have here the letter they address you at this auspicious moment and I will read them out to you.

This is from Casely-Hayford:

Voice I: Men and women of the Dawn of the New Era—greetings. I send you my congratulations on this great day—the greatest in the annals of our history. This is the day other patriots and I laid down our lives for. Remember that Independence is meaningless if you fail to consider equally West African solidarity and the welfare of peoples of African descent all over the world. The fight is hard but fight on—all the forces of good are on your side.

Mother Africa: And this from Aggrey of Africa:

Voice II: My people of the Dawn of the New Era—greetings. Once again I say to my people—Africa, my Africa. A new day has really dawned and my people of Africa, accept my congratulations. I remind you of my black and white keys—I remind you also of the need for peace and unity among all tribes on basis of true Christian principles. Make the New Era an era of religious revival. You are eagles—don't be content with the food of chickens. Stretch forth your wings and fly—fly—fly.

Mother Africa: The third is from Tete Quarshie:

Voice III: Men and women of the Dawn of the New Era—greetings. Accept my heartiest congratulations. From the day I brought the seed of cocoa to the Gold Coast, I knew I had paved the way for my peoples' economic freedom. All the same, that's not enough, my people; it's not safe to place all your eggs in one basket. Expand your agriculture and relate your scale to the world economy. " Go back to the land " must be a slogan with meaning. Accept this great challenge of

	political and economic self-determination and work hard to that end. You have the men. Goodbye.
Mother Africa:	Lastly, the message from Yaa Asantewa:
Female Voice:	My peoples of the Dawn of the New Era—greetings. Accept my heartiest congratulations. I wish to address myself particularly to the women of the Dawn. I shivered with delight when news reached me here that women are eagerly seeking equal status with the men; and that women appear in almost all types of work and shoulder heavy responsibilities. Bravo! Organise and be of help to each other. Come forward therefore and take over leadership where men fail. Goodbye.
Mother Africa:	These therefore are the messages from some of our people yonder; they all share with you your joys.
Statesman:	Mother Africa, words fail me to express our deep gratitude to our heroes for their words of inspiration. We ask you, with all due reverence, to carry back to our ancestors and fathers our best wishes and thanks. We promise to work hard to meet their aspirations; we promise to eschew all deeds that will make them feel ashamed of us, and when, finally, we lay down our tools and join them in their triumphant host, we hope we shall have tales of joy to tell.
Mother Africa:	Thank you, Statesman, I will carry your words along. Now I say this last to all of you—be of good cheer, have confidence in yourself and trusting in the might of God, march on boldly in your path to Independence. Now—we shall spend the day with feasting.

The Meaning Of Independence
By R. K. Gardiner

The campaign is over. The campaign started when some of our fellow countrymen chose death rather than go aboard slave-ships some two hundred years ago. In spite of our protests, the support which was given us by other parts of the world, our people were carried away to live in captivity, humiliation and discrimination. But despite all this the struggle went on.

When the late Asantehene went into exile, the whole of the Gold Coast agitated for his return; and we all rejoiced when he came back to us to restore one of the important traditional landmarks in our society.

Our fathers, before us, organised the Aborigines Rights Protection Society to protect our lands and to prevent the development of plantations which would have rendered the workers of this country wage-earners on the estates of big commercial concerns. Less than a generation ago, our leaders protested when attempts were made to fossilise our institutions through the systems of Indirect Rule. We have never ceased to agitate for self-government. The West African Congress, the Gold Coast Youth Conference, the United Gold Coast Convention, the Convention People's Party, the National Liberation Movement, are all indications of our people's determination to attain and to secure freedom.

During the campaign, we have had our differences and our frictions. Some will recall frictions which occurred in the Fante Confederacy and also in the Aborigines Rights Protection Society; the disappointment of the leaders of the West African Congress when they felt that their delegation to London had been betrayed; the bitter criticisms levelled at the protagonists of the Provincial Council of Chiefs; the differences which led to two separate delegates being sent to London in 1934; the differences between the United Gold Coast Convention and the Convention People's Party on points of timing, tactics and strategy; and finally the fears of those who have felt that political changes might needlessly obliterate traditional institutions.

Our differences and frictions should have taught us many lessons. We now know that it is possible for our honest convictions to clash. In such circumstances clever political moves solve no problem. If we shut our eyes to inconvenient facts, we only show our weakness. The constitutional lawyer can resolve a political problem only if the people are willing to accept a solution. We shall need to draw upon this experience in managing our affairs as a sovereign state.

It would be wrong to give the impression that in our struggle we never received sympathetic support from people outside this country. The Anti-Slavery and Aborigines Rights Protection Society has assisted many delegations which have gone to the United Kingdom to plead the cause of African territories; the Churches have always assisted; many voluntary organisations have also championed our cause. Individual scholars, politicians, newspapermen and explorers like Livingstone, drew attention to what was happening in Africa during the days when we seemed absolutely helpless. Let us record our appreciation and gratitude to those we remember and also to all those whose efforts will always remain anonymous.

We owe a debt to British statesmanship which over the years has attempted to consider our aspirations and has today granted our demand in full. It is not a common practice for a ruling authority to transfer power so peacefully. The British tradition of statesmanship has made this possible; and so we enter the field of international politics, not as total strangers. We find ourselves in the company of old friends who have faith in us. This is a definite psychological advantage.

Yes, the campaign for freedom from alien rule is over. Two things have happened: at least one source of friction has been removed; but our common objective, an important unifying factor, no longer exists. Unless our vision of self-government goes beyond the negative aspects of freedom, namely, the removal of hindrances, we shall discover that we have been chasing a mirage. Now that the restraints have been removed, we are called upon to concentrate on the content of freedom. This is no easy task.

During the last part of the campaign, we sometimes saw ourselves as a nation divided by differences which, apparently, no act of man could bridge. When we were sunk in this mood, the Secretary of State for the Colonies came and discovered fundamental unity among us. Sometimes we pictured our opponents as mischievous and even treacherous individuals. Fortunately, this attitude only represents a momentary emotional outburst. In an open democratic society there must be room for healthy differences of opinion. The idea of an adversary in good faith is a necessary condition for clear thinking and responsible action in public affairs. We were even tempted, on occasion, to lose faith in ourselves and to question our own competence for self-government. These doubts, fears and snarls and suspicions will continue to haunt us but we should be prepared to cope with them.

The period of daydreaming about what we would do or what a sovereign independent Ghana would be like is over. Our country is expected now to lead the responsible life of a full member of the world society of nations. We individually and collectively are expected to deal justly with our own people and honourably with the outside world.

The task of leadership is now much greater than ever; for
No other touchstone can test the heart of a man,
The temper of his mind and spirit, till he be tried
In the practice of authority and rule.

A leader's lips cannot be sealed by fear of his supporters or the opposition; nor can he put his loyalty to his friends or relatives above his duty to his country. Because:
Our country is our life; only when she
Rides safely, have we any friends at all.

What of us all, as individual citizens of Ghana ? We are now in direct contact with the outside world. We shall be doing business with individuals and organisations with many years' experience and good reputation. We should endeavour not to forfeit the trust they have in us. Integrity in all dealings is a necessity, not a luxury in the affairs of sovereign states.

Mushroom organisations run by shady characters will make their appearance here. Some of us in our ignorance or innocence may be tempted to enter into questionable deals with such swindlers. The citizens of Ghana who get involved in such ventures will lose in almost every case. But apart from their personal losses, they will do harm to the credit of this country and drive away honest industrial concerns.

This is an opportunity for us to look at ourselves afresh. In the United States, people of African descent have shone in various fields—scholars, artists, distinguished medical specialists, educators, top-ranking officials in international organisations. The Caribbean and Latin-America have a similar record of achievements. We have a chance during the celebration of independence to meet some of them. The performance of people of African descent abroad, in spite of the handicaps under which they labour, is proof of our latent capability. Thus, out of our group adversity we can now draw some inspiration for the future. More important still, these men have a love for the home of their ancestors and anxiously look forward to our success in independence to vindicate their claim to equal treatment and full citizenship.

We are also acutely aware of other parts of this continent where Africans dare not hope for self-government. What is happening here may sound like a fairy tale to them. We must not let such people down. I am not suggesting that we should carry a chip or a sharpened stick on our shoulder and begin to talk about "manifest destiny", the ' sacred mission of Ghana.'

But we ought to be aware of the fact that by our deeds, not only ourselves but other Africans and people of African descent, will also be judged.

We have then every reason to be proud of our achievement in the campaign, to rejoice and to face the future confidently. In our joy let us remember all our public men who by their labour and sacrifices have contributed towards this achievement. We are fortunate to be alive to see this day. Let us never forget the dark nights through which we have passed. James Weldon Johnson, the Negro Poet, has put into words the prayer which I am sure is in all our hearts today:

God of our weary years,
God of our silent tears,
Thou who hast brought us thus far on our way,
Thou who hast by Thy might
Let us into the light,
Keep us forever in the path, we pray;
Lest our feet stray from the places, our God where we met Thee,
Lest, our hearts drunk with the wine of the world, we forget Thee.

NATIONAL ANTHEM
(To a tune by Philip Gbeho)

Lift high the flag of Ghana,
The gay star shining in the sky,
Bright with the souls of our fathers,
Beneath whose shade we'll live and die !
Red for the blood of the heroes in the fight,
Green for the fruitful farms of our birthright,
And linkèd with these the shining golden band,
That marks the richness of our Fatherland.

We'll live and die for Ghana,
Our land of hope for ages to come !
Shout it aloud, O Ghana,
And beat it out upon the drum !
Come from the palm-lined shore, from the broad northern plain,
From the farm and the forest, the mountain and mine,
Your children sing with ancient minstrel lore:
Freedom for ever, for evermore !

This be our vow, O Ghana,
To live at one, in unity,
And in your strength, O Ghana,
To build a new fraternity !
Africa waits in the night of the clouded years
For the spreading light that now appears
To give us all a place beneath the sun—
The destined ending of a task well done.

The Contributors

Geormbeeyi Adali-Mortty was born in 1916 at the village of Gbledee among the mountains on what is now the French Togoland border. He was educated in the Roman Catholic School at Kpandu, and at Achimota. He worked as a teacher for nine years after leaving school, and in 1946 became a social worker, transferring to the Institute of Extra-Mural Studies in 1949. He has written many articles for the newspapers, and for bodies like UNESCO, and an unpublished manuscript on life in Gbledee is awaiting consideration. He confesses to being a lover of English literature, but a stranger to English. These poems were inspired by a recent visit to Ceylon.

Joyce Addo was born in 1932 at Sekondi, of a well-known Accra family (her father is Town Clerk). She started writing at the age of 16 while still at Achimota. In December 1951 she entered the Government Statistician's Office, transferring to the Broadcasting Department in September 1955 as an announcer. Her first poem was broadcast in November of that year. In June 1957, she wrote her first radio play *The Mother-in-Law*.

Adolph Kwesi Afordoanyi Agbadja was born in 1928 at Dzodze on the French Togoland border near the Coast. His father was a road overseer, his mother a trader. He was educated at the Roman Catholic Mission in Peki Blengo and the Nsawam Methodist School where he obtained the Primary School Leaving Certificate in 1944. For five years he worked for John Holts, then for another five years as a *colporteur* of the magazine *Psychology* (of which he sold about 1,000 copies a month, with other publications). He started writing short stories in 1954, after a correspondence course, and under the inspiration of the B.B.C. programme *West African Voices*, and particularly of the Nigerian writer Cyprian Ekwensi. About 18 stories, in English and Ewe, have been broadcast by Radio Ghana, which he joined in February, 1956.

Samuel E. Archibald-Aikins was born in 1932, the son of a teacher, and educated at the Methodist Senior Boys' School at Cape Coast. He is at present working as a clerk in the Ghana Broadcasting System at Sekondi.

O. H. (Kwesi) Brew was born in 1928 at Cape Coast of a well-known Fante family. At an early age, he was left an orphan, with guardian K. J. Dickens, " to whom I owe everything ". He went to school in Cape Coast, Kumasi, Tamale, and Accra. He later took a degree at the University College, where he played the lead in *Dr. Faustus*. In 1953, he entered the Administrative Service, working as Government Agent at Keta Krachi for nearly two years. He then went as Assistant Secretary in the Public Service Commission, transferring to the Foreign Service. While still a student, he won a poetry competition organised by the British Council.

Peter Kwame Buahin was born in 1931 in the State of Assin Apemanim, the fourth son of the chief of Assin Anyinabrin. He was educated at the Roman Catholic Schools at his home town and at Fosu, and entered St. Theresa's Minor Seminary at Elmina in 1946, going on to the Major Seminary in 1952, where he read a preliminary course in Thomistic Philosophy, and started other disciplines in 1954. In 1955 he became a teacher at St. John's Day Secondary School at Sekondi, moving to Accra in 1956, where he is now teaching at the Odorgonno Secondary School. He has been active in youth movements. His work has been published by the late Methodist Magazine *New Nation*, as well as by Radio Ghana.

Dr. Seth D. Cudjoe was born in 1910 at Lome, then capital of German Togoland, and received his education at Lome, Adjimah, Kano in Nigeria, and Mfantsipim School at Cape Coast. His medical training was at Edinburgh and Glasgow from 1932–1939, and he subsequently practised at Chesham, Ilford, and in London, until 1955, when he returned to Ghana. His wide art interests, both creative and critical, include musical composition, painting and poetry, and the study of Ewe music, drumming and dancing. He has published a short book, *Aids to African Autonomy*.

I. B. Dadson was born in 1920 at Kintampo, the son of a Postmaster. He was educated at Mfantsipim School, and joined the Civil Service in 1939, specialising in Accountancy. While in Kumasi, he translated *Julius Caesar* and the *Merchant of Venice* into Fante, and these versions were staged successfully. An attempt to produce *Romeo and Juliet* failed when he was transferred to Accra.

A. B. Derimanu was born in 1918 in the Compound of the Gulkpe Naa in Tamale. He started his Koranic Education in 1925, but was forced to enter the new Government School the next year, in place of his elder brother, who escaped to the village of a grandparent at Gbondzon. He still recalls the terrifying impression made by a pile of canes, and a number of boys awaiting punishment. In 1927, the School moved to a new site on the Bagabaga Ridge, under the Rev. J. S. Candler, In 1936, he completed his Seventh Standard and won a scholarship to Achimota, where he was one of a picked group, including the Tolon Naa, Ebenezer Adam, Imoru Egala, and L. R. Abavana. In 1940, he gained a 2nd Class Teachers' Certificate, and worked at Kpembe, Tekyiman and Tamale, leaving teaching 1950 to become Registrar of the Gulkpegu N.A. Court at Tamale. He joined the Broadcasting Department in 1955.

S. A. A. Djoleto was born at Somanya in Manya Krobo in 1929, his father being headmaster and catechist in charge of the Presbyterian School and congregation. He was educated in Accra, Teshie, Ada, and Christiansborg, and remembers that he had a strong liking for English. Even at the age of four, he came home one day determined to teach his mother to say " The sun is up ". He received his secondary education at the Accra Academy, and won a Government Scholarship to St. Augustine's Roman Catholic College at Cape Coast in 1951. At school, he never learned mathematics, but did a great deal of private reading, and took part in the debating society, and in sports, but broke a right arm and injured his thigh. Before going to St. Augustine's, he was an unpaid reporter on the defunct *National Times.* At the school, he wrote his first poem, and his first story at the University College, where he is now studying for a degree in English.

M. Cameron Duodu was born in 1937 at Asiakwa in the State of Akyem Abuakwa. He was educated at the Presbyterian Primary School, and at the Government Middle School in Kibi, which he left in 1953, at the age of 16, on the death of his uncle. He then taught for two years and studied by correspondence for the General Certificate of Education, which he passed in June 1956. In September of that year, he joined the *New Nation* with many contributions under the name of Kwadwo Duodu. In April 1957, he joined the News Staff of the Ghana Broadcasting System, but continued private studies, and passed the General Certificate of Education at the Advanced Level. He is particularly interested in religion, and international affairs, with his favourite authors varying from Shakespeare to Leslie Charteris.

Robert Kweku Atta Gardiner was born in 1914 at Kumasi, of a well-known Anomabu family, his father, P. H. D. Gardiner, being a business man, and his mother a daughter of George Ekem Ferguson. He was educated at Adisadel College, Cape Coast, and Fourah Bay College, Freetown. In 1937, he went to study economics at the University of Durham, next year going to Selwyn College, Cambridge, where he gained a masters' degree in economics and anthropology in 1940. He was then appointed to research posts at Nuffield College, Oxford, and the London School of Economics. In 1942, he was given a Phelps Stokes Fellowship to study American educational centres. In 1943, he married an artist from Jamaica, and took up the post of lecturer in economics at Fourah Bay. He became an area specialist in the Trusteeship Department at the United Nations in 1946, returning to Africa in 1949 as Director of Extra Mural Studies at Ibadan. In 1953, he returned to the then Gold Coast, as Director of the Department of Social Welfare and Community Development. After a spell in the Ministry of Housing, he is now Establishment Secretary. He is also Chairman of the Kumasi College of Technology, and of the Vernacular Literature Board.

Joseph Ghartey was born in 1911 at Cape Coast of a family well known in Winneba. He was educated at the Government Boys' School, and joined the Administrative Service in 1929. In 1937, when broadcasting was started in Kumasi, he was put in charge of the local news bulletins in English, and began to develop other programmes. He had been interested in theatre since his school days, and scored a great success in writing and producing several plays in Fante, starting with an adaptation of *A Basket of Flowers*. Two of these plays have been translated into English and Ga for radio and the stage. In 1947, he was transferred permanently to the Broadcasting Department, and in 1949–50 given a Government scholarship to the United Kingdom, where he took courses in linguistics and translation at the School of Oriental and African Studies, as well as working at the B.B.C. Staff Training School. In 1954, he was appointed a member of the Editorial Committee of the Vernacular Literature Bureau, where a number of his plays and poems are awaiting publication.

G. R. Hagan was born at Cape Coast in 1927, losing his mother at the age of five. He was educated at the Methodist School and Mfantsipim, where he took the Cambridge School Certificate. After leaving school, he worked for three months in his uncle's store at Sekondi, then taught for six months at O'Reilly's Educational Institute in Accra, where he was also organist. In December 1949, he entered the Civil Service, which he left in 1953 for the University College, returning in 1955. Apart from several short stories in English, he has written two plays in Fante, *Suban Bon N'ahyese* (*The Beginnings of Bad Character*) and *Sika Enyiber No Nsunsuando* (*Lust of Money and its Consequences*).

Lebrecht Hesse was born in Christiansborg in 1933 of an ancient family dating from the days of the Danish occupation. He was educated at the Presbyterian Boarding School in the town, and at Odorgonno Secondary School. In 1954, he went to America on a scholarship for the *New York Herald Tribune*. He is at the moment recovering from a serious illness.

Israel Kafu Hoh was born at the village of Afiadenyigba on the coast of Eweland in 1912, his father being an evangelist. He was educated at the Evangelical Presbyterian Infant and Junior School, then in the Senior School at Keta, at the Teacher Training College at Akropong, and in the Seminary at Ho (1932). He has taken certificates including Standard Seven, Teachers' Certificate " A ", and a Diploma in Advanced English. In 1933, he became a teacher, working at Amedzofe, Keta, Peki, Keta again, Anloga, and as band-master, choir leader and scouter. In 1945 he became a Head Teacher, and in 1953, he was transferred to the Administration, as Assistant Education Officer at Abor, Anloga, and, at the moment, Dabala. His first poem, *Henabaeta*, was written in 1929. Since then, he has produced a great deal of work, not only poetry, but dramas and a biography.

L. K. Idan was born in 1921 at Winneba. He was educated at the Methodist School in that town, then at Adisadel College, Cape Coast, the School of Art at Achimota, and the College of Technology at Kumasi. He has been a textile designer for a Cape Coast store, an arts and crafts assistant at Adisadel and is now assistant art master at Achimota. He is the author of four unpublished plays and a number of poems.

Bossman Laryea was born in 1910 at Accra, and joined the Civil Service in 1930. He is a member of the Ga Society, and is on the executive of the Accra Amateur Football Association. He has written several short stories, as well as critical articles.

J. K. O. Lindsay was born in 1933 at Cape Coast, and was educated at Mfantsipim School. He was trained as a teacher at Kumasi College of Technology, and is now completing a degree in Economics in London. He has contributed a number of articles to the *Daily Graphic* and *Sunday Mirror* in Accra, and to the weekly *West Africa* in London.

E. K. Martey was born in 1935 at Accra. He was educated at Africa College, and is now working as a Laboratory Assistant at the Medical Research Institute. He has contributed articles and poems to the *Methodist Youth News Sheet*, and to *New Nation*.

Albert Kayper Mensah was born in 1923 at Sekondi, of a Shama family, his father being a trader. He was educated at Mfantsipim School, Achimota College, Queen's College, Cambridge, and London University. He holds a Master's Degree in National Sciences (Cambridge) and a Diploma of Education at London. Since 1950, he has been a teacher at Wesley College in Kumasi. He is the author of many plays, several of which have been broadcast, and a large number of poems. In 1956, he won the Margaret Wrong Prize for literature, and he also gained a British Council prize for a play.

G. M. K. Mensah was born in 1935 in the village of Agbozume-Amukoe in Keta district, his father being a carpenter, and now a weaver of *Kente* cloth, and his mother a baker and a brewer of *Liha*, a drink made from malt (*Ahali*). He was educated at the Some National School, and then at the Government Secondary Technical School at Takoradi. He has worked as farmer, fisherman, and weaver, but is now attached to the Ghana Broadcasting System as a Youth-in-Training.

J. V. Mensah was born in 1935 at Elmina. He explains his late schooling (he did not go to the Abosso Roman Catholic School until he was 11) to the fact that he was unable to pass the traditional test of maturity—touching both ears with his hands placed behind his head. He later attended the Roman Catholic Boys' Schools at Tarkwa and Elmina. He has contributed occasional journalism to the *Standard*, a Catholic newspaper published in Cape Coast. He secured a certificate of merit in an essay competition organised by the United Kingdom Information Office in 1956.

J. H. Nketia was born in 1921 at Ashanti Mampong, and was trained in Presbyterian Schools at Mampong (1928–36) and Akropong (1937–41). He was appointed to the staff of the Training College at Akropong in 1942, and won a scholarship to the School of Oriental and African Studies in 1944. On the completion of his course in linguistics, he was appointed an assistant for three years, at the same time taking an Arts degree at London University. He returned to Akropong in 1949, and took up his present appointment as Research Fellow in African Studies in the Department of Sociology in University College in 1952. His publications include 12 books in Twi—traditional literature, a play, fiction, some translations and two books of original poems, *Anwonsem*. He has also published a book in English on *Funeral Dirges of the Akan People*, and many articles in learned reviews. He is an accomplished musician, and has written a number of original songs, which have not been published, although several have been performed over the air of Radio Ghana. One of them, *Yehwe Ono Ara*, is the signature tune for the weekly literary programme, *The Singing Net*.

Frank Kofi Nyaku was born in 1924 at Ho, his father being a teacher in the Evangelical Presbyterian Church. He went to school at the age of six, and graduated as a teacher from Achimota in 1943. In 1945, he took a year's course in theology in the Seminary at Ho, and in 1949, a music teachers' course at Achimota. In 1952 he was appointed an Assistant Education Officer, and he was promoted in 1956. He has published three school text books in Ewe—a biography of Dr. Aggrey, an anthology of stories and poems, and a novel, *Kofi Nyameko Nutinya*. He has also composed a number of Ewe songs recorded by Radio Ghana, including *Wo bada ku badae* (Horrible death usually ends reckless lives) and *Miva kpo dzidzo* (Come, let's be merry).

Henry Ofori was born in 1924 at Oda. His father was a Schoolmaster who came from Anum—the family is in fact Guan, of a people who were the first settlers in the country, before the Akans. He was educated in the Government Schools at Sefwi Wiawso and Accra. In 1940, he entered Achimota, taking the Cambridge School Certificate in 1943. He worked at the R.A.F. Base in Takoradi in 1944, and for $2\frac{1}{2}$ years as a Soil Analyst at the West African Cocoa Research Institute at Tafo. In 1948, he took a post-secondary course at Achimota (this has since become the University College), leaving next year for the Government Secondary Technical School at Takoradi where he taught physics until 1954. In 1955, he joined the staff of the *Daily Graphic* as a columnist, and last year (1957) became Editor of *Drum* Publications. His career as a writer really started in 1949, when he won the prizes for poetry and prose at Achimota. In 1950, he contributed a column *Bushman Comes to Town*, under the pseudonym of Carl Mutt, to the *African National Times*, then under the editorship of Ako Adjei. He kept his pseudonym on the *Graphic*. Mr. Ofori is married with two children.

Andrew Amankwa Opoku was born in 1912 at Bechem in Ahafo, Ashanti, of an Aburi family, his father being a Presbyterian Minister. He grew up in Bompata in Ashanti, where he learned most of his forest lore. His father died in 1920, and the family moved back to Aburi, where he attended the Middle School, going on to Nsaba and Akropong. Here he was trained as teacher and catechist, and began his academic career in 1935, at Middle schools in Anum, Abetifi and Aburi. In 1945, he went back to the Training College for a year's special course, and taught for 18 months. Then he engaged in the timber industry in the Western Province at Twifu. In 1948, he was appointed Headmaster at an Infant's School at Akwasiho, going on to the Middle School at Mpraeso. In 1951, he was seconded as Twi editor to the Vernacular Literature Bureau, from which he joined the Ghana Broadcasting System in 1956. He has published four books for the Vernacular Literature Bureau, a guide to correct thinking, a Yam festival play, a book on travel, and another on food. He is a sculptor, belonging to the group called the Akwapim Six. He also maintains a farm outside Aburi.

S. K. Otoo was born in 1910 at Otuam (Tantum) on the coast near Saltpond. He was educated at Wesleyan Methodist Schools at Tantum, Tarkwa, and Saltpond, and at Wesley College at Kumasi. He became a teacher at Saltpond, and then a Headmaster at schools at Elmina, Tarkwa and Shama. He joined the Vernacular Literature Bureau as Fante Editor, and has published a number of Fante books on fishing. Since 1954 he has been a Member of Parliament (Independent, now Convention People's Party) for the Ekumfi-Enyan-Breman constituency.

F. E. K. Parkes was born in 1932 at Korle Bu, his father a Pharmacist from Sierra Leone and his mother a Fante from Winneba. His grandfather was a West Indian, J. C. E. Parkes, who was Secretary of Native Affairs at the time of the Baibure rising. At the age of three, he was taken back to Freetown, returning to the Gold Coast in 1941, where he attended the Accra High School. He ran away from this establishment, and took up odd jobs in the soldier's camp at Winneba, but returned in 1942. In 1944 he went to Adisadel College, and passed London matriculation in 1949, but failed the Intermediate Bachelor of Arts degree in 1950, which he attempted at the age of 18. In 1951, he was a reporter on the *Daily Graphic*, the year after tried clerking in the Deeds Registry, and next year edited two short-lived Cape Coast papers, the *Monitor* and the *Eagle*. He won a short story competition, but was out of a job when in 1955 he "got involved in Broadcasting".

H. K. B. Setsoafia was born at Anloga, on the spit of land east of the Volta, about the year 1920, the son of the *agbotadu* or linguist of Chief Zoiku II. His father and mother were first cousins. He attended the Presbyterian School at Anloga, but failed to reach the Training College at Akropong, on account of financial difficulties on the death of his father. He accordingly worked at Adeiso in Akwapim with relatives in a store, and then for two years as a clerk in the French firm C.F.A.O. at Nsawam, Suhum and Accra. In the capital, he was fired with ambition by the lectures and writings of the Nigerian leader, Nnamdi Azikiwe, then working in the Gold Coast, and started private study for the Cambridge School Certificate. The 1938 " cocoa hold-up " shattered hopes of making money in cocoa near Hohoe in Togoland, and, still in quest of his ambition, he entered the Regis College, founded by Father Dogli, where he taught in the middle school and studied in the short-lived secondary department. In 1940, he was recommended to the Rev. F. K. Fiawoo, who had founded Zion College in Anloga, and studied there for four years on a scholarship basis, matriculating in 1944. Next year he passed the Teacher's Certificate "A" Examination, and taught at Tsito, Anfoeta Gbogame, Gbi-Vegbe, and Kpandu. He resigned at the end of 1948 to study for a degree at Fourah Bay College in Sierra Leone, where he later gained a Gold Coast Government scholarship, but he was forced to return to Anloga for health reasons in 1950. Here he re-joined Zion College, where he worked until 1956, going in that year to the Broadcasting Department as a Senior Programme Assistant. He is now (1958) once more in the teaching field.

Mr. Setsoafia's dramatic experience dates from his days at Zion College, where he assisted in staging *Julius Caesar*, Galsworthy's *Strife*, and Dr. Fiawoo's play, *The Fifth Landing Stage*. He translated into Ewe *Julius Caesar*, *King Lear* and *Richard II*, as well as Chaucer, *Don Quixote*, and Booker Washington's *Up from Slavery*. Of these, *Julius Caesar* and the *Clerk's Tale* have been published, the former reaching a third impression. His first original play, *Fia Agokoli* (Chief Agokoli), was written in 1945, his first play *Kato Fiayidzi-he* in 1948. The comedy, in English and Ewe, *I Married a Been-To*, written at the end of 1957, was a great success when broadcast over Radio Ghana, and the present play won the first prize in a competition for radio plays, which attracted an entry of 40 manuscripts from all parts of Ghana, many of a high quality.

J. Aggrey Smith was born in 1921 at Cape Coast, and received his education at the Government Boys' School, and Adisadel College. He joined the Customs and Excise Department in 1941, and in 1951 passed the Intermediate B.A. examination by private study. In 1953, he taught at Abuakwa State College at Kibi, and at the Aggrey Memorial Zion Secondary School at Cape Coast. In 1956, he was ordained a Minister of the A.M.E. Zion Mission, and continued teaching at the Cape Coast School, where he is now Chaplain.

Kenneth Donald MacNeill Stewart is the only non-Ghanaian in this collection, by right of residence of thirty-five years. He was born in 1905 in Trinidad of mixed African and Scots ancestry. At the age of nine, he was sent to England, to the moors of Woodvale, near Formby in Lancashire. His first poem was written when he was eleven, and by the time he was thirteen, he had published poetry in *Pearson's Magazine, Time and Tide, Pall Mall,* and the *Africa and Orient Review.* For a time, he attended St. Paul's School in London, but at seventeen, the young man moved to the then Gold Coast. Here he has lived ever since. For a time he worked in commerce. Then he edited the first daily paper, the *Times of West Africa,* followed by the *Echo.* With the help of Dr. J. B. Danquah, he published poetry in 1939 under the title *If I had Wings,* while a collection of war poetry was published by the Government under the title *The Gold Coast Answers.* At present, he is living on his farm at Oterkpolu in the idyllic landscape of Yilo Krobo, where he is a member of the Local Council.

Efua Theodora Sutherland (née Morgue) was born in 1924 at Cape Coast, of a family that hails from Anomabu. She was educated at St. Monica's Training College at Ashanti Mampong, and taught there, until she got a teachers' scholarship at Homerton College at Cambridge in England. She then worked for a time as a demonstrator in the School of Oriental and African Studies in London. Returning to Ghana, she taught for a time at the Fijai Secondary School. She has published several poems in the Journal of the Royal African Society, *African Affairs,* from which translations were made for the German publication *Schwarze Orpheus.* Some of her short stories and plays (original and adaptations) have been broadcast by Radio Ghana. She is married to an American, and she has three children.

F. K. Chapman Wardy was born in 1924 at Saltpond on the coast, where he received his elementary education. In 1940, he entered St. Augustines Roman Catholic College, and passed the Cambridge School Certificate in 1945 with grade one distinction. He joined the Civil Service, where he now works in the Accountant-General's Department. A short story, *Ofori Gave Me a Ring,* appeared in the *Sunday Mirror* in 1955.

E. Archie Winful was born in 1922 at Saltpond. He was educated at Mfantsipim School and graduated in the Honours School of English at the University College of the South-West at Exeter in England in 1947. He then worked at the School of Oriental and African Studies, and trained as a Book Editor at the Oxford University Press. Since 1949, he has been variously employed as editor, schoolmaster, and officer in the Administration.

GP/W1852/2,050/11-57